BUYING
A PIECE
OF PARIS

BUYING A PIECE OF PARIS

A MEMOIR

ELLIE NIELSEN

ST. MARTIN'S PRESS NEW YORK

www.stmartins.com

Library of Congress Cataloging-in-Publication Data

Nielsen, Ellie.
　　Buying a piece of Paris / Ellie Nielsen. — 1st U.S. ed.
　　　　p. cm.
　　"First published in Australia by Scribe Publications" —T.p. verso.
　　ISBN-13: 978-0-312-38355-8
　　ISBN-10: 0-312-38355-X
　　　　1. Paris (France) —Description and travel. 2. Paris (France)—Social life and customs. 3. Nielsen, Ellie—Travel—France—Paris. 4. Nielsen, Ellie—Homes and-haunts—France—Paris. 5. Real property—France—Paris. 6. House buying—France—Paris. 7. Apartments—France—Paris. 8. Aliens—France—Paris—Biography. 9. Australians—France—Paris—Biography. 10. Authors, Australian—Biography. I. Title.
　　DC707.N65 2009
　　944'.361084092—dc22

2008035284

First published in Australia by Scribe Publications Pty Ltd

First U.S. Edition: January 2009

10 9 8 7 6 5 4 3 2 1

In memory of Bebe

One

I blame the butcher's shop — the one across the street from the first apartment we rented in Paris. Every morning I stood in the window of the apartment, mesmerised by that shop. It was so elegant, so classical, so unlike a place that just sold ... flesh. I was dazzled by the graceful, tangled curves of art nouveau writing on the windows, by the door's fine framed-glass panels, and even by Monsieur who slowly polished his white-marble bench as though he was caressing a thigh. But this butcher's shop flaunted its insensible beauty only to mock me. In this shop there were no pre-packaged, take-home, pop-straight-in-the-microwave meat solutions. Here there were real animals — with fur and heads and eyes — meat that looked dead rather than not living. This was meat that demanded experience. French experience. It was experience that excluded me.

It's true. I didn't understand French meat. And what I wanted, more than anything else in the world, was to walk into that butcher's shop and buy a piece of paradise. I wanted to say, 'Bonjour, monsieur' and have Monsieur say, 'Bonjour, madame'. And I wanted to be able to tell him, calmly and with some authority, that I would like half a rabbit (no, I don't need the head) and a few pieces of canette (female duck's legs) and some andouille. Whilst thanking Monsieur I would purse my lips, shrug a shoulder, and outline my weekend cooking-plans in flawless French.

Of course, this could never happen. For a start, I am not in the habit of eating rabbits, headless or otherwise. When I purse my lips I look comical or intoxicated (depending on the time of day), and I cannot speak French. I am, however, greatly in the habit of imagining myself in all manner of situations that are outside my real, everyday life. So that day, almost four years ago, as I stood at my window, willing the street beyond to leap up two floors and embrace me, a plan popped into my head. It was a perfect plan, one that involved daring, danger, and a ridiculous amount of money. It was a plan that would show that butcher's shop who was who. I decided to buy Paris. Well, just a tiny bit of it. I'm not totally irrational.

My husband, Jack, doesn't always see things the way I do. He would, for instance, prefer to listen to the cricket than to one of my brilliant ideas. We were back home in Melbourne driving to a friend's house for Sunday lunch when Waugh hit a six, and Jack hit the steering wheel and turned the radio up even louder.

'That's it,' I said. 'You never listen to a word I say.'

'Yes I do.' But his attention remained fixed on the cricket. 'You were talking about Paris.'

I sighed rather than answered. It was mystifying the way Jack always knew what I was talking about even when he wasn't listening. He turned the radio down a bit and raised an eyebrow at me.

'Well', he said, 'I think you're right. I think we should look at buying an apartment in Paris.'

'What? What do you mean "look at"?' I squinted at him. The sun was criss-crossing the car.

'Alright. Buy one. I think that maybe we could buy one. A very small one.'

'Really'? I let the sun embrace me. Very small was perfect. More than perfect. We could buy a very small apartment in Paris. There was magic in that sentence.

'It's not as crackpot as some of your ideas,' said Jack grinning, pleased with his surprise. 'But,' he continued as he lent to turn the radio up again 'it'll be up to you. You'll have to do all the work. See the agents. Work out the system. We'll be there in six weeks. You can have a go at it then.'

I took my sunglasses off and smiled across at him. He beamed back at me. 'Even our accountant thinks it's a good idea.'

'Wow.'

'See,' he added 'I was listening.' He turned the cricket up to screaming point.

I sat staring straight ahead thinking, this is it. This is one of those moments I'll remember for the rest of my life.

Two

It doesn't feel like a Monday. When you're in a foreign country the days of the week are not yours. But I know it is Monday because I have earmarked a Monday to begin my foray into the French real estate market. So that's why I'm sitting here now, staring across at the pretty girl in the apartment opposite, the one who wears a sort of bright pyjama-type outfit while squeezing lemons with a metal lemon-squeezer, and debating what to wear to the real estate office. I don't know whether to opt for a French or Australian look. I can't imagine how I'm going to do it — what I'm going to say. A sudden attack of nerves and I'll forget both English and French. I run a diffident eye over *De Particulier à Particulier*, the French real estate guide where property is sold privately without an agent. Although this guide has an excellent reputation and provides a less expensive way to buy an apartment, I don't have enough confidence in my ability with the French language to use it. The thought of making a rendezvous, noting an address, or exchanging those polite, formal pleasantries fills me with dread. Maybe I had better go in disguise. If you go down to the woods today. This is not a good time for the Teddy Bears' Picnic song to distract me. I choose a pale pink skirt, white cotton shirt, and flat-healed shoes. It's not exactly haute couture, but I've no real idea what the dress code for this sort of endeavour is.

I step outside our rented apartment on rue Vieille du Temple, straight into the noise and clamour of a big demo, a grande manifestation. I suppose it's the actors again. I take that to be a good omen. For some reason, I feel encouraged by the sight of actors demonstrating. The street is blocked off at the rue de Rivoli end, so I turn heel and bounce down rue Rambuteau towards the Centre Pompidou. I stop bouncing outside the first real estate office I come across.

Immobilier Marais. This looks like a good place to start. Okay, let's see what they've got. The window is papered with ten or twelve bad photographs of beautiful apartment interiors. These photographs are accompanied by brief descriptions of the apartments, the buildings they're in, and the prices. Some are singled out as beautiful buildings — des beaux bâtiments. How wonderful that sounds. Good morning. I would like to buy a beau bâtiment, s'il vous plaît. Certainly, madame. I press my face closer to the window and try to decipher the rest of the text, but all I can see are the prices. They seem a lot more expensive than my study of *De Particulier à Particulier* led me to believe. Maybe Parisian agents' fees are exorbitant. Well, there's only one way to find out. I take in a big gulp of Paris' summer sky and push open the real estate office door. After all, you can't tell by looking at me that I've never done this before. Can you?

'Bonjour.'

There are four people in the open office. They look up at me and stare. They stare because, with one little hello, I've declared myself a foreigner. An immaculately dressed young man in his middle twenties responds softly, 'Bonjour, madame'.

They wait. They wait to see what sort of foreigner I am. Am I the sort who can speak the language or not? That's the problem with me. I look a lot more competent than I really am. I used to be an actress. It's an occupational hazard. There's no point worrying about that now. Insouciance — that's what's needed here. Insouciance and backbone. It's curious how those two don't sit that well together.

'Je cherche à acheter un ... (I'm stumbling already. I'm not sure if apartment is masculine or feminine, then I think I remember something called the double-vowel rule, so I stick with the masculine) ... un appartement à Paris'.

No one laughs. Instead, the young man, who I have now mapped as charming, stands and says, 'Oui, madame. Dans le quatrième?'

'Oui', I echo, 'dans le quatrième.' I detect the ever-so-slightest exchange of looks between him and his colleagues.

'Combien de mètres carrés, madame?'

I look at him blankly. The energy in the room intensifies. A brave voice inside my head urges — go on, go on.

'Um. Avec deux chambres.'

Eyes flash around the bureau. Monsieur pulls at his impeccable shirtsleeve and explains, in very, very, good English that 'apartments in Paris are sold by the square metre. They have one, two, or three pièces. If you want one pièce for a bedroom — that is for you to decide, madame.'

'Oh'.

He smiles at me. 'It is as you want.'

His smile is both sympathetic and contemptible. The rest of the bureau resumes work.

'Oh', I say again. 'I'm sorry I didn't know that. I'm Australian.'

'Ah. Australienne. Ah.'

The bureau lights up again. Everyone seems to be smiling now.

'Oui, je vois,' says the lovely young man. (He's back in my good books). 'Australienne. I see. Alors. Perhaps I do have an apartment I can show to you.'

'Now?' I ask. 'C'est possible ... to see the apartment now?' Forget insouciance. I'm suddenly heady with possibility. The endless possibility of tall French windows, of parquetry floors, of mirrors soaring above slender marble fireplaces. And views. Glorious vistas of sky and chimney pots and graceful statuary smiling benignly on Paris' privileged inhabitants. Living in Paris. Working in Paris. Perhaps I could work in an office just like this one. Perhaps ...

'Non,' says the young man. There is a loud movement of papers on desks. 'Non. Ce n'est pas possible maintenant.'

Maintenant. Now. Of course it's not possible now. Not right this minute. These things take ...

'C'est possible à seize heures.' He leans over his desk, and scribbles the time on a card and hands it to me. 'Seize heures,' he repeats. 'It is four in the afternoon.'

I spend the hours until seize heures trying to curb my excitement, wandering, imagining. I sit in cafés and peer up at beautiful, untouchable apartments where secret Parisian life takes place. 'That's me', I murmur as a waiter looks straight through me. I don't mind. I'm used to my lack of language rendering me invisible. C'est moi. Invisibility is exciting, too. It's exciting to sit in a café sipping coffee, aware that no one knows where you came from or what you came for.

'S'il vous plait, monsieur.' Everyone but the waiter looks in my direction. Why is it so hard to pay the bill in Paris? I consider leaving five euros on the table, even though my coffee cost half that, but only a tourist would leave such a tip. I'm not a tourist. I'm … well, it's hard to say exactly. Maybe I should spend the change on another coffee. Of course. That's brilliant. 'S'il vous plait, monsieur'. He looks up at me as I point into my empty cup. I lean across my tiny tabletop and feel success sparkling on my face.

The demonstrating actors are still snaking along the rue de Rivoli. There are voices on loud speakers booming down the street. There seems to be a bottleneck near the Palais Royale. Maybe they're going to storm the Comédie Française. I consider joining in, and then I consider getting arrested and missing my appointment at seize heures, and so I reconsider. The street is crowded. People everywhere are ducking and weaving. Cramming themselves through tiny people-pockets. Progressing steadily like snails. Strange, though, how they look pretty much the same as people walking down a busy street in Melbourne. But I ignore that. I always ignore anything that is contrary to my imagined Paris. I try to take my mind off it by practising my lip pursing, but two coffees are making my blood race. Seize heures still seems an eternity away. That's okay. Eternities are easy to imagine here.

'Hello. Hello.'

I stumble on a stretch of uneven footpath as a beggar outs me. Again.

'Hello,' he cries. 'Vous êtes Américaine.'

Close enough. (Why are the beggars of Paris so bloody observant?) I try to cast a look of polite French disdain. It doesn't work. Instead I blush and hurry past in case some other Parisian discovers me for the imposter I so clearly am. I turn a corner and take refuge in a small cobbled street. There's no need to panic. That won't happen to me again. Not when I have my own apartment. Not when I become a real Parisian. But where am I now? Rue des Blancs Manteaux. White Coats Street.

That's one of my favourites. Its secluded doorways and tiny shops are great for stealing in and out of. I walk for a while until my heart rate returns to normal, and again I'm face to face with a real estate agent's office. Agence immobilière. I roll the words around in my mouth. I get all the Es and Is mixed up. I stare at the small coloured photos of ancient Marais apartments. Two pièces, three pièces. 30 square metres, 75 square metres. Why haven't I noticed those measurements before? Très calme, très clair, cuisine Américaine, double séjour. Le balcon. At least I know what that is. Pierre. Pierre? Isn't that a boy's name? La poutre. They nearly all mention that. I whip my notebook from my bag and write it down. Whatever it is, it must be important. It always makes it to the top of the special-features list. I catch my reflection in the shop window. I look a bit disappointed. That can't be right. I've only just started. I'm probably just a bit nervous. I need to be more philosophical. I need to find a park, somewhere I can sit quietly and concentrate on my vocabulary.

I wander along to the Place des Vosges. I sit in the shade of the plane trees and gaze across at Victor Hugo's beautiful, quiet house. The exquisite symmetry of the square revives me. Multi-coloured tumbles of children play in the enormous sandpit. A small boy stands behind my seat, his hands covering his eyes, counting while others hide. Six, sept, huit, neuf. Numbers. At least France and Australia both use the metric system. I'm grateful for that.

I open my notebook and stare at the list of apartment words. Why does language take so long? I've had two years. I've nearly completed a course at the Alliance Française de Melbourne, bien sûr, and still I can't remember eighty or seventy. Quatre-vingt: four times twenty. Soixante-dix: sixty plus ten. I've watched the French news. I've listened to French songs. I've eaten too much Brie, doused myself in French perfume, downed too many Beaujolais, and still I struggle. I close my notebook and squeeze it between the palms of my hands. Why can't you learn a language by osmosis? I'm sure that's how I learnt English. A scream goes up from the sandpit. A woman leaps to her feet and grabs a small, dark-haired girl by the arm. She keeps hold of her as she remonstrates with her for throwing sand at her brother. She remonstrates in sonorous, lilting language. I smile. C'est la vie. See, I can't think of anything original in French.

Small white gravel clicks a happy song under my feet as I head towards the exit. I lift the latch and open the dog-proof gate. C'est la belle vie! This is the life! Did I say that? I almost skip through the passage that leads to rue Saint-Antoine. I didn't even know I knew that. C'est ma belle vie! C'est incroyable. There's another one. Just like that. Maybe I have a natural hidden talent for languages. I turn onto Place du Marché Sainte Catherine and order a Perrier. The waiter brings me a beer. I thank him profusely. A Perrier is a lot more expensive than une bière. There's no point dwelling on trivialities when you've got your eyes on the big picture. I flatten my notebook on the tabletop. Hmmm. Now what exactly is a square metre?

Time for two new entries:

1. Buy a tape measure.
2. Learn how to pronounce Perrier.

Three

Monsieur Real Estate Agent walks purposefully down the street. He seems taller out of the bureau. I have to run to keep up. He greets me warmly but briskly (a combination I can never manage), and carries on a monologue which I presume is about the apartment; but because the only word I really pick up is l'appartement, I can't testify to that. We turn into rue des Blancs Manteaux. Et voilà! The apartment is in this street? I don't believe it. Of all the streets. I try to share my enthusiasm with Monsieur, but I recognise his glazed smile. It's the same one I answer the French with when I have no idea what they're saying.

'Je vois,' he says.

I know he doesn't, but I make a mental note to memorise that. Je vois. I see. Now, that could come in handy. We continue along the street at a slower pace. Its familiarity encourages me. I decide to call Jack. After all, this is the first one, le premier. He ought to be here, too. I ask Monsieur for the street number. The sentence goes likes this: 'Le numéro, monsieur. Mon mari.' He looks at me and then, as understanding dawns, gives me the number. Thirteen. Number thirteen rue des Blancs Manteaux. Hmmm. I wasn't really expecting thirteen. I don't know why not. For all I know, thirteen might be lucky in French. Treize. Treize sounds nothing like thirteen. It's much more poetic and positive. Zs are always positive. It strikes me that numbers — not just square metres — but all kinds of numbers are going to play a crucial part in this endeavour. Street numbers, telephone numbers, the numbers for times, dates, and rendezvous. The list is endless. I shake my head and look up at Monsieur cheerfully.

'Désolée, monsieur, mais je suis complètement nulle avec les numéros.'

To my horror, a flirtatious grin pulls at my mouth because,

even though I have confessed to being hopeless at numbers, I'm secretly congratulating myself on my sentence construction. Self-congratulation always makes me flirtatious.

'Je ne vous crois pas', he says gallantly. Our eyes smile. Of course he doesn't believe me. He thinks I'm an accountant. I drop my eyes. What he's really wondering is why I'm tainting candor with sarcasm. Parisians always distract you from the big picture by making you look at the small.

I call Jack on his mobile but, after waiting for what seems like an eternity, a female voice tells me that the number I am calling has never been heard of in the whole history of telephone numbers and, judging by her tone, I gather that it never will be. I click the phone off and try the number again. It's getting hot. My mobile starts to perspire in my hand. I pull at my shirt; it's defenceless against Monsieur's unrelenting crispness. This time (even though I'm sure I've dialled the same number as before) the phone's mournful ring-tone sounds in my ear. Jack answers, and I tell him in a rushed and incoherent fashion that the apartment is just around the corner and perhaps he would like to come and see it, too. I continue to talk to the dead phone after he hangs up. I'm trying to buy some time, some composure — trying to think of how best to convey these new developments to Monsieur.

'Okay,' I say. 'Yes, that's fine. Okay. Five minutes.' I snap the phone closed.

'Cinq minutes,' I say with a dramatic nod of my head, as if world peace starts then. 'Mon mari dans cinq minutes.'

Monsieur turns and looks at me. For the first time he actually looks at me. His eyes smile as he nods. He continues to look at me. The warm wind turns into a sauterne-sweet breeze. Of course I can do this. This is not difficult. Just be yourself. That's what everyone says. That's the key to everything. Just as well there is Monsieur and a breeze and the task at hand to divert me from continuing in this vein. The problem is, the 'be yourself' idea has never really worked for me. I generally pretend to be some other, better person. I'm quite good at that. Only, at this moment, no one really springs to mind.

'Cinq minutes,' I say again. Monsieur nods, and we consult our watches in quiet unison.

Jack assails us further along the street, looking fresh and infuriatingly French. Monsieur greets him with a smile and a handshake as Jack regales Monsieur with some badly accented pleasantries. Now it's *on y va* and we're off again, marching up the street in single file. I thought the French were supposed to saunter.

The apartment is at the top end of the street close to the corner of rue du Temple. This end has suffered neglect, and is currently undergoing a face-lift. There is scaffolding and noisy jackhammers, and the crash of bricks and mortar escaping to the ground through dusty plastic tunnels that curve from the top of the building to the footpath below. Monsieur throws his head in the direction of the building works.

'Très bien pour le quartier,' he says.

Jack and I nod and raise our eyebrows at each other. No matter how much inconvenience is afforded by the noise and detritus of progress, what's good for the quartier is fine by the Parisians. They don't see dust, noise, and debris. They see progress. Improvement. A brighter future. It's that sort of determined optimism that keeps you looking crisp.

Monsieur points across the street to another faded apartment-building. It sits next to an enormous open door which leads to a rambling, faded courtyard. This courtyard is home to two cars, numerous bicycles, and lots of mismatched pot plants. Sturdy iron stairs run along the building's exterior. This apartment is nothing like the one that's inside my head. That apartment has a hidden courtyard and an internal staircase. C'est la vie. I'm happy to compromise. I follow Monsieur up the stairs to the second floor. I overhear him telling Jack that all the car spaces are taken, but there's plenty of room for our bicycles.

'Bon,' says Jack in a loud voice, even though he's terrified of bicycles.

Monsieur looks happy at this. 'Follow me,' he says enthusiastically.

'Suivez-moi,' says Jack.

Jack loves translating what the French have said in English back into French. And, inexplicably, the French love it, too. Monsieur laughs as he wrestles a key into a peeling white door at the end of the landing. The door gives in easily.

'Et voilà,' says Monsieur, moving aside to let us enter.

We step over the threshold and peer through the dust.

The apartment, our very first apartment, is big, dark, hot, and derelict. There is a long corridor that divides it in two. Down one side runs (in this order) the toilet, bathroom, kitchen, and a nice-sized room that could be used for a bedroom. Monsieur throws open door after door, clearly relishing the opportunity to show off so much Parisian apartment space. Down the opposite side of the corridor, on the street frontage, there are two large living rooms. A double salon. So that makes the apartment ... trois pièces? Quatre pièces?

'C'est un quatre pièces,' says Monsieur.

Thank God I wasn't trying for inscrutable. I nod and translate needlessly, 'Four rooms.'

'Mais,' says Monsieur authoritatively, 'si vous …' and he bashes his flat hand against an adjoining wall. Bits of plaster and slivers of chipped paint leap up and rush to escape through the window he has opened. 'Si vous …' he hits the wall again, 'trois pièces.'

'I suppose that's the good thing about buying an apartment in this condition,' Jack says. 'You can do anything you like to it. Knock a wall out here or there.'

'Oui. It's as you wish,' says Monsieur. He leaves the wall, and flings open another window and gestures outside. His personality matches his clothes in that they are both impervious to the loud, dusty surroundings they find themselves in. He turns back to us and makes a grand gesture with his arm.

'Allez,' he says.

We sidle out into the corridor. We stand there, held in the gloom, not sure which room to venture into. This is not what I expected. It's not what we expected. I steal a look at Jack. I hope that this first experience will not dampen his spirits. I try to look enthusiastic. 'It's in a great spot,' I say.

'Yes,' he says slowly.

'And the rooms are … (I struggle for the right description) in good condition.'

'Yes.'

'And it gives us a good idea.'

'Of what?'

'Of size.'

'C'mon. Neither of us have a clue how many square metres this place is.'

That's true. My enthusiastic look is wearing my face out. I step back into the crumbling salon. 'Excusez-moi, monsieur, mais combien de mètres?'

'Soixante-cinq. Soixante-quinze.'

Damn! It would have to be one of those soixantes. I mumble

the numbers in my head as I return to find Jack in the kitchen.

'It's either sixty-five or seventy-five.'

The measurement means nothing to us. We stand together in silence. We are not thinking about measurements. We are thinking about this kitchen, and how pretty it would be with freshly painted cupboards and curtains on the window and an aromatic coq au vin cooking slowly in the oven. We are also thinking how futile this is. We can't renovate. We don't live here. We barely speak the language. We don't know what's going on. A car reverses out of the courtyard to a flurry of amiable farewells.

'It would be nice, though, wouldn't it?'

'Of course it would,' says Jack. 'And it's probably a pretty good buy at three hundred and fifty thousand, but you know we can't manage a start-from-scratch job.'

We stare out at the courtyard. Deep-red geraniums stare back at us. I make a mental note to add them to my wish-list.

We rejoin Monsieur in the front room. His pursed lips and nodding head rob us of the need to speak.

'Malheureusement …'

'Oui, oui, je vois,' says Monsieur with an accompanying open hand gesture that seems to symbolise opportunity lost.

'C'est grand,' I manage.

'Oui, c'est très grand,' agrees Monsieur.

'Oui et …' I struggle to squeeze out another adjective.

'Clair,' suggests Monsieur.

'Oui et très clair.'

Monsieur nods reassuringly. Of course, it isn't clear or light. The windows shake in time to jackhammers, and scaffold casts strange shadows on the walls, but Monsieur appreciates my attempt at a positive appraisal.

'Pas de poutres,' I add, emboldened by his encouragement.

'Des poutres?' Monsieur looks at me surprised and then lifts his head to the ceiling. 'Non. Pas de poutres.' He shakes his head, repeating the words under his breath as he heads towards the front door. Jack and I follow.

'What did you say?' whispers Jack as we sweep down the corridor.

'No beams. I think I said there are no beams.'

'Well, he doesn't seem too impressed.'

'No. I think I've offended the building.'

Out on the street, Jack escapes the scene (ostensibly in search of a newspaper), leaving me to walk back to the bureau with Monsieur.

'Je suis désolée, monsieur.'

I seem to have nailed the language of disappointment. Excusez-moi, monsieur. Malheureusement, monsieur. Monsieur looks down at me with … what? Disdain?

'C'est normal, madame.'

Why did he say that? What's normal? He's still looking at me, expecting some response. I smile. I'm starting to hate smiling. Every inane I-don't-have-the-vaguest-idea-what-you-mean-or-what-you're-talking-about smile carves an indelible mark around my lips. With each pretence, these etch themselves deeper into my face.

'Oui,' he says again, 'C'est beaucoup de travail.'

Travail? Ah. Work.

'Oui,' I say with loud relief. I want to say, 'Yes, it is,' but I don't even know how to say 'it is' in this context. 'Très travail,' I say instead. Very work? But Monsieur doesn't seem to notice that most of what I say makes little sense. He nods his agreement and quickens his pace. I run along beside him, grateful that I chose flat shoes. He doesn't mention the apartment again. Instead he launches into a monologue that I think is something like his life story. It's something about how he's not really a real estate agent. Well, he is now, but not for long or he hasn't been for long.

I have no way of discerning any of the nuances. I do manage to glean that he used to work for Air France, but something happened and something else happened and then something even bigger happened after that. I'm supposed to know what this something is, because he cries, 'Vous connaissez, vous connaissez' and waits for my response. Do I know? No, I don't. Still I nod and frown and hope that this comes across as thoughtful and add, 'Oui, je vois.' He seems happy with that. He continues on at a purposeful pace. I continue my facial gymnastics, even attempting a lip purse as his monologue continues. Then I allow myself a smile. It occurs to me that I have passed another milestone in my pursuit of the French language. Both my ability to comprehend what is being said and my ability to fake comprehension have improved expeditiously.

Monsieur holds the door open for me as we step inside his bureau. No one looks up as we enter. He offers me a seat, and when I fail to take it he returns to my side of the desk and holds the chair out for me. A phone rings. The woman at the neighbouring desk answers it and speaks animatedly into the receiver. Monsieur throws a manilla folder onto his desk, opens it, and peers inside. Just as quickly he snaps the folder closed, places both his hands on its cover, as though trying to stop something from escaping its interior, and says, 'C'est tout, madame. Si j'ai quelque chose, je vous appelle.' He claps his hands together and stands.

I try to keep up. The woman on the telephone is conversing in an inexhaustible series of 'oui's. These range from short and sharp to slow, elongated ones that take three or four seconds to finish.

So Monsieur will call me? He hasn't actually asked for my name or telephone number and here I am again, dwelling on trivialities. Madame on the telephone lets out a series of oui, oui, ouis, followed by a surprised intake of breath. Wee, wee, wee, all the way home. I shake my head. I must concentrate. But Paris is full of so many delightful distractions.

'Ça va?' Monsieur is holding me in his gaze with a tired, patient look.

'Désolée,' I begin, but Monsieur raises a hand against my apology. 'Oui, ça va,' I say instead.

'Très bien.'

Everyone in the bureau looks up and smiles. Nothing too dramatic. A bureau full of lip smiles. No teeth.

'Au revoir, madame.'

'Au revoir, monsieur.'

'Bonne journée.'

'Bonne journée à vous.'

Goodbye, madam; goodbye, sir; good day, madam; and good day to you. It's all so cordial. I could go on making exchanges like this forever. Everyone in the bureau is looking and smiling at me. Clearly they are impressed. Buoyed by a rush of confidence, I curb a wayward urge to blow them a goodbye kiss. Even waving in this context would be a grave breach of protocol. Instead I sashay towards the door and say, 'À très bientôt.'

Monsieur's face clouds a little. The eyes in the bureau move from me to him. Madame on the telephone holds her hand against the receiver so that she is nearly inaudible. I flash them a big Australian smile. Don't worry, I'm not about to 'see you soon'. Paris is full of agences immobilières. I'll practise on someone else tomorrow.

I skip all the way back to our apartment. I fly through the front door, but the apartment is empty. C'est la vie. I make my way to the fridge and pour myself a glass of wine. A toast: to our first apartment, to day one, to Mondays. I stand at the kitchen window, watching rue Vieille du Temple bustling below me. How beautiful Paris bustle is. And today I stepped — *bof* — right into the very heart of it.

Four

Jack is sitting at a pretty café on rue François Miron. He waves as I round the corner. He looks relaxed and content in the warm morning sun. Our son Ellery sits next to him, covering himself and the table in pain au chocolat.

'Bonjour, ma chérie,' says Jack, folding his copy of *Paris Turf* in half and turning to grin at me. 'How was your walk?'

'Great. I found the most brilliant stationery shop.'

'I thought you were supposed to be looking for real estate agents.'

'That's easy. They're everywhere.'

'That's true,' says Jack. 'There's another one across the street.'

I steal a piece of Ellery's pain au chocolate and squint in the direction of Jack's outstretched arm.

'Agence de Saint-Paul. They've got one that looks promising.'

'In Saint-Paul? Can we afford Saint-Paul?' A small sliver of chocolate slips down my throat. I love eating chocolate for breakfast.

'It's not in Saint-Paul. They've got an apartment in our street.'

'Our street?'

'Rue Vieille du Temple.'

I leap up and cross the street. A neat white blind covers the door and tells me that the office is closed. Damn.

The agency window is dressed with eight or ten beautiful clear photos of beautiful apartment interiors. One of the photos is of a large living room with big French windows awash with glorious, flowing white curtains. The words 'In the heart of the Marais, rue Vieille du Temple' are typed underneath the photo. I stand and marvel. Bâtiment unique. Trois pièces, grande cuisine, deux salles de bains. I feel my heart start to quicken. It looks perfect. Trois pièces. That's room enough to make two bedrooms. Two bathrooms, too. Big kitchen. No price mentioned. It probably costs a fortune. Très calme, très clair, bon état général. I fossick in my bag for my dictionary. État: state. Generally in good condition. I wonder how accurate the descriptions are. Jack and Ellery join me, and together we stand and peer at the photograph.

'Which one is our apartment, Mummy?'

'None yet. We're just looking.'

'But I thought you said we were going to buy one.'

'Well, we are, but it's not as simple as that. It takes a long time.'

'How long?'

'I'm not sure.'

That's nearly a blatant lie. Although I don't know how long it takes, I do know exactly how long we have — two weeks. That's it. I don't dwell on this small detail. In fact, I try not to think about it at all. Instead I point at the photograph.

'It's this one here.'

Ellery balances on one leg and looks up at it.

'Do they let you buy the photo, too?'

'Probably.'

'Looks pretty good, doesn't it?' says Jack.

'It looks pretty expensive. How much do you think it is?'

'Wouldn't have a clue. We'll come back later and find out.'

'You're going to come with me?' I turn to look at him.

'If we can get Julia to look after Ellery, I might as well come.'

Well, this is contrary to the plan — the one where I do all the ground-work — in Jack's frenzied time-frame. It seems that the possibility of owning a little bit of the Marais is bewitching him, too.

I take his hand. 'It's exciting, isn't it?'

'Hmmm,' he says smiling at me, wary of conceding too much, too soon. 'Paying for it's going to be even more exciting.'

We laugh at ourselves standing here, together, in Paris. The sun is bright in the sky. Everything glows. The street, the real estate window, and us — we're glowing, too. It's an omen. There's something about this one. It's a world away from yesterday's apartment. Is it possible to find the perfect apartment in only two days? Of course it is. Magical transformation is an everyday occurrence in Paris. You only have to look at a hand-cut square of chocolate or inhale the scent of a single pale rose to know that.

'C'mon,' I say. 'There's a park near here that has ping pong tables.'

'Ping-pong tables,' cries Ellery. 'For everyone?'

'Yep.'

He takes my hand and smiles up at me. 'I love it here, Mum,' he says softly.

'So do I, darling. So do I.'

The afternoon is gloriously sunny. I stand looking at myself in the mirror. I'm caught in the grip of another what-to-wear panic. Maybe white. Something to make me look calm and confident.

'Do I look alright?' I step out of the bedroom at attention.

'Fine. You look fine.'

'That's not very good.'

'Darling, they're not going to worry what you look like.'

Why do men always say that? Of course they do.

Julia breezes in around noon, and dumps her impossibly big bag on the kitchen table.

'You look great, Elle, but didn't you tell me the apartment you're going to see is all white? You might disappear.' She throws open the door to the fridge. 'Any Gini?'

'I think there's one there. Late night?'

'Seriously late. We had a gig at that place on the rue de la Roquette. We played for three hours. It was cool, though.' She opens the soft drink and perches on the kitchen bench. 'I wish there was a beach in Paris. It's such a St. Kilda day.'

'It's twelve degrees in Melbourne, Jules. I think you'd better settle for the pond at the Jardin du Luxembourg.'

She throws me one of her lip-quivering smiles and yells across the apartment for Ellery.

'I think I'll try and speak in English,' I say to Jack as we head out into the hot afternoon sun. 'Just until I get the feel of things.'

'Don't worry so much,' says Jack, 'You're trying to *buy* an apartment. It doesn't matter how much of the language you speak; they're still going to be keen to sell you one.'

'Hmmm.' That sounds okay in theory, but in practice I'm not convinced. I've visited Paris enough times to know that my right to purchase a Camembert will be jeopardised if I seem unable to consume it properly.

The real estate agent is a woman. She is alone, sitting at the only desk, writing with a fountain pen. She looks up slowly and watches me enter her office.

'Bonjour, madame.'

'Bonjour, madame.'

Madame is in her early forties. She wears a light grey suit with a soft white shirt underneath. She sits in her hot, unairconditioned office with her jacket on. Her shoes are perfect, black sling-backs with a small bow on each side and tapered, pointy toes. She has matching black hair which is neat and flat and bounces to just a hint of a bow at either side of her cheeks. Her fingernails are perfectly manicured and unvarnished. She smiles at me efficiently and half raises an eyebrow. It's my turn. I take a deep breath.

'L'appartement dans la fenêtre.' I turn towards the window and wave my arm around in an uncommitted sort of way. I thought I was going to speak in English — what am I saying?

'La fenêtre?' she says, puzzled.

As I turn back towards her I can already feel the blush beginning to seep out from under my protective white clothing.

'Oui.' Wrong pronunciation? Wrong gender? Window was one of the first words I learnt. I remember it clearly. The names of things in a room: la table, le placard, la fenêtre. Nouns. I love nouns. You know where you are with them. They're not mercurial like verbs. I pride myself on being good at nouns. This memory encourages me to have another stab at it.

'Ici la fenêtre.'

'Here the window ...' is not a brilliant sentence. But I'm hoping it will do the trick. Madame manages not to smile by biting her bottom lip.

'You speak English?' she asks. I nod. 'Oh, you're American,' she says confidently.

'No, I'm Australian.' Madame looks just the tiniest bit disappointed, but masks this by rising from her desk and moving towards the window.

'The window,' she says. 'In French, this window is not a window. She is not la fenêtre; she is la vitrine, the shop window.'

'Oh,' I say and then repeat 'shop window' because I can't think of anything else to say.

'Oui,' she says, warming to her subject. 'You would say "l'appartement affiché dans la vitrine".'

Captive in her bureau, I have no choice but to participate. 'La vitrine,' I say.

'Très bien. Par exemple, she is "la vitrine de l'agence immmobilière" ou "la vitrine du boucher". Boucher, he is a shop for meat.'

'I know. It's very close to English.'

Madame raises two eyebrows this time, as though this information is highly doubtful. I decide not to continue along this track. I could point out that the two words have only one different letter and that they're pronounced in much the same way. I could also point out that a butcher's shop is not he — it is it. But that seems a bit impolite and complicated. I'm not here for a language lesson. Madame remains standing next to me. She meets none of my real estate agent expectations. She is calm and sanguine, and seems to have very little interest in the apartments advertised in her vitrine.

'I'm interested in the apartment in the … the one in rue Vieille du Temple.'

'Rue Vieille du Temple.'

Her eyebrows knit together. 'Rue Vieille du Temple, she is not in Saint-Paul.'

'Oh, I know where it is,' I say enthusiastically.

She looks puzzled at my response.

'I'm staying in an apartment in the same street.'

Madame regards me a little more closely. She moves back towards her desk and gestures me to the chair in front of it.

'Sit down, please,' she says. 'You want to buy an apartment in Paris?'

Finally. 'Yes. Oui. I want to buy an apartment in Paris.'

'Why?'

Why? Why is she asking me why? She leans across her desk expectantly, as though I am going to deliver a lecture on the secret relationship between women and real estate.

'Well, because I love Paris and we spend quite a bit of time here and …'

'Everybody loves Paris.' She throws her hands in the air. 'Everybody.'

Clearly this is not a reason in Madame's eyes. She sizes me up as someone incapable of explaining herself in any language, then she lowers her hands, leans across the desk, and whispers conspiratorially, 'But does Paris love you?'

She waits. I can see this is not rhetorical. I fidget around on the desk.

'I don't know,' I murmur, but she has fixed me with a gaze that makes me want to confide in her. It makes me want to tell her the real story — all the details of my unrequited love affair with Paris.

'No,' I say eventually. 'I don't think she even knows I'm here.'

'Of course not. Paris loves no one but Paris.'

What? That's a bit harsh. Now I'm blushing again, because you can't say 'fair go' to someone as perfectly Parisian as Madame. Her relationship with Paris is established. She can afford to be dismissive. Her eyes flash at me. A faded dimple holds her smile in check. I give up.

'I just want to be here,' I say at last. 'It's as simple as that.'

'Simplicity is always the hardest,' she says.

I nod, exhausted at our exchange. What am I doing? I'm in a real estate agent's office. It shouldn't be this hard. My back is aching from perching on the edge of my chair. I feel as though I have been in here for hours. I steal a look at my watch.

'It is half after thirteen,' says Madame. She rises and moves to the window and retrieves the photograph of the apartment. She places it on the desk in front of me. 'It's a very nice apartment and not too expensive.'

'It looks very nice.'

'Saint-Paul, is of course, better, but this is a nice one, too.'

'How many square metres?' I ask. She looks up, impressed. 'It is very big. Seventy-five square metres with two bathrooms.'

'And three salons.'

Madame smiles. 'You want three salons?'

'We have a young son. We need two bedrooms.'

'Quel âge a-t-il?'

I hesitate. I'm unprepared for the switch into French. 'Il a six ans,' I say finally.

'Six ans. C'est un âge très mignon.'

'Oui.'

'I have a — what do you call them — nephew who has six years.'

'Ah.' Now it's my turn to 'très mignon.' Buoyed by this micro conversation, I decide that perhaps a language lesson is, after all, what I'm here for. I ask questions about la cuisine, les salles de bains, l'etat — anything I can think of. I imitate Madame's eyebrow gymnastics. I steal her words to finish my sentences. We start to speak the same language.

'Oui, oui, oui. Trois pièces. C'est parfait pour vous.'

She seems certain of that. 'Parfait,' I repeat. I would like to say something a little more sophisticated like, 'Well, we'll see after we have seen it' or 'Well, it might sound perfect, but let's not jump to any conclusions'. But 'parfait' seems more appropriate, given the circumstances.

'You want to see it this afternoon?'

'This afternoon?'

'Yes. The owner is in Paris at the moment. Of course, I will have to call her, but I think perhaps you can see it today.'

'Oh! That would be wonderful.'

'You are very enthusiastic.'

I counter-claim with a grimace. I must stop being so enthusiastic. I'm never going to get anywhere with that attitude.

'You want to bring your husband? And your son, of course.'

'I'll bring my husband. My son is at a ... friend's.'

'You have friends in Paris?'

'Yes.' I'm not sure that this is the right answer. Madame twirls her fountain pen around her fingers and looks at me. 'Just a couple. Mostly Australians.'

'Très bien.' She takes up the photo and taps at a new manila folder. 'We will open a dossier.' She stills her fountain pen. Is it my imagination, or has she become just a little more business-like? I suppose she has other work to do. After all, I've already been in here for at least twenty minutes and I've yet to give her my name.

'Name?' She holds her pen poised over a clean, stiff sheet of buff paper.

She's going to handwrite? I look around the office. It's the first time I notice the lack of a computer.

'J'ai. I have ...' I fumble around in my bag and produce a small white printed card with my details on it. 'Et voilà,' I say, handing it to her.

She peers at it. 'Nielsen,' she says. 'It's Scandinavian, no?'

'Yes,' I say, pleased with my foresight. These cards save me from pronouncing all those impossible i's and e's.

'You are Australian and Scandinavian?' She looks at me accusingly.

'Well, yes, sort of. Not really. Everyone in Australia comes from somewhere else.'

Madame looks at me disbelievingly. 'That must be very confusing,' she says.

'No. Not really. We're all used to it. In fact, that's one of the best things about Australia. People from all over the world live there.'

'And they all speak English?'

'More or less,' I say. She begins to copy my details onto the sheet of paper. 'You can keep the card.' She doesn't seem to hear me. A funny story pops into my head. 'Once,' I say, 'I had an English professor' — she looks up at me — 'when I was at university, and we were talking about which language would become the world's language. Everyone thought it would be English, of course.' Madame looks at me intently. 'But my professor said that that was only half right. He said that the world's language would instead be very *bad* English.' I beam across the desk. 'And, to some extent, I think he might be right.' I burst into laughter. Madame looks back at me, horrified.

I run across the road to the café and bounce into the chair next to Jack.

'I've done it,' I yell. The other coffee drinkers wince at my volume.

'I should hope so. You've been gone long enough to buy ten apartments. Monsieur probably thinks I'm going to put in a bid on this place.'

'You're allowed to sit at a café all day in Paris if you want to.'

'Well, I don't want to,' Jack says. 'What happened?'

'The apartment sounds perfect. We're going to see it at seize heures.'

'How much is it?'

'Pardon?'

'You heard me.'

I fiddle with the drink coaster. 'I forgot to ask.'

'I don't believe it,' Jack says, sighing into his empty cup.

'I'm sorry. The question did pop into my head several times, but the whole thing was very complicated.'

The waiter balances at the edge of our table, a hurried 'Madame' escaping from his closed lips. I order 'un café,' and he disappears without looking at me. Jack's looking at me, though. I decide to give a précis of the complications.

'The apartment's vacant. But the owner, who has left Paris, is back today. Apparently you can't look at an apartment without the owner being present.'

'Sounds a bit strange.'

'What does?'

'Well, that the owner happens to be in Paris, the place being vacant. How long has it been on the market?'

'I don't know. Madame said she thought it would sell very quickly.'

'Without even telling you the price.'

The waiter brings my coffee. I'm grateful for its diverting aroma.

Five

We rendezvous outside our apartment at four o'clock precisely. Madame, whose name I now know to be Véronique, greets us warmly and directs us away from the rue de Rivoli in the direction of the 3rd arrondissement. We walk for about ten minutes. The apartment is further away than I imagined. Then again, you can cover a lot of ground walking around Paris for ten minutes. We stop fleetingly outside the Hôtel de Sully.

'This,' says Véronique proudly, 'is the Musée Picasso. You have been here?'

'Oh, yes,' we chorus.

'Très bien,' she says.

We pass a Moroccan restaurant with low-hanging coloured lights and soft sofas around the tables. I take a quick note of the name.

'Beaucoup de restaurants,' says Véronique. Clearly she has eyes in the back of her head.

We walk a few more blocks. It's much quieter up this end of the street. It's more residential. Fewer tourists. Fewer cars. I try to imagine us living here. I look around for a métro station and a boulangerie and a quaint café. I find a drycleaners, a small hardware store, and a furniture shop. Well, once we've bought an apartment we won't be swanning around cafés all day anyway. That's when we'll really have work to do. Véronique comes to a sudden halt and points at a large building that floats impressively at the intersection of three converging streets.

'Voilà.'

We stand silenced by this grand example of Haussmannian architecture. The triangular-shaped building sits in the middle of the intersecting streets. It looks like a huge ship at the confluence of several seas. Véronique allows us to stand and be amazed. Jack leans into my ear and whispers, 'That's not a building; it's a wedge'. I pretend not to hear him. Instead I move to congratulate Véronique on leading us to this magical place, but she has turned away to greet a slight, fair woman who slowly walks towards us. The women exchange kisses and small pleasantries. 'This is Madame Martin,' says Véronique.

Bonjours from everyone. I even manage an 'enchanté'. Why not? Enchanted — that's how I'm feeling. Madame Martin spins around to face me. 'You speak French?' she asks abruptly. I pause.

'No. Not really. I'm just learning.'

Madame Martin's eyes find Véronique. Surely she can't tell just by looking at me that I'm murdering her language.

'On y va,' says Jack, coming to my rescue. Bemused looks all round, and then we're off across the street.

We come to a halt at a giant, carved oak door. An enormous key is produced, which turns perfectly in the equally enormous lock. The door opens onto a well-preserved parquetry entrance hall. A sensual, curved staircase leads up to the light — up to the sky perhaps. Véronique breaks our awed silence with a solemn 'très beau'. Oh yes. It's definitely très, très beau. We climb the stairs. There's no lift. That doesn't matter. You don't need a lift for the third floor. Just think how fit we'll get.

At the top of the third-floor stairs we assemble in front of an imposing wooden door. Et voilà! This is the apartment. It occupies the entire floor. Madame Martin turns two keys in different barrels several times before the door springs open. We step gingerly through it. It looks like one of those doors they have in apartments in New York. Not the real New York — the New York you see on television. Those doors that are really thick with heaps of different kinds of locks and steel bolts and chains.

'Très blindée,' says Véronique when she sees me staring at it. 'Très, très blindée.'

Obviously, that's secure or reinforced. Reinforced? It's an armoured door. And what's wrong with that? Why wouldn't you have an armoured door at the top of a sweeping stone staircase and honey parquetry?

Inside the room I forget all about the door. Now I can only see windows and curves. Tall, elegant windows dressed in swathes of white, billowing material dominate the bright, oval-shaped room. Véronique notes our surprise, and swings a satisfied arm into the air to guide us through the main features: the marble fireplace, the soaring ceiling, the herring-bone parquetry floor. It's all très original. Très charmant. Jack wants to know if the chimney works. Véronique drops her arm. She explains that it is summer. Madame Martin nods, either in answer or agreement — it's difficult to say. She says something else about flowers and then takes her leave.

The kitchen is in need of work. But, despite the chipped, dirt-brown tiles, the broken latches, the ageing Laminex, and dozens of impossible-to-reach cupboards, it's a big room with two long, beautiful windows.

'Paint,' says Véronique cheerfully. 'She can be completely transformed with paint.'

I turn my back on the ancient stove and its towering chimney flue, and try to imagine white walls and billowing curtains and croissants and coffee for breakfast. 'It looks like it needs a lot more than paint,' says Jack. 'It's pretty run-down.'

Véronique smiles and leans into me. 'Men, always thinking of the franc and now the euro,' she turns, and addresses the stove. 'Always thinking of the money.'

'Someone has to,' says Jack, only half under his breath. 'And while we're on the subject — what is the asking price?'

There is a small fluttering silence. I move over to one of the windows and peer out. The traffic below crawls around the building silently. The double-glazing blocks out all the noise. The quiet conversation between Jack and Véronique about the price keeps me pinned and staring at the street below. I'm always uncomfortable talking about money. Perhaps it's a legacy of growing up without any. Perhaps it's guilt at now having some. The kitchen window faces another. A man wearing nothing but a large pair of white shorts vacuums his living-room. He moves about briskly, vacuum hose in one hand, cigarette in the other. If he notices me staring at him he doesn't acknowledge it. I look up past the vacuuming man to the ceiling above my windows. There are no blinds or curtains.

The room is very open. For all its beauty, it would be hard to live a secret Parisian life in an apartment like this, with windows everywhere and the world outside always inside. Jack is saying, 'I just want to be clear. Is the apartment four hundred and twenty thousand euros or four hundred and ten thousand?'

'Now it is four hundred and ten thousand,' says Véronique. 'It is a very good price. You will see.'

The bathroom is a surprise. It's spacious, modern, and newly refurbished, and houses a deep, luxurious-looking bath. Jack and I exchange a smile. This is more like it. Now we're back on track. Véronique notes our approval.

'It is new. You see from the bathroom what you can do with the kitchen.'

She has a point. Yes. Now I can see it. A sparkling new kitchen. Something with all those beautiful, work-of-art appliances the Europeans are so good at.

'Oh, yes,' I say, always a willing victim of an active imagination. 'I see what you mean.'

'Is plumbing very expensive in Paris?' asks Jack.

'Of course,' answers Véronique, throwing Jack a glimmer of an impatient look. 'Plumbing is expensive everywhere.'

The main bedroom is large, too, but it's made small by the biggest, blackest, ugliest built-in wardrobe I've ever seen. I suppose it's difficult to place furniture in a round room with no wall space and only windows. I try to imagine the apartment with beds, tables, sofas, a television. It's not easy. I suppose that's why the French have so many brilliant decorating solutions. French flair. I wonder if it's genetic. We move back into the salon and cross to the second bedroom.

'The bedroom for your son,' announces Véronique.

Sadly, it is also dominated by another gigantic black wardrobe. It's exactly the sort that would scare any six-year-old half to death.

'A perfect room for a child,' declares Véronique, gesturing around the room, around the wardrobe. Maybe it is best to overlook the wardrobe. Wardrobes can be got rid of. Although how exactly you would get either of these monsters down the stairs is a mystery. Véronique talks us through the opulence of a second bedroom of a second bathroom, too, bien sûr. We nod and concur. Très biens fall from our lips. So even though the second bathroom is really a tiny shower poked inside a small cupboard, we acknowledge it as the luxurious feature it is meant to be.

We're back at the New York door. Véronique is smiling at us indulgently.

'Have another look. I will wait here. We have five minutes before we meet Madame Martin.'

Five minutes? We've only been here seven at the most.

We retreat to the kitchen.

'Well, what do you think?' I whisper. We stand, inevitably, in front of one of the windows.

'Well,' Jack says, 'it's nice.'

'It is, isn't it?' Of course it is. What am I thinking? Be positive, insouciant. 'It's lovely.'

'Well, I wouldn't go that far. But the building is nice, and there's plenty of room and lots of light.'

'And heaps of potential.'

'Don't get carried away,' warns Jack. 'It needs a lot of work.'

Hmmm. Perhaps it's a mistake to stand discussing the apartment's good points in the worst room in the house.

'But, on the other hand,' Jack continues, 'Véronique is right. Paint would work wonders.'

'Yes, it's amazing what paint can do'. I feel as though I'm endorsing a product for a television commercial. There's something unreal, even surreal, about this whole experience. I mean, is this all it takes? You pop in, have a quick tour, and then put your hand up to buy? Just like that? I suppose the realities of a dream are never equal to the dream itself. The vacuuming man is looking at me. I move towards the stove.

'What's the matter?'

'There's a man there. Leaning out of that window across the street. Don't look,' I whisper. 'He might see you.'

Jack laughs. 'Of course he's going to see me. He's standing a couple of metres away. He looks harmless enough.'

'I didn't say he was dangerous. I just don't like him staring at us.'

'He's not staring at us. He's talking on his mobile phone.'

'Don't be ridiculous. You know what I mean.'

'I know our five minutes is ticking away. We'd better have a quick last look.'

I'm happy to leave the kitchen. We tiptoe across the salon back to the main bedroom. I steal a glance at Véronique but she, too, is talking on her mobile phone and doesn't seem to notice us.

'That cupboard is dreadful,' says Jack.

'Shhh.'

'Well, it is. How anyone in their right mind …'

'Maybe it's because there isn't a bed.'

'What's that got to do with it?'

'I don't know. I'm just trying to …'

'Darling, if you don't like the place, I'll tell Madame and we'll go.'

'Nooo,' I say, horrified. Véronique must have heard me. We stand frozen in the small silence that follows. The dull rise and fall of her phone conversation reassures me. 'It's not that I don't like it. I do.'

'Then why are you grimacing?'

'I'm not grimacing. It's just that there's something odd about it. Maybe it's the front door.'

'What's the matter with the front door?'

'Didn't you see it? It's got hundreds of locks and it's about a metre thick.'

Jack laughs. 'All the doors in Paris are like that. The French are very security conscious. So what do we tell her? Thanks but no thanks?'

'That's a bit hasty.'

Jack raises an eyebrow at me.

'I just need to think about it somewhere else. Somewhere squarer.'

'Okay. I'll tell her we like it, and organise a time for a second look.'

'Are you sure?'

'No harm in that. We're not buying the place today. It's only the second one we've seen.'

'That doesn't mean we can't buy it.'

'No. I'm not saying that. But, for now, I think we'll tell Véronique that we're interested, and then take it from there.'

'Oh, my God. It's so exciting.'

'Hold on,' says Jack. 'I thought you said …' He looks at me and shakes his head. 'Anyway, even if we think it's the best apartment in Paris we still have to find out about stamp duty, rates, agent's commission.'

Véronique coughs lightly. We take this as our cue to come out of hiding. Too late. She already stands in the doorway.

'You are ready to leave?' she asks pleasantly.

We return to the salon without protest. Our five minutes is up. We've probably gone over time. We stand awkwardly, not meeting Véronique's gaze. She doesn't seem to notice.

'So, you want to make me an offer?'

We stare at her disbelievingly. What? Right now? She can't be serious. She must know we need time to discuss it. Time to tease apart all the pros and cons, to do the sums. Like you would in Melbourne. Only, we're not in Melbourne. There are no 'open for inspection' signs. There is no freedom to inspect without a real estate agent in toe; no opportunity to return to the property again and again. Well, of course, every country — every city sells their buildings differently — but je crois pas. No one in their right mind would just up and spend nearly three-quarters of a million dollars (even Australian dollars) on something they had seen for just five minutes. I regard Véronique sceptically. Is she playing us for fools? She looks at us optimistically, but there's also a hint of challenge in her eyes. Is that what makes her look so fabulously French?

'No,' says Jack finally. 'There are a few questions I would like to ask first.'

'Of course.' Her challenging eyes lock us in her gaze. 'What do you want to know?'

'The cost of stamp duty and the rates.'

'The rates? For the municipalité? They are not very expensive. A few hundred euros. And the other?'

'Stamp duty,' repeats Jack.

'If it is the tax, it is 10 per cent.'

'Of the purchase price? The tax is 10 per cent of the purchase price?'

'That is right. You find a notaire. You know what is a notaire?'

'I suppose it's a notary.'

'Yes,' says Véronique. 'He will work out the price of the tax. Do you have a notaire?'

'No. Not yet.'

'It's not a problem. I can get a good one for you.'

It's all sounding pretty neat so far.

'And the agent's commission,' asks Jack, 'it's included in the purchase price?'

'Correct,' says Véronique, as deftly as a quizmaster. 'It is the same in Australia?'

'Pretty similar,' says Jack.

'That is very good for you. No?' asks Véronique, knowing.

'Still means you have to part with a lot of money for an apartment, no matter which country you're in,' says Jack good-humouredly.

'It is true. But in Paris the apartments are still reasonable.' Véronique lowers her voice and presses a kiss-curl to her cheek. 'It's not like in London, you know.'

'Oh, I know.' For some reason, we sound terribly English as we chorus this. The words hang in the air. Signal relief. How fortunate we are to be in Paris, not London, where real estate is absurdly expensive.

'So,' says Véronique, taking full advantage of the diversion, 'so, now you want to make me an offer?'

'Now,' says Jack, 'we would like to go and talk about it and then see the apartment again later in the week and then …'

'It would be best if you made an offer now,' interrupts Véronique, a determined look settling on her calm face. 'That way,' she continues, 'you can decide after seven days.'

'This is only the second apartment we've seen,' I say, appealing to reason.

'The apartment I am living in now, it was the first that I saw.'

'The first?' I can't think of a better response.

'Yes. I knew straight away. The moment I saw it. It was the same as my list. Everything on my list was in that first apartment. It is often like this in Paris.'

C'est toujours comme ça à Paris. I love that sentence. I drift along with her cadence, her accent, into an imaginary scenario.

Véronique and I are close friends. She is standing at my kitchen window, leaning on the iron railing telling me about the Australians: a charming couple who bought the apartment next door to mine. She is sure they will be very happy there. The apartment is elegant and spacious. Perfect for them. She tells me that it was the first apartment they saw. They snapped it up. They were worldly, urbane. They knew immediately that this was the one. Such spontaneity. Such esprit. She is thinking of inviting them to dinner.

'We don't have a list.' Jack's voice breaks my reverie.

'You don't have a list?' Véronique moves towards the door. 'You must have a list. Otherwise you waste everyone's time.'

'Really?' says Jack.

'Ce n'est pas grave,' says Véronique, struggling for patience. 'But if you don't make me an offer — I have some Americans who are also interested.'

'Not the Americans.' Jack looks so serious I have to turn away and stifle a laugh.

'Yes. From New York. I think they will make an offer today.'

'Well, good for them.'

'But,' continues Véronique, 'if they make an offer first …'

'That's a risk,' says Jack solemnly, 'we'll have to take. *Que sera sera.*'

He's enjoying this. The sun streams in the windows and dances on the worn wooden floor.

'It would be a shame to lose such a beautiful apartment,' says Véronique. We all look around the room and sigh in agreement.

'Why is the owner selling it?' I ask more abruptly than I mean to.

Véronique looks a little taken aback but tells me, with a slight pout, that Madame has moved to a very small place in the Luberon called Albi. She doesn't volunteer why. Or maybe she doesn't get a chance to, because I leap in with, 'Albi is a gorgeous town.'

Véronique eyes me suspiciously.

'Toulouse Lautrec. Lapérouse.' I don't really need to add this. The French are brilliant at their history. 'It's really pretty with lots of little restaurants and great shops.' Véronique looks a little thin lipped. 'In fact, I bought this shirt there.'

'Ah bon,' she says. 'Trés jolie.' She doesn't sound it. She unbolts the door and holds it ajar for us. I turn and take a last look at the sunny, oval room. A last thought pops into my head. 'The door,' I say. 'Is there a problem with burglars?'

'Burglars?' Véronique looks lost.

'Les voleurs, madame,' says Jack, helping out.

'Ahh. Les voleurs. Non.'

'Then why is the door so ... so ...'

'Blindée?'

'Yes. Blindée.'

'Because it is better. It costs a lot to have a door like this.'

'Oui. J'imagine,' I say.

'Après vous.' Véronique ushers us through the expensive door and turns the key in the lock with a satisfied click.

'We'll be in touch,' says Jack as we shield our eyes against the low-lying sun.

'It is as you wish. You can ring me, of course, but ... the Americans. It is a woman. About your age. She comes to Paris often. She is an artist, I think. And ... ah, Madame Martin.'

We look up the street. Madame is standing at the door of a tiny overflowing florist shop talking to Monsieur le Fleuriste. She holds an enormous bunch of yellow roses. Véronique whips her mobile phone from her pocket and says cheerily, 'I will phone you tomorrow at ten o'clock.' She swans off towards Madame Martin.

'We have to start thinking more like the Americans,' I say.

'And how do you think they think? You've never even been to America.'

'You know what I mean. They're decisive. Sure of themselves. That apartment would be perfect for them.'

'You're beginning to sound like Véronique. There are no Americans, darling. That is not the sort of apartment they would buy.'

'Why not?'

'Because Americans wouldn't live in a wedge.'

'Hmmm.' He sounds so certain it seems churlish to pursue the matter further.

Six

We walk around the perimeter of the building. There's an expensive furniture shop on the ground floor. That's a bonus. You know where you are with a furniture shop. Furniture shops don't play loud music till three in the morning. My mind drifts back to the first apartment we rented — to the thrill of discovering the neighbourhood, the way we felt so at home there, and the joy of turning into 'our' street at the end of the day despite the bar on the ground floor pumping music into our sleep all night long. We coped with the music and the noise and the late-night reverie on the street below. We coped because it was French music, French noise. It's hard to be critical when your desire for approval softens every rebuke. Even when the music finally stopped, we could still hear it.

I wondered then if the butcher lived above his shop. I wondered how he coped, the sole provender in the midst of bars, cafés, and clothing shops. There were never many people in that butcher shop, but every morning he was there at his counter, amongst the ducks and rabbits and endless sausages. I stand back and look at the building again. Jack's right. It is shaped like a wedge.

We retrace our steps down rue Vieille du Temple, locked in contemplation. The Marais-blue door at La Belle Hortense is pushed open. We walk inside and stand in front of the parchment-coloured novels. Opposite the books runs a long zinc bar. Wine and books — now there's an irresistible combination. At La Belle Hortense you can buy a book or a glass of wine, or both. I'm always torn between the pleasures of standing, musing over the books' covers, and sitting, drinking wine at the bar, imagining myself involved in the life here. I often note the names of the writers on the blackboard and see myself somewhere in the future at some lecture or other, attentive in the crowd, asking questions, chatting to the speaker over a glass of wine at the night's end. At the moment I have to be content to sit at the bar anonymously. Without language I am not privy to that kind of intimacy. Once I asked if I could buy the CD that was playing here. Monsieur, containing his embarrassment, told me softly that La Belle Hortense was not a music shop. It sold books. He told me the name of the CD three times until, finally, I asked him to write it down. I didn't ever buy the CD, but I still have the piece of paper, ripped from a small notebook which reads: 'Parle Avec Elle — Almodóvar'.

Today, Monsieur pours us chilled Chablis. We take our glasses and look pointedly into each other's eyes. 'Santé.' We can never do this with a straight face. The French are adamant that you look directly into the eyes of all those toasting. Failure to do so gets you seven years' bad sex. Given that we hadn't heard of this belief until recently, neither of us thinks there can be much in it. I put my wine aside and wrestle my notebook and pen from my bag. I place them importantly on the bar. I try to look professional. Perhaps Monsieur will think that I'm a foreign correspondent, rather than just foreign. I flick my pen between two fingers. I write the word 'offer' in my notebook, and decorate it with doodling.

'Do you think we can do this?' I ask quietly.

'Do what?' asks Jack and then, as if to answer his own question, says, 'We don't have to buy it.'

'I don't mean that. Maybe we're not ready. Maybe it's too soon.'

'It's now or never. Prices are only going to go up. If we don't do it now, we'll be priced out of the market.'

'Perhaps we should have made an offer then.'

'We need to know more about the system first. Whether there's a cooling-off period. The difference between the asking price and the real price. That sort of thing.'

'How are we going to do that?'

'No idea.'

We sit and drink our wine in happy ignorance. Monsieur is looking at me. That's probably not true. I'm almost certainly looking at him. Trying not to stare at his long, brown hair, his deep, hollowed-out eyes, or his eccentric hat. He only wants to know if we'd like more wine. He always asks this question wordlessly. He likes to pretend, as we do, that we understand each other.

'I think I'll start the list.'

'That's the way.'

I wave my pen above the paper. The only word I can think of is 'hat'. That's ridiculous. What about 'window'? That's a better word. I stare down at my notebook. I don't need to put window in a list. Of course the apartment has to have windows, even if they are proving to be complicated. Wooden floors. That's probably a given as well. Two bedrooms. That's better. Large living room. Kitchen. That's obvious. Renovated kitchen. Good, and the bathroom, too. Fireplace.

'What do we want a fireplace for?' asks Jack, looking over my shoulder.

'They look nice. Can you think of anything else?'

He runs an eye over the list. 'What about beams? All the apartments in the Marais have beams. Even here.'

We look up at the ceiling. Ancient wooden beams hold it in place, have held it there forever.

'You pay an extra fifty or sixty thousand euros for those,' I say.

'Strike that from the list. What we need is a lift, a dishwasher, and a view.'

'You don't want much. What do you want a view of?'

'A métro stop and a boulangerie.'

'Everything in Paris is close to a boulangerie.'

'Not any more,' says Jack wryly.

This is fun. We should have done this earlier. You can put anything you like in a list.

'Quel étage?' I ask brightly.

'What?'

'What floor?'

'Not the ground.'

'No.'

'Not the sixth. Too hot. The first?'

'Too close to the ground.'

'What about the fourth? That's a good compromise.'

'Okay.' I add quatrième étage to the list. 'Parfait. Now we only need to get a better idea of square metres. I think I'll phone the agent and ask him the size of our apartment.'

'He might think you want to buy it,' warns Jack.

'That would save a lot of trouble.'

We finish our wine, bid Monsieur a bonne soirée, and step out onto the street. The local beggar turned artist (or is it the other way around?) has set up shop right outside the doorway. We almost collide.

Monsieur le Painter lies sprawled across the footpath, more languid than asleep, clutching a large whisky bottle in his right hand. His painted canvases stand up against the wall of the neighbouring building. Dozens of paint-brushes with paint-covered handles stand in empty paint pots beside them. Monsieur lives here on the street, a couple of metres from the entrance to our apartment. I live in fear of making eye-contact with him. This is because he wakes us every morning, at six or seven, screaming and cursing on the street below our bedroom window. Some mornings I lie awake listening to him, trying to make out what he's saying. But he wails through the early morning in a language I can't understand. Wails? Rails is a better word. There's an energy to his cries that's unsettling, because he doesn't appear to rail against a personal injustice. He's not the self-pitying kind. Quite the opposite. His monologues mix despair with delight. Energy buzzes around him like a force field, and compels people, French people, to stop and admire his work.

But I never stop, never admire, and never look at him directly. He snaps things at me as I walk past. He snaps and waits for my response. When I pretend to ignore him he throws back his head and convulses with laughter. He continues laughing and shouting after me as I hurry past. He makes me fumble the door code. He is even louder when I try the code again. Next door, at L'Etoile Manquante, the outdoor patrons look lazily in my direction. It's mortifying to be seen quailing at your own Parisian front door.

'That painter's outside again,' I say as I burst into our living room.

'Why wouldn't he be?' says Julia. 'He lives here.'

'I got eleven sticks on the horses, Mum.'

'Eleven? Wow.'

I look down at Ellery's Orangina-stained face, and remember the first time we took him to that merry-go-round at the Luxembourg gardens. The concentration of those tiny children, as they sat on their mounts and held their sticks at right angles, like mini-lances, ready to capture the rings held by Monsieur of le manège, commanded respect. When the horses stopped galloping, Monsieur silently retrieved his rings. No winner was announced. Le manège is a private contest — a quest that every child I saw then and have seen since participates in with the conviction of a white knight.

'Lucky legs eleven,' I say, bending down to kiss him. 'I wish I'd seen that.'

Julia sits at the dining table nursing a glass of wine. Jack has taken Ellery down to the playground at Saint-Paul for a helicopter ride. I'm flinging opening the living room windows trying to explain the wedge. It's difficult. Je n'ai rien à cacher. I saw that once. It was written on a shopping caddie that was coming towards me down the boulevard Saint-Germain. I have nothing to hide. Isn't that what Parisian living is all about? Apartment life and street life intertwined, overlapping, moving from one to the other and back again? You fling open a window, lean over a balcony. Lights on. Curtains open. Nothing to hide. You wash dishes. Vacuum floors. Turn on the television. Talk on the phone. You do all these things in full view of the city. And when you are certain that Paris is your audience, you stand in the window and slowly draw your curtains.

'The real estate agent told us we should make a list.'

'What sort of a list?'

'Of all the things we want in an apartment.'

'That idea's worth a koala stamp,' says Julia.

Julia has a sense of humour that I never associated with musicians until I met her. Not that I really knew any musicians before Julia. This was more by choice than accident. Studying at the Victorian College of the Arts, you couldn't completely avoid musicians. The School of Drama was in its infancy in the early 1980s when I was a student there, so for every actor there were about ten musicians. At least that's what it felt like. The musicians were seriously cool. (Even though cool had yet to make a comeback.) This meant they wore a lot of black, spoke very little, smoked a lot, and wore their hair long and unkempt. They were self-consciously unfunny. The actors, on the other hand, were vibrant, loud, exuberant, and willing to find humour in just about everything — especially themselves. They fashioned their hair into elaborate and complicated styles. They wore hats and scarves and anything that separated them from the crowd. There was not a great deal of cross-pollination, so to speak. Most musicians seemed happier making love to their instruments than to other people. All that's changed, apparently. Julia is a fund of information on what's changed. She stops fiddling with her long, curly hair and lays her hand flat on the tabletop.

'And?'

'Well, it had walls and plumbing and there were no building works out the front. Maybe we should have snapped it up. What if it's our only chance?'

'There's no such thing as an only chance. You're always telling me that.'

That's true. I'm an appalling hypocrite when it comes to advice. I'm always telling Julia to be brave, to follow her passion, and to believe in herself. That's what I'd like to do. Instead I'm forever diverted by doubt. I smile and look down at the table. 'Buying your way in. That's what I'm trying to do, Jules. It's not honourable.' I trace my finger around an ancient burn-mark on the tabletop.

'Nobody does honourable anymore, Elle.'

I drain the last of my wine. Well, they should. I fiddle with my empty glass. I suppose that does sound a bit overblown. Why is it so difficult to explain doubt? Why can't I say that this afternoon's inspection reminded me of my first day at work? Reminded me of the interview where I was confident and funny. I never thought they'd actually give me the job. Who in their right mind would employ a fifteen-year-old kid with a broken education and a 25-words-a-minute typing speed to work somewhere as prestigious as a solicitor's office? When they hired me I was so grateful I couldn't function. I spent five years there with my head down and my tail up. They spent five years wondering what had happened to the sparkling girl they interviewed. It's the same with the apartment.

'Alright. I don't feel as though I deserve it. It's as though the grand, audacious plan was the interview, and now I've got the job I'm overwhelmed by it.'

'That's Paris. That's why I'm living here. I love being overwhelmed.'

Of course you do (I think to myself). You're young. I used to love being overwhelmed, too. Lately, I think I loved only the idea of it. I also thought that Julia reminded me of my younger self. As I look across the table at her now, I realise that that's not really true either. Julia reminds me of the younger self I would like to have been — witty, beautiful, and blessed with the most wonderful where-with-all.

'So what do we do? Buy this apartment just because we can?'

'You don't have to decide tonight.'

I leave the table and walk over to a window facing the courtyard. The courtyard is large and green. It's home to several tall slender trees, and to unruly grass that never looks properly cut. On the opposite side of this courtyard is the most beautiful apartment I've ever seen. It's full of antiques and books and important-looking chairs. If that was the apartment we were considering we would have made a decision to buy it hours ago.

'The real estate agent told us that some Americans are interested. They're going to decide tonight.'

'Did she tell you that in French or in English?'

I turn away from the open window and look at her. She returns my look with a smile playing at the corner of her lips.

'Why don't I take you to see it? It's only ten minutes from here.'

'Sweet,' she says, and slings her bulging, black canvas bag across her chest.

It's peak hour. People in bars and cafés are jockeying for position. Cars and motorcycles and bicycles squeeze along the narrow, one-way street. We pick our way happily amongst them. I point out the Picasso Museum, the Moroccan restaurant, and the joys of the quiet end of the street. The nearer we get, the more I'm enjoying myself and the more I can't wait for Julia to see it.

'There it is,' I shout as the intersection comes into view. 'There, on the third floor.'

'Wow,' says Julia. 'It's awesome.'

She turns to me, her eyes alight. 'Elle, it's so French.'

'French?'

'It's an island. Like the île de la Cité.'

She sounds so certain. Possibility squeezes through me. Of course it's French. Quintessentially French. Très clair, très calme, très lumineux. A soft breeze tugs at my hair, and I catch my reflection in the furniture-shop window. For a moment I'm held there, suspended in space, looking at myself looking out at Paris. Then there's a sudden lurch in my chest. What if it's too late? What if the Americans …?

Seven

It's Friday, and it's raining. I pick my robe up from the floor and wrap it around me. I hadn't thought about rain. Now it lashes the awning, spits inside, and trickles down the wall. I close the window and stand looking out at the street. The denizens of rue Vieille du Temple are nowhere to be seen. I press my face to the pane and see if I can spy Monsieur le Painter. I'm relieved at his absence, then worried. Where does he go when it rains? I suppose if you live on the streets you always consider rain. What about his paintings? I make a mental note to ask Yoann when he comes to dinner tomorrow tonight. I strain up between the buildings for a piece of sky, and find a slate-grey patch being buffeted by big, bullying clouds. All the windows across from mine are closed tight against the weather. There are no doors flung open, either. No chairs on the street. I bend down and pick up my watch. It's eight forty-five. Still early.

I sit on the edge of the bed. It's a mess of real estate brochures and guides. I pick one up and open it at random. The brochures are not what I expected. They're cheaply produced and lacking any hype. The wind outside pushes the rain erratically across the window. Perhaps someone invited the painter into a warm, dry home. People do that in Paris. I think I was expecting more properties to be on the market. Of course there are hundreds; but then again, there are thousands, maybe millions, of apartments here. Perhaps summer is a bad time to buy. I can't imagine how he copes in winter. Yoann once told me that a homeless person came to live with him. He didn't say 'homeless'. That wasn't how he saw him. He was just someone without shelter. When I asked why, he shrugged at me. He told me that he met a person without a home and he gave him one. That was the beginning and the end of the story. My eyes drift to a sunny photo of a small château somewhere near Aix-en-Provence. It seems inexpensive in comparison with the fourth arrondissement. People are always asking about his paintings. People with satchels and handbags and briefcases. Young people. Older people. People dressed in suits and jeans. Once I saw him addressing a group. He spoke in earnest. It took me back to my university days. I contrived to stand within earshot, but I didn't understand a word he said.

The front door bangs. 'Mummy. Mummy.' Ellery's voice climbs the stairs to the bedroom. 'Croissants are here and I've already had an Orangina and it's only breakfast time.'

I fasten my robe and walk downstairs. 'Did you get wet?'

'No. We took the parapluies. That's umbrellas.'

'Très bien,' I say beaming at him. He looks lovely with his ragdoll hair flying around his face.

'Coffee won't be long,' says Jack. 'What's this morning's plan of attack?'

I pick half-heartedly at a croissant. 'I think I'll go over to the left bank.' What I'd really like to do is spend the day in the Musèe d'Orsay, or run a bath and lie in it and listen. Rain is the best listening there is. Of course, I'm not going to get a Parisian life wandering around museums or lying around listening to the rain. 'I might as well see what's over there. I'm not having much luck on this side.'

'It's a bit wet for exploring, isn't it?,' says Jack, clearing a space on the table for his coffee and the papers.

I glance at a headline. The tourist numbers are down. The Americans aren't coming. That's not true. One or two of them are here right now, signing up for an apartment in this very street. That's probably overstating things a bit, but the travails of the last two days have made me wonder. Perhaps our decision (or Jack's decision — this morning it's beginning to feel as though I was coerced into agreeing with him) not to make an offer on the wedge was a bit rash. In the past two days we've combed the Marais, les Halles, the Bastille, some parts of the République, and even l'île Saint-Louis (though that was just for fun, an excuse to fantasise about apartments with museum-like proportions and sweeping views of the Seine). The response was more or less the same wherever we went. 'Desolé, madame, but we have nothing at the moment.' Nothing? Not one small apartment with two bedrooms, a kitchen, and a fireplace? Non. 'Je n'ai rien à cacher.'

And that seemed true enough. What's in their windows is all there seems to be. What's pictured in the brochures is mainly in the suburbs or the countryside. Maybe we should have made an offer on the wedge like Véronique urged us to — because what if that was our one and only chance? What if there are no other apartments, no more rendezvous, no jolting lurches in the chest. I wish Jack trusted in chest pain like I do. Instead, he's happy to risk the Americans. He wants to wait until we find something else — one other apartment, at least — with which to make a comparison before we make any offers on anything. My eyes stray to the open window. 'I think it's easing a bit, and since we're not buying the wedge …'

'It's early days yet,' says Jack, his head already inside the *Herald Tribune.*

The rain has eased a little. I splash down the lovely rue du Pont Louis-Philippe as Jack's 'early days yet' phrase keeps repeating in my head. How can he be so insouciant? When you have only two weeks to do something that matters, there are no 'early days' to be had. I walk determinedly past my favourite jewellery shop and cross over to the Seine. What Jack wanted was a holiday, and traipsing around Parisian real estate offices wasn't his idea of one. I don't suppose it was mine, either, but I was prepared to give that up. I was prepared to do whatever it took. So the plan was, we'd spend six weeks holidaying in the French countryside, and then we'd devote our last two weeks to Paris and the search. It was that or nothing. Those were the terms and conditions. Of course, they had seemed absurd, but perhaps a compact with absurdity was what it would take. If this impetuous plan worked, if we really did find an apartment in only two weeks, our dream would be transformed into destiny. But this morning's reality — of only nine days to go, and nothing even on the horizon — doesn't feel anything like destiny. At this moment, standing on the Pont Saint-Louis, struggling to keep from blowing into the river, our plan feels more like a futile waste of precious Paris time.

I push my way through the back of Notre-Dame and the hordes of tourist buses. They're full of exuberant Italians who are not in the least daunted by the weather, who don't really look as if they could be daunted by anything. I continue up the rue des Bernardins, past the youth hostel (the one I thought was a gym until I met someone who was staying there), and in fifteen minutes I'm standing in the fifth arrondissement on rue des Écoles. The left bank, this less familiar Paris, stretches out before me. It feels more residential than I remember it. Maybe we should have begun our search on this side. Maybe it is 'early days' yet. I linger outside a pretty, *dry* café, wondering which way to turn. Of course, left seems the perfect choice. Walking left will also take me past the Brasserie Balzar and, if things work out, if the expectation slowly rising in me leads to promise, I may even have time to have lunch there.

The last time I ate in a brasserie alone was seven years ago at Les Deux Magots on boulevard Saint-Germain. I remember walking past it several times, trying to decide whether to sit outside or inside, trying to summon the courage to walk in and sit down alone. A waiter made the choice for me. He was suddenly outside ushering me into the empty restaurant. He thought I'd like to sit at the table occupied for so many years by Simone de Beauvoir. I remember the thrill of squeezing onto her banquette. Simone de Beauvoir probably ate here alone all the time. Reading the names of the restaurant's literary clientele on the plaques on the walls, it was hard to be convinced of that. It was hard, too, to concentrate on the menu. Champagne was the only thing I could think of — that and the fact that I was then four months pregnant. My baby-to-be and I watched as Monsieur zigzagged the cake trolley towards us. Together we chose a tiny mille feuille. Monsieur handed us a history of the brasserie. To read, he said, and to keep. He had the most beautiful smile in all of Paris. I ordered a little champagne. Une coupe de champagne. And that's how it came, sparkling up and over the glass's wide, smiling brim.

The streets are getting progressively busier. I twist my map, my *Plan de Paris,* left and right and left again. I ought to head over to rue Monge to find Immobilier Extra. The name's not very promising, but this agency produces a weekly tabloid that advertises apartments all over Paris. That's what I need — a real estate agency that networks. It's too time-consuming tracking down dozens of tiny, independent places.

Zut alors. That's a lot of money. I stop outside an enormous window. No one says 'zut alors' any more, according to Julia. Why don't they? Good heavens. How on earth! Well, I'll be damned. How could something so expressive be obsolete? It's the only phrase that accurately describes my surprise at the prices listed before me. Deux pièces: 650,000 euros. Trois pièces: 800,000 euros.

Trois pièces: 875,000 euros. Are these apartments bigger than the ones in the fourth? The photographs are certainly bigger. I stand in the drizzle staring at the advertisements. A pretty young woman steps in beside me to shelter in the little alcove of the doorway. She gently opens and closes her umbrella, shaking it dry. She looks like a pale-feathered bird freeing its wings of water. She smiles at me apologetically, and says something about the weather. I smile back and say, 'Il pleut beaucoup.' She looks at me quizzically as she drifts backwards through the office door. Should I have said 'aujourd'hui'? Il pleut beaucoup aujourd'hui. No, I tell myself. You got that one right. It makes sense either way. I note the address of the agency. If Immobilier Extra proves disappointing I can always come back. I continue towards rue Monge, better to keep en route than to think about those exorbitant prices.

Immobilier Extra is on a corner, covered in metal mesh. No wonder I couldn't find it. A man arrives. He eases the security door up out of the way. I hurry towards him, then change my mind and cross the street. I stand outside a florist's, staring across at him. I'm not sure why I think it's better to lurk on the opposite side of the street rather than approach the office like a normal person would. Getting the lie of the land, that's what I'm telling myself, when Madame la Fleuriste scares me half to death by sneaking up behind me, ostensibly to see if I would like to buy some flowers.

'Voulez-vous des fleurs, madame?' Her sharply raised eyebrow lassoes me to the footpath.

'Merci madame, mais non.' She was not expecting this. Emboldened, I continue. 'Non, je regarde, seulement.' As I say this, I realise that I haven't given her flowers a second look. Now their colours and range surprise me. If I'd completed my day's work I would buy some, even though I don't know if the apartment has a vase. I would have taken the risk, had things been different. 'Très jolies,' I say, after what I realise could be construed as a lengthy pause. Why doesn't she just go back inside? Surely she doesn't think I'm going to steal something.

'Monsieur,' she says slowly and patiently, 'monsieur, il s'absente encore.'

What? I spin around to face Immobilier Extra. Monsieur clicks the iron-shutter door into place and marches off purposefully down the street. An 'Oh, no' escapes from me before I have time to check it. Madame la Fleuriste looks concerned.

'Vous avez un rendez-vous?' She jerks her head towards Monsieur's hurrying figure.

'A rendezvous?' I turn and look at Madame wide-eyed. A rendezvous. Of course, that's it. That's the way the French like to organise things. Go into the bureau and make a rendezvous. A proper appointment where my details can be noted and my list considered. That's what I've been missing. A rendezvous will make me look prepared, serious. A woman with where-with-all. I nod and turn towards Madame, smiling happily. Of course, that's what I must do. How perspicacious Madame is. 'Je cherche à acheter un appartement à Paris,' I say. I notice that the rain has nearly stopped.

'Ah bon?' Madame looks me up and down.

I don't always look like this. Only in the rain. Everybody looks dishevelled when they're soaking wet.

'Et mon mari,' I add to reassure her.

Madame folds her arms across her chest. 'Ça c'est le plus beau quartier de Paris,' she says imperiously. I mould my face into a concurring look. 'Vous connaissez Monsieur Hulot?'

Do I know Monsieur Hulot? Of Jacques Tati fame? That can't be his name. I squint up at Madame to see if she is making fun of me. She looks back at me, waiting. I shake the thought from my mind. Why on earth would Madame la Fleuriste want to make fun of me?

'Il est très sympathique,' she says candidly. 'Très sympathique.'

I nod again and try a slight frown. Madame nods, too, and we stand like this on the footpath, nodding and contemplating Monsieur the très sympathique agent immobilier, for what seems like ages. I'm at a lost as to how to end this ... what? Encounter? Perhaps I should buy some flowers. It does seem discourteous to have taken up all Madame's time and not buy something. I take a deep breath and try in an exquisite French way to convey that I am about to do what I intended doing all along. 'Madame, en fait, je pense que je vais acheter des fleurs.' Perfect. It's amazing how easy French can be when you're not being rushed.

'Pourquoi, madame?'

Because I'm trying to be nice, that's why. I can't say that. I look out vaguely from under my umbrella. It's stopped raining. A pale sun nudges the clouds.

'C'est pour offrir?'

I knot my eyebrows into an expression of I'm-not-entirely-sure-about-that.

'C'est un cadeau?' This time, Madame speaks slowly and directly.

Because they enjoy the art of instruction, Parisians insist upon being understood. If, for example, you are being counselled on the finer points of pronunciation, or how best to cook duck à l'orange, or which métro route to take you from Place Vendôme to boulevard de Clichy, they stand firm until you get it right. Madame is standing firm now. She looks serious. Language is a serious business. Paris will not brook a slap-dash attitude, and neither will its citizens. Madame tries again.

'C'est un cadeau, madame, pour votre mari ou ...'

I've got it. 'Oui, madame. I mean non. Ce n'est pas un cadeau.'

Madame looks a little suspicious at this. I try to reassure her. 'Les fleurs sont pour moi.'

'Non,' she says flatly.

It's apparently bad form to cart your own flowers to a real estate office rendezvous. Madame tells me I should make a rendezvous and then buy flowers. That is the order of things. She also tells me about another, très bien agence immobilière further along the street. She ends with a monologue about her sister's daughter (I'm pretty sure that's right, even though I don't know the word for niece) who took three years to buy an apartment, and someone else she knew who took a year to buy or sell an apartment on the Champs-Élysées. Our parting is warm and cordial. I saunter off down the street feeling pleased with myself. It's a matter of practice, that's all. When we have our own apartment we can come to Paris and practise whenever we want. It'll be wonderful and très, très bon pour ma pratique. Only yesterday, a young girl of about seventeen told me that I'd confused the gender of a salad. She thought this was hilarious. I hadn't thought about it before, but calling a salad 'he' when it ought to be 'she' is pretty funny. We laughed away together. Her eyes were still smiling at my mistake as she handed me my takeaway salade niçoise.

'C'est très bien pour mon pratique,' I said, trying to prolong our conversation. Now she started giggling. Not only had I made a mistake with 'salad' but with 'practice', too. It's ma pratique. I'm sure I'd been saying mon pratique for at least two years, and no one had ever corrected me before. Obviously, I'm looking more approachable. Apartment or no apartment, things are going well. Imagine the day when I'll be able to regale Madame la Fleuriste with a tale such as that. Imagine the day when I'll be able to imagine in French. I look up at the sky. It seems so very far away.

Eight

I trip along rue Monge, looking at the shops and the cafés. Now that the rain has stopped, waiters are busy lining up chairs on the footpath. But I don't have time for lunch. I'm on a mission. I stop myself detouring into a kitchenware shop that sells robust saucepans made of cast iron and hundreds of different-sized frying-pans. On my next visit I'll be in and out of shops like this all the time, searching for things for my own Paris kitchen. The cafés are filling up. I quicken my pace. Some offices close at lunchtime.

I'm back at the Brasserie Balzar. Diners are lined up in twos, tearing bread apart, talking over grilled steak and pommes frites. That's the trouble with Paris: its beauty is everywhere. How do you choose between one arrondissement and another? I push my hands deep inside my nearly dry coat pockets and count the numbers. One hundred and six, one hundred and four. There it is. One hundred and four bis. Immobilier Catherine. I stare at the door and its elegant, twisted door-handle. I can see the outline of a woman sitting at a long glass desk at the back of the small bureau. I shake my hand through my hair, turn the handle, and walk expectantly inside.

Madame looks up at me pleasantly. 'Bonjour, madame.'

'Bonjour. I would like to make a rendezvous, please.'

'Bien sûr. Please take a seat.'

She gestures to the small white chair in front of her desk. It certainly helps to have a recommendation. It would be prudent to tell Madame of my acquaintance with Madame la Fleuriste. I run a couple of ideas for this sentence around in my head, but none of them seems right. The room is in silence. I realise that Madame is waiting for me to continue. 'I would like to make an appointment to buy an apartment in Paris.' That wasn't exactly the sentence I had in my head, but Madame understands.

'Ah bon,' she says, as if it's all in a day's work. She opens a draw, whips out a file, and smoothes it out on the desk in front of her. 'Votre nom?'

'Nielsen.'

She snaps the lid off a bright red ballpoint and writes it down. 'Prénom?'

'Ellie.'

'Où habitez-vous?'

'À Melbourne.'

She looks at me tolerantly. 'In Paris? Where do you stay in Paris?'

'Oh. In a rented apartment on rue Vieille du Temple.'

'Très bien.' She looks up at me approvingly. It's nine out of ten so far. A pretty good score, but now her face clouds a little. I try not to smile. I know there must be a tricky one coming.

'Dans quel arrondissement?'

Too easy. 'L'appartement est dans le quatrième arrondissement. I also add 'the fourth' just to prove I can manage numbers in French and in English.

'This is the fifth,' she says.

'Yes. I know that.'

'Apartments are more expensive in the fifth than the fourth.'

'Really?'

'Mais oui.'

'Oh, that's alright,' I say airily.

She looks reassured and holds her pen poised above the page. 'Donc. How many square metres do you want?'

'Soixante,' I say instantly. Madame Catherine looks at me doubtfully over the top of her glasses. What's wrong with sixty? 'Or seventy.' Seventy doesn't help; she's still looking at me.

'Ça c'est très grand,' she says.

I smile apologetically. It's warm in her office. I'd like to take my coat off, but I'm not sure of the protocol. Is it too familiar to remove your coat in a real estate agent's office? I press on. 'We need something with two bedrooms. We're Australian.'

'Australienne, ahh oui. Je vois.'

Her office breathes a sigh of relief.

'Are you going to work in Paris?' she asks.

'No.'

'Then why buy an apartment? It is cheaper to rent one.'

There does seem to be some logic to this line of thinking. But then again, logic has very little to do with my wanting to buy an apartment in Paris. 'It's because …' I pause. This explanation is always difficult. 'It's because, mon mari et moi …'

Madame sits opposite me impassive, waiting. It's because I want to live in a fantasy world. I can't say that, but right at this moment that's what it feels like. Why does this question make me cringe? Is it because I don't know the answer or because there are too many answers to give? Madame is not interested in that. She doesn't want to know that sometimes Paris makes me feel beautiful and joyous. That's not the sort of thing you tell people. 'J'adore Paris et je pense que c'est une très bonne …' I love Paris and I think it's a very good …. idea. I should have added the word 'idea'. That would have made all the difference. Oh, well. C'est pas grave. Madame Catherine looks a little puzzled, but continues on bravely.

'What kind of apartment are you looking for?' she asks.

What kind? A French one. Something quintessentially French. How do you say that? I fiddle with the button on the top of my coat, praying for one intelligent sentence to pop into my head. 'Something with parquetry floors,' I say eventually.

'Ah.' Madame's face lights up. 'You want something charming.'

Charming? Of course I do. That's exactly what I want. 'Oui, madame. Quelque chose charmant.'

'And old,' continues Madame, 'something old and charming and with character.'

'Oui, madame, avec du caractère.' I can see it now. I've seen this apartment a thousand times in magazines, in books. I'm after a quirky, original, and cleverly decorated apartment — the kind of apartment that exudes character and style.

'Caractère,' Madame says again.

We both know we've found a winner. Character is the key to finding an apartment. It's obvious.

'I have an apartment exactly like this.'

'Really?'

'Oui. It is completely charming, close to here, and it has two bedrooms.'

'Really?'

'Mais oui. It is full of character because it is a little bit unusual. It is shaped like this.' Madame, makes a sort of cathedral-window shape with her arms. I study her movements carefully. A diamond. That's what she's drawing in the air. Imagine an apartment that's shaped like a diamond.

'It sounds perfect,' I say, and immediately regret it. Don't be so effusive. This is a very small office. I clasp my hands together on the desk. 'Is it possible to see the apartment, Madame?'

'Oui,' says Madame in that slow, elongated way that means of course, by all means, why not. She pulls a large, black appointment-book towards her and flips it open. 'I have a key because the apartment is vacant. You can see it tomorrow morning.'

'Perfect,' I say again, overjoyed. I never learn. 'Tomorrow morning. I'll bring my husband, too.' I stand ready to leave. One more syllable and my head will burst. À demain, that's all that's needed now. I prepare for my magnificent departure but 'à de …' is as far as I get. That's nowhere near magnificence.

'Madame, you do not know the time.'

Shame shrinks my face. The time. Hadn't we mentioned that? It's so hard to know what order things have happened in when the language is not your own — when mundane details masquerade as crucial information. Madame reads my disappointment.

'Ce n'est pas grave.' She consults her book for a suitable time.

Well, it's not serious for you. You could do this with your eyes shut. But for me it's très, très sérieux. I have to listen with every pore of my body just to understand the edges of what is being said. I miss so much. I miss subtlety, complexity, and nuance. I had no idea how complicated simple language could be. Madame looks up from her appointment book.

'The time,' I say, defeated. We smile and shake our heads at silly old time.

'À onze heures?' queries Madame.

Onze heures. Onze heures. I run the number around in my head. Eleven. Yes, I'm sure that's eleven. Madame mistakes my confusion for contemplation.

'Or ... ,' she searches her pages for another possibility.

'Onze heures, c'est bien.'

'Très bien.' Madame notes the appointment and hands me her card. 'Charmant,' she repeats as I stand to leave. I turn the white card over in my hand. Her name is printed across the top in fine, black letters. Madame Catherine Garcia. Garcia? Isn't that Spanish or Portuguese? How could someone who is not French seem so French?

'I think it could be perfect for you,' she says.

The interview is over. 'À demain, madame. Au revoir.' I slide through her door. Until tomorrow and tomorrow. I've done it. Another appointment. An appointment to see a charming apartment. That, of course, ought to have been my criterion all along. It's funny how often the things you think you know are the things you don't know at all.

I walk down boulevard Saint-Michel wondering why there's no photograph of the charming apartment in her window. It's probably just been listed. I turn her business card over and over in my coat pocket. Madame Catherine Garcia. Garcia might be her married name. That makes sense. She married a dashing Spaniard, married him for his name alone. That's unlikely. I stop in the middle of Pont d'Arcole and look out across the racing water. I should see if Monsieur Hulot has returned. See if he has something, anything. My heart's not in it, though. My heart is here on the bridge, watching the Batobus and les Vedettes du Pont-Neuf sail under me. Watching the passengers exclaiming at exterior Paris, knowing it's interior Paris they're really imagining. Through their camera lenses, they see themselves stealing through the archives at the Louvre, starving in the dungeons at the Conciergerie, and gourmandising at La Tour d'Argent. That's the sort of thing I imagine when I'm sailing down the Seine. It's easier to imagine that than explaining the day's events to Jack. I'm not sure they'll sound as promising in the retelling. And then there's the shape; a diamond is very close to a wedge. I didn't come apartment-hunting with shapes like that in my head. Rectangles, like the apartments that line the Seine, like the ones I'm looking at now: that's what I came with.

Nine

We stand dripping all over the floor as Catherine eases herself into a beige Burbury raincoat. We're five minutes early, but she doesn't seem to mind. 'Il pleut très fort,' she says pleasantly.

'Oui,' we nod happily.

I've been having weather conversations with myself all morning and now that I'm here, in situ, at onze heures, the words inside my head (as usual) prefer to stay there. The only thing I can think of is, 'Il y a beaucoup de vent,' but it isn't. There's no wind. It's wet and sticky.

The apartment is about fifty metres away in a small street off rue Monge called rue d'Arras. It's in a flat, whitewashed building with tall, narrow windows. The windows on the second floor have shutters. These are wooden and peeling, and sit flat against the wall of the building. The building is old and faded. Charming? I suppose old and faded equals charming. It's odd, though, how the word 'neglect' keeps tapping at my brain. How unimaginative to see neglect where charming lies. I look harder. Yes, I suppose it has a sort of lived-in beauty, and that's very French. The old shutters are nice. I hope that one's ours. There I go again — seduced by possession.

Inside, the hallway is unexpectedly spacious and bright. We close our umbrellas and shake ourselves dry on the enormous, worn flagstones. Monsieur le Guardien emerges out from behind some large potted plants, and shuffles out to open the glass security-door. Catherine greets Monsieur warmly. We stand in the background, noting the soaring ceiling and the patina of the stone staircase. Monsieur disappears into his apartment for a few seconds and returns with a very impressive-looking key — the sort of key you would expect to open a vault or a metre-thick door in a château. Jack and I steal a look at each other. What a surprise. But then you can't tell what's inside by looking at the outside. And here, that goes for buildings, too. We follow Catherine up the stairs.

'Quel étage, madame?

'The fifth,' she says. 'The last one.'

She leads the way, her brown ballerina-style shoes gliding easily from floor to floor. The fifth. That's a lot of stairs. Yesterday I was so carried away with charming that I forgot to ask about a lift.

Doesn't matter now. C'est pas grave.

'There's no lift,' says Jack absurdly.

'Non,' replies Catherine. 'Mais … there is a gardien. Not many apartments have guardians today.'

That's true. A guardian is becoming a rarity. They're being replaced by thickened-glass security doors and electronic keys. Prams and bicycles now reside in the tiny ground-floor dwellings that were once home to these caretakers.

'C'est très bien for the security,' says Catherine, 'and très pratique.'

Paris and practical have a close relationship. This surprised me at first, but now I can see the advantages in that. Being practical frees you up to do less practical things.

'I thought a guardian was called a concierge,' says Jack.

'Non,' says Catherine without missing a footfall. 'The gardien is called the guardian.'

Put like that, it seems indisputable.

The higher we ascend, the darker the building becomes. By the fourth-floor landing the staircase has narrowed considerably and the walls are in desperate need of paint.

'Nearly there,' sings Catherine. There's no catch in her voice. I suppose I'd be fit and sleek, too, if I ran up and down five flights of stairs every day. We stop on the tiny fifth-floor landing. It's dark and airless. We can just make out two tall wooden doors that stand at right angles to each other. Wordlessly, Catherine turns the enormous key in the one on our right. The door pushes open. More darkness. Catherine strides through the room and snaps open the shabby, creamish roller blinds that cover two tiny dormer windows. A pallid grey light casts a pall over the room.

'That's better,' she says. 'When there is sun it comes in there.'

She points at the windows. They face a blank, grey wall. I stand on the edge of the room feeling like I need to hold onto something. Where is charming? Where's character? Where is the precious diamond shape? This is squalid. How can an apartment in Paris be squalid?

Catherine stands on the yellowy, stained floorboards pointing out the apartment's features. The walls are in very good order. Then there's the shape of the room. Très original. What's original about a corridor of a room with a kitchen down one side and cramped windows down the other? We must look closely. It is easy to be fooled by an old kitchen. We must look beyond age — to what? The water pressure. Catherine turns on a tap. The water pressure is excellent. It's hard to find water pressure this good in Paris. Jack, whose resilience in the face of life's disappointments never ceases to amaze me, follows Catherine's every move. He raises his eyebrows in surprise. He concurs with her assessments. He nods sagely. I'm trying to adjust. How could this have happened? I blame myself. Clearly, I misunderstood everything.

Catherine points at the small door down the other end of the room. 'Through there,' she says, 'are the bedrooms. Deux chambres. It is rare in the heart of the fifth. Rare for such a good price.'

'And what is the price, madame?' I ask, not caring if she says two dollars or two million. Jack looks at me, surprised.

'It is only three hundred and eighty-two thousand euros.'

We stare at her. She repeats the amount slowly and then adds, 'I think you could offer three hundred and seventy-five thousand.'

'So that really is how the offers work,' says Jack, showing an annoying degree of interest.

'Yes,' says Catherine. 'You make an offer, and wait for a response in seven days.'

'And then what happens?'

'And then the propriétaire decides if he will take the offer.'

'What happens if he doesn't?'

'Then the offer is finished.' Catherine looks at her watch. 'I will show you the bedrooms now.'

We move through the living room to the first bedroom. It is also rectangular, but narrows considerably at the farthest end, where a small door forms the greater part of the wall. The floor is covered in some musty-smelling grass-type material. There is one tiny window, the same as those in the living room. Speckled mirrored tiles line the wall opposite the window.

'Good size,' says Catherine as we hurry through to the second bedroom. La deuxième chambre is little bigger than a large cupboard. Its two side walls run together to form a point down the other end of the room. It's a musty, claustrophobic triangle with a recently added matchbox-sized window. I struggle to hide my disappointment.

'Very nautical,' says Catherine confidently. She misreads our blank looks. 'It's the shape; the shape is like a ship.'

'Oh.' We look dolefully around.

'Je ne pense pas,' I begin.

Catherine leaves me to catch up. She has returned to the first bedroom and is pulling on a door-handle, hidden in the middle of the speckled mirror. It opens up part of the wall. She gestures for us to take a look. We stick our heads through the doorway. Although it's not possible to stand in the bathroom together, it is surprisingly fresh. There's a new shower, a tiny hand-basin, and a toilet all squashed in together.

'Very practical,' says Catherine.

I can't think what she means by this. We back out of the secret bathroom and into the gloom of the living room. We stand lined up along the kitchen bench.

'Regardez,' says Catherine enthusiastically, 'the sun.'

We turn and look towards the grimy windows. A long stream

of sun crosses one of the panes. It makes no attempt to come in.

'Well,' says Catherine, 'it is exactly the kind of apartment you want. Charming and full of character.'

She can't be serious.

'Of course, it needs a coat of paint. You always need to paint. Even if the paint is new, you may not like the colour and then you will need to paint.'

She waits for our agreement. We manage half-hearted nods. What is going on? We don't seem to be looking at the same thing. What she sees and what we see are worlds apart.

'Oui. Je vois, madame, mais …' I begin.

Catherine looks at me impatiently.

'Mais …' My reticence is not buying time; it's only prolonging the agony. 'This apartment is not really what we're looking for.'

Catherine refuses to believe us. 'But it is exactly as you want,' she says. 'It has charm and character and two bedrooms. It is quiet and full of light. Of course, it needs some work. All apartments need some work, but you must use your imagination.'

She is more challenging than persuasive. The more I look around, the worse it gets. Imagination? This place would benefit from nothing short of a miracle. 'I'm sorry,' I say, 'but I'm afraid …'

'So,' Catherine interrupts me, 'does this mean that you are not going to make me an offer?'

'No,' says Jack firmly, 'we're not.'

'If,' says Catherine, snapping off lights and pulling down blinds, 'if you have no interest in this apartment, then I do not know why you want to look at it.'

We stand in the airless, unhappy apartment, staring at the fading laminate on the kitchen bench. How do you answer this? It seems self-evident that the only way anyone can decide whether or not they have any interest in an apartment, or anything for which they are about to pay a fortune, is to look at it.

'It is a waste of my time if you tell me this is the sort of apartment you want, and then you don't want it. If you don't want character, you should not tell me that you do.'

I look at Jack helplessly. This is the third inspection that has ended with us offending someone or something. I try to salvage the situation.

'Je suis très desolée, madame, but this is not the kind of character we're looking for.'

Catherine regards me with contempt. 'This is Parisian character,' she says. 'There is no other kind.'

My heart sinks. I take a last look around the room. No, I refuse to believe it. This apartment has less Parisian character than yesterday's baguette.

We sit in a café sipping coffee. Jack is unusually quiet. He's over it. I'm sure he's over the whole idea. I know he only really agreed for my sake. With or without Paris he'll still be happy. He's happy in most places.

'I think,' says Jack, looking up at me resignedly, 'that we're going to have to pay more.'

'What?'

'The cost of apartments has risen more than I thought. There's no point buying a place we don't like. It's not necessarily a bad thing — if the market continues to rise.'

'Since when did you know anything about markets?'

'I'm serious, darling.'

Oh-oh. We're not usually serious at the same time. One of us always keeps a lighter perspective. That's how we work so well together.

'There might be a bit more money than I thought. Once everything's sold.'

I stare out of the window at the slow, sticky, summer's morning. It's not the sort of weather in which I usually think of Bebe. My memories of her usually rush in during wild, volatile days, those days when the sun dashes in and out of the clouds, and wind tears at the trees. Jack's mother, Bebe, died a year ago. She was a woman of great intelligence and energy — a woman whose spirit, wit, and brilliant bloody-mindedness would have been more than a match for Paris and any of its formidable real estate agents. She left us bereft. She also left us money. It's her money that's buying Paris. I don't know if she knows about it, but I'm sure she would approve. In her final suffering years she drank French champagne every single day.

'You miss her, don't you?'

'Of course I do.'

I reach for Jack's hand. 'Why don't we just buy the wedge?'

He looks at me apprehensively. 'I didn't think you liked the wedge.'

'It's not that I don't like it. It's just that, I don't know, compared to that hovel' — I wave my hand in the air as though the apartment is sitting at the next table — 'the wedge is perfection itself. You're the one who wanted to make a comparison.'

Jack sighs and finishes his coffee. 'That may have been a mistake. Anyway, what's her name, Véronique, she didn't ever call back, did she?'

'No, she didn't.'

We stare out at the street again. Neither of us feels strong enough to mention the Americans.

Ten

Jack has put apartment-hunting on hold for the rest of the day. It's Saturday, after all. Yoann and Athina are coming over for dinner. We're going to rescue Julia from her ping-pong match with Ellery, have some lunch, and then shop for tonight's dinner. My expectations are too high. I have to be patient. Take some time out. I know he's right. My expectations are wearing us out.

Ellery runs towards us, waving his ping-pong bat in the air. He's had great fun. Julia is hopeless at ping-pong apparently. She gives me a sideways look as she dashes off to catch the métro.

'Je t'appelle,' she yells as she rounds the corner.

I don't have to tell her that the diamond turned out to be a fake.

We head back to rue Vieille du Temple. The street is loud with Saturday lunchtime activity. Strong streaks of sun follow us down the steamy footpath. I walk along, blinking into the glare. Ellery wants a pain au chocolat. He persuades Jack to join the queue at the pâtisserie. I wait outside, feeling a little conspicuous in my raincoat, wishing I had my sunglasses instead. I hear Monsieur le Painter before I notice him, on the opposite side of the street, talking to a young, business-dressed couple. He is waving his arms around flamboyantly, describing his paintings with the flair and drama of an auctioneer at Sotheby's. The couple hang on his every word. They nod and frown and look earnest. Now Monsieur looks earnest, too, and something else. There is something else emanating from him. He turns and looks in my direction. His face is washed in a gentle smile. He looks unlike himself. He looks like someone who knows that every moment of life is valuable. I turn away, even though I'm sure he hasn't noticed me. He has his paintings and an audience and himself for entertainment. He doesn't need me. He may not need anything more. I move further along the street. I move closer to him. I want to see what everyone else sees. I want to see his paintings.

The couple are looking at the biggest one. It's nearly two metres tall. It's yellow and orange and red; the colours are thick and rich on the canvas. There are circles circling themselves and fat, sensual curves that look like sad smiles. Monsieur grabs hold of the painting and thrusts it at the couple. They struggle down the street with it. Monsieur tucks the money from the sale into his pants' pocket and pulls a bottle of something from his coat. He looks along the street. Our eyes lock. The smile on his face has gone, but radiance still clings to him. I wonder if he's sober, and immediately reproach myself. He unscrews the top from his bottle, waves it in my direction, and then throws it to his lips.

Monsieur is not very old. I haven't noticed that before. I look at him bending down, now fiddling around with his paint tins. He's in his early thirties. Thirty-five at the most. Even accounting for the way he lives, he still looks young. The way he lives. What would I know of the way he lives? What would I know about the way any of them lives? Somewhere in the distance a church bell chimes. An in-love, jeans-clad couple move past me. A bicycle rings its bell. 'Putain!' Me? Please don't swear at me. I'm just trying to be part of it. There are little pieces of me that belong here, too. Little pieces that need to be set free. I can feel the sun beating down on the back of my neck. It feels like home. Home? Why does it take so long to buy a pain au chocolat? Monsieur le Painter has disappeared. Again? What is he made of? A motorcycle mounts the footpath and drives perilously close to my foot.

'Mum. Mum.'

Ellery stands at my side, waving his chocolate-coated hands in my face. 'Mum. Why are you talking to yourself?'

'What?'

'Dad's been looking for you. He's at the Missing Star. We're ready for lunch.'

I try to focus on Ellery's waving hand. I'm further away than I thought. I'm on the corner at rue du Roi de Sicile, standing on the edge of the road. I squint along the street. 'I thought you'd come down this way instead,' I say, sneezing. I sneeze a second time. Ellery looks up at me. 'Have you catched a cold?'

'It's the sun. It's so bright after all the rain.'

'You look sad, too, Mum.'

'Sad?' I try and laugh. 'Why would I be sad? I was just feeling a little bit … homesick.'

'What's homesick?'

'It's a sickness you sometimes get when things remind you of home.'

'What reminds you of home here?'

I look down at him. 'You do,' I say, 'and the changeable weather.'

'That doesn't make sense, Mum, because how can I remind you of home if I'm already here?'

'I know. Come on, we'd better go and find Daddy.'

'You're weird, Mum.'

'Thanks.'

'Good weird. Not bad weird.'

He takes hold of my hand, his chocolate one in my sneeze-sticky one, and together we walk away.

Eleven

Athina and Yoann arrive at our door with a bright bunch of orange tiger lilies. They've always shared their Paris with us. They've introduced us to their family and friends, to their special restaurants, and to their local markets. They've taken us to see fringe theatre and little-known museums and the midnight lights running up and down the Champs-Élysées. We've stood around their piano on Christmas eve and sung carols and tied balloons to the roof of their car, and driven around the shimmering Eiffel Tower at New Year. Now, as Jack wrestles with the cork on the champagne and I rummage through the kitchen cupboards searching for a vase, it seems so much longer than a week ago since they met us at Charles de Gaulle airport and drove us to our apartment.

A tall plastic jug is all I can find. 'It spoils them,' I say, disappointed.

'N'importe quoi,' says Athina gaily as she takes the flowers and their makeshift vase, and places them on the mantlepiece. 'Et voilà.'

She's right. Their beauty still shines through.

We're drinking champagne and talking over the top of each other when a siren's wail interrupts us.

'It's for the painter,' says Yoann matter-of-factly.

'The painter?' I rush to the window. An ambulance blocks the street and the view. 'Is he alright?'

'Mummy hates that painter,' says Ellery.

Now Athina and Yoann look injured.

'Of course I don't.'

'But you said …'

'I didn't mean I hated him. I just find him …' I look down at Ellery's frowning face, 'a bit …' The only word that pops into my head is 'homeless'. That doesn't make sense. How could it be his homelessness that perturbs me?

'I think,' says Yoann slowly, 'that he fell and hurt his arm. There were a lot of people helping him. It is not the first time.'

'That's good. I mean, it's good that he's okay.' I smile anxiously. I'm worried about the lamb.

'Yoann likes the painter's work,' says Athina.

'I do, too. I was looking at his paintings just this afternoon. I thought we could buy one for our new apartment.'

'Let's just buy the apartment first,' says Jack.

I'm still not used to them coming to us for dinner. It has always been the other way around. I often think of myself standing in their small Paris kitchen, getting in the way, watching them whip up terrines and salades and tartes. They never rush. They always make everything from scratch, in their own time. They do things when it suits them. Like looking for lemons at midnight or kneading pastry at two in the morning.

I'm serving tarte au citron tonight, too, but I didn't whip it up all by myself. I took a philosophical approach to the vexed question of dinner. I went to Picard. There's no point losing your sang froid fretting about meat and vegetables. *Bof* — to spending hours wrangling with chou pastry or straining consume or waiting for asparagus season to make a mousse. Picard has it all. It sells everything from everywhere, and all of it is frozen. It's the ultimate in pre-packaged, take-home, pop-straight-into-the-microwave cooking. There's no fur, no heads, and no eyes. (Well, none for sale, anyway.) At Picard you trade experience for know-how. So this afternoon I joined the know-how men and women who moved up and down the aisles whipping stiff cold boxes into their tartan shopping trolleys. So now the terrine is ready to serve. The lamb is in the oven and the tarte au citron sits defrosting on the kitchen bench. Everything is under control; even so, preparing dinner for these accomplished cooks makes me a little bit nervous.

Jack's exaggerated version of rooms too small to stand up in and windows as big as postage stamps amuses everyone. We open a second bottle of Sancerre rouge. The dinner has been a great success — the lamb especially so. It's the first time Athina and Yoann have eaten New Zealand lamb. They think that going to Picard showed great esprit. Esprit! I would have been happy to settle for savoir faire.

We talk around the wreck on rue des Blancs Manteaux, and the wedge, and the strategy for week two. Yoann thinks our search is too narrow. He suggests we try the sixth and the seventh and even the fourteenth.

'The fourteenth,' says Jack determinedly, 'is too far away.'

We disagree about that. It's not that far away. Up the boulevard Saint-Michel, past the Jardin du Luxembourg, and you're practically there. The fourteenth is residential and authentic. It's where real Parisians live. Athina and Yoann live there. Their apartment is where I imagine I am when I'm imagining myself in Paris.

'Ellie must be the only person on the planet who could think that buying an apartment in Paris would be easy.'

Athina protests for me with a slight shrug. 'It's not that difficult, Jack,' she says, 'with help and some luck. Luck plays a big part, too.'

I know she's right. Some Parisian know-how is useful, but luck is what you really need. Athina and Yoann were lucky. They found their apartment straight away. They found each other straight away, too. Athina is pouring herself some water and smiling encouragingly at me. Maybe Paris is her destiny alone. After all, she was equipped for Paris — she came bearing gifts.

I met Athina eleven or twelve years ago when we were students at Monash University in Melbourne. We met on stage. I was playing Cleopatra in Shakespeare's play, and she was writing an essay on the production. I'd taken the easy option. It wasn't too difficult to be cast in a leading role in a university production with a diploma in acting in my kitbag. The daughter of hardworking, immigrant parents, she was fluent in four languages and had a competency in three or four others, including Japanese. She was also gifted in English literature, was a talented actress, and could parallel-park her dad's orange Valiant with her eyes shut.

She decided to continue her studies in Paris. I sort of followed her — not to study (although I've always wished I could do that, too), but to enjoy a Parisian life vicariously. I've accompanied her to the Sorbonne. I've read her conference papers and parts of her doctoral thesis. We've been to opening nights and closing parties at Yoann's theatre, and spent days and weeks talking our way around politics and art and the mysterious way that life works. I've coveted the Parisian life of my Greek–Australian friend even as I recognise the irony of her return to Europe and all that she misses about the country she was born in.

'I agree with Athina,' says Jack. 'We need some assistance. A bit of back-up.'

'What about luck?' It's a rhetorical question. I know Jack's not a great believer in luck. Of course, Athina has volunteered to help. She always does. She always takes time from her busy work-schedule to do things for us. That's the problem. I'm concerned that I rely on her too much. I worry that, if I can't manage to do this on my own, I won't be able to cope afterwards when the real work starts. When I have to cope with solicitors, notaries, and bankers. When I have to deal with the gas people and the phone people and the body corporate. I can see the hurdles I'll have to clear just to get the apartment furnished. I've already made a study of bed linen. It's a nightmare. All the sheets are sold by measurement. By the square metre, for all I can tell. There's no such thing as a double bed or a queen-size bed. I understand the French not having queen size, but even so you need a mathematics degree just to get the top and bottom sheets to fit the same bed.

'I don't know. I feel like I ought to be able to do this by myself.'

Jack feigns offence. 'So what am I doing here?'

Yoann purses his lips and fiddles with a tear-shape of wax that has fallen onto the table. 'All the apartments you have seen have been empty. Normally they would have furniture.'

He pours himself some more water. Has anyone ever studied how much water the French consume? They drink water like a nation continually parched.

'If an apartment is empty,' continues Athina, 'it's probably been on the market for some time. It's possible that because you don't know anyone …'

'They try to palm them off onto foreigners,' says Jack. 'I'd probably do the same if I had to sell a hovel.'

'That's not quite true.' Yoann's calm voice floats across the table. 'It is just that the agent must be cautious.' He takes a sip of his water. 'Claude says it's impossible to find the right apartment without the right real estate agent.'

'Impossible?' I reach for the wine.

'She has a friend she can introduce you to. It is better if the agent knows you. It is important to have trust.'

'In a real estate agent? How would that work?'

'Yoann has spoken to his Aunt Claude,' says Athina, ignoring Jack. 'She knows you. Of course, she is happy to help.'

It's difficult to make a dream come true. You have to be able to stand firm and bend all at the same time.

'Alright, let's ask for Claude's help. It would be nice to see an apartment with furniture in it.'

'She will be at the theatre tomorrow to hear Vladimir Nastase play. Why don't you come, too? You can talk to her then.'

'Me? She doesn't speak English,' I say, horrified.

'You'll be fine,' says Athina. 'Claude is charming.'

That's indisputable. She's charming, urbane, generous, and intelligent. She's also the most Parisian *Parisienne* I've ever met, and that intimidates me. 'She won't be able to understand a word I'm saying.'

'N'importe quoi,' says Athina confidently.

That's the point. If I have to explain myself in French to Claude, it's bound to sound just like nonsense.

Twelve

The aroma of good cooking seeps out of the buildings and reminds me of our Greek neighbours in Melbourne. It's my first trip to Alfortville in the daytime. I'm surprised at how different this suburb is from the Paris I know. The buildings I pass are sad and dilapidated. The modest shops are stocked with ordinary things. They sell electrical stuff, discount clothes, and hardware. There's a petrol station and a few struggling cafés. I pass young people dressed in dull, synthetic tracksuits, talking on mobile phones. Mothers are grappling with children and babies. Elderly people are sweltering at bus stops. I hurry along the streets, anxious to reach the theatre. It's a bit too real out here.

Le Théâtre-Studio is a converted wine cellar similar to the Malthouse Theatre in Melbourne, only smaller. It's intimate, but feels spacious thanks to a soaring beamed ceiling and the lack of hidden wings. Yoann is the theatre's administrator. It's his job to implement the diverse and ambitious programme that includes new work by English playwright Edward Bond, emerging playwrights from Eastern Europe, and innovative children's theatre. Musicians, poets, and street-kids-turned-actors all tread the boards here. Le Théâtre-Studio is subsidised by the government, and locals can attend for free. If there are any here today I can't tell which they are. I can see Claude, though, looking calm and elegant, leaning against a pillar, talking to Athina.

We were first introduced to Yoann's aunt when we were staying at his grandmother's house in Brittany a couple of years ago. At the end of this visit, Claude invited us to dinner at her apartment in Paris. I remember being delighted by the apartment's comfortable chic. I noted the details carefully: the restrained harmony of small antiques with objets trouvés, the baby grand piano, and the confident, red colour scheme. I remember us sitting on small chairs that were dotted about the living room, sipping champagne, listening to Claude introduce us to the other guests as Athina's Australian friends. She lent across the top of the baby grand and gave a précis of our three-month tour. There were polite très biens all round, but some mild surprise, too. What reason could Australians have for spending so much time in France? However did we manage with the accents? Jack surprised everyone when he said he found it easier to understand the accents in the provinces than those in Paris. I said I found the opposite. We started a debate. There is no better debut.

Dinner in the all-white dining room was relaxed and elegant. I sat back and watched myself enjoying every moment of it. This was the Paris of my dreams. I had long dreamt of red rooms and harmonious chairs, of leaning across tables and pianos. Any visitor could delight in public Paris. What I coveted was the élan, the exactitude, of private Paris. Claude had this Paris in abundance. Hers was the inner sanctum — not the Paris you could be privy to by chance.

Now, as I look at Claude, a study in intelligent interest, I'm still acutely aware of this. Despite all my efforts, I've never befriended a Parisian by chance alone. All my intimates here are the friends or family of friends of foreigners like myself. I'm hoping that buying an apartment will change that; but, as I battle along with my stop-start language, explaining the bâtiment unique and the wedge and the diamond, I wonder why I'm always setting hope against reason.

Claude's advice is not to worry. Her real estate agent friend, Josephine, is trustworthy, professional, and happy to help. She will find us the right apartment, an apartment near amenities. Position is very important. Bien sûr. You can't argue with that. That's a real estate maxim everyone understands. You want to step out of your door and have everything at your fingertips. That's what it is to live in Paris.

'Mais ...' Claude lowers her voice. She cautions us that good positions are scarce. We must find a street that is quiet and in the midst of everything, too.

'Oui, je vois,' I say confidently.

Athina and Claude exchange a look. They're not sure if I appreciate the difficulties involved, but at this moment I'm not worried about those; I'm revelling in the way I'm keeping up with Claude's monologue.

Athina suggests I tell Claude where we'd like our apartment to be. I start with the fourth. The Marais always meets with everyone's approval. We also like the fifth. Très bien. The fifth is close to everything. And the third. Claude's not sure about the third.

The fact that it's close to the Picasso Museum doesn't sway her. Donc. What about the fourteenth? I like it, but Jack's not so sure. Claude's sure. It's her view that the fourteenth is not for foreigners. Athina murmurs disagreement. Claude is adamant. The fourteenth arrondissement is not where you live if you're just visiting. This is where real Parisian living happens. Visitors are not interested in real Parisian life. They would be bored to death in the fourteenth. Josephine has an apartment in the seventh. That's where we ought to be looking. She will phone tomorrow to make an appointment to show it to us.

The performance is due to start. I thank Claude for her assistance. I'm grateful for her advice and her encouragement. I'm grateful for her comprehension because I know that listening to my meagre sentences is not easy for her. Claude is a perfectionist. That's why she doesn't speak English. Her command of her language is brilliant. Why undermine brilliance? The desire to embrace a foreign culture puzzles her, too. To leave or somehow drift away from your place of birth is a folly that Claude cannot countenance. She encourages travelling, of course, but not giving your heart away — there's no decorum in that. Maybe it's hard to maintain your Parisian identity when you're a long way from Paris. Australians don't have that problem. For the most part, we wear our history lightly, happy to be identified by who we're not rather than by who we are.

In the auditorium, I'm surprised to find that most of the seats are already full. The audience squashes up to make room for us on the long wooden benches. No one seems to mind the struggle to secure a place. Yoann introduces the musician. Vladimir Nastase is tall with a thin, expressive face and fat, long, brown hair. He sits on a small wooden chair at the front of the stage cradling a violin. The audience leans forward as he says something inaudible to Yoann, smiles, and readies himself to play. The lights dim as music, soft and yearning, fills the theatre. His playing is intense and joyous and transporting, as only music can be. I forget all about apartments, and abandon myself to it. I'm grateful for the respite. I love the theatre, and even though I swapped my imagined illustrious career as an actress for another imagined illustrious career as a professor of English, I still feel at home in one.

The musician is on his feet now and smiling broadly, delighting in his own performance. He plays faster and faster. The music resonates with life and possibility. He breaks a string and then another. The more strings he breaks, the more joy he plays with. His joy is fierce and passionate. The music reaches a crescendo. Tears — the warm, wonderful tears that beauty brings — fill my eyes and slide down my cheeks. My applause stings my hands. I collapse back into my seat. I thought I came to hear a Romanian playing Ravel. Instead I heard the music that comes of living something that you love.

After the show I stand on the edge of a group waiting to meet Monsieur Nastase. Animated conversations about art and the elections and something about the change to post offices flow around the auditorium. The Romanian's eyes light up when Yoann tells him I'm Australian.

'You speak English?' he asks.

'Oh yes,' I answer as someone refills my wine glass, 'but I'm trying to speak French, too.'

He looks pleased. 'I try also, but I speak better English. French, it is …' he looks up to the ceiling. I follow his gaze.

'I agree. It must be up there somewhere.'

Vladimir laughs softly. 'Australia is a very beautiful country,' he says, 'and very big.'

'Yes it is. Big and beautiful.'

'Then why are you in Europe?'

'Pardon?' I heard his question. I just wasn't expecting it. I don't really think of France as being in Europe. And Paris, well, I seem to think of it as a continent all to itself. 'Um. Well ...'

He looks at me intently and waits. Yoann waits, too. We all stand, waiting for something to spring from my mouth. Fortunately there's no need to answer questions quickly here. I swallow some more red wine.

'Paris ...' That's always a good word to start with. 'In Paris ... I feel happy and sad, too.' I screw up my face. Now I seem to be having trouble with English.

Vladimir laughs again. 'Don't you feel that everywhere?'

'No. Not as much as I do here.'

He brushes his long fringe from his eyes. 'I understand,' he says. 'It is the same for me with Romania.'

He smiles at me. My heart skips. I want to sit down and tell him everything. The whole story. His face is mapped with a million stories. Together we could spend hours talking through our lives.

'Life,' he says unexpectedly raising his plastic cup, 'and our beautiful countries. I hope they will not be too sad without us.'

We all raise our glasses.

'Don't worry about that,' I say gaily, 'my country never misses me. I don't think he ever misses anyone.'

'Aren't countries feminine in English?' asks Yoann.

'Usually.' I down the last of my wine. 'Not Australia, though. Australia is definitely a man.'

Out on the street, I say goodbye to Claude. She suggests we look in the newspapers, too. It hadn't occurred to me that Paris would have classifieds. That'll be fun — circling all the possibles in thick, red pen. I lean against the wall of the theatre and watch Claude walking away to get her car. A slight breeze tries to cool the air. I ask Athina whether she thinks Josephine will speak English. She shakes her head. She tells me I was fine this afternoon. I followed conversations, made replies. I smile resignedly. Claude's white dress disappears around the corner. Athina is wearing white, too. I'm in black. Black for summer in Paris? Where did I think I was going? Carlton? I sigh and look at the ground.

'It gets harder, not easier. I wasn't expecting that.'

'N'importe quoi,' says Athina, kissing me au revoir and then hopping in the car beside Claude. 'Bon courage,' she sings, waving goodbye.

I walk back towards the métro with her words repeating in my head. *Bon courage.* I suppose that's exactly what it takes.

Thirteen

On the long métro journey back to the Marais I'm hot and tired. A boy of seventeen or eighteen, ably led by a large, long-haired German shepherd, gets on at Ourcq. Smoking a cigarette, he walks through the carriage asking people for money. Some, including me, oblige him. I'm too intimidated not to. Most people get off at the next stop or change carriages. I can't tell which. I wonder if I should move, too, but I'm drifting lazily in and out of a jumble of thoughts, and can't summon the energy. Confused images of Parisian suburbs, Romanian musicians, thin dogs, and fate play inside my head. I try to replay Vladimir's Ravel, but my memory produces something more atonal than asymmetric. Isn't atonal the devil's interval? The sort of music Stalin would have banned.

I read somewhere that if you are found guilty of a crime you can be banned from entering Paris. I suppose it's a modern form of banishment to find yourself imprisoned in the suburbs. The boy is saying something to his dog. His voice is hoarse and low, and there's something else that strains into my head, an awkward vulnerability. He disappears at the next stop, leaving the stench of cigarette smoke behind him.

A tall man of indeterminate age gets on and stands in the middle of the carriage. He holds on to the centre pole. He wears a slightly short-for-him dark jumper, even though it must be close to forty degrees underground. He's one of those men you try not to look at but know you ought to keep your eye on. He flicks down one of the fold-up seats. The noise makes me jump. He turns to look at me. I pretend to examine the métro map on the back of my *carte orange*. That will fool him. Only locals carry weekly transport passes. Why that should make a difference to him, I'm not sure. The map is tiny and difficult to read in the moving train. I count the stops until my stop, Bastille. There's still a long way to go. A girl gets on at Laumière. She's in her mid-twenties and tall and willowy. She reminds me of my friend Davina. The man stands up and holds onto the pole again. She takes a quick look at him and walks over and sits down one seat from me. She smiles quickly at me as she does so. He's outnumbered now. Not that that always makes a difference.

Davina came from Wynouiomarta. Eighteen years ago I'd yet to travel to New Zealand, so I had to ask her the name of the town again and again before I could remember it. We were en route to Russia and met, by chance, in a transit lounge in Taipai. We became close friends, and travelled on and off for six or seven months. I remember being thrilled when she finally agreed to come to Paris with me. A proud Anglo-Saxon, she wasn't the least bit interested in Paris or the French.

We stop at Stalingrad. What sort of a name is that for a French métro station? A handful of people move into our carriage. The French Davina continues staring through her thin-framed glasses into the middle distance. The man at the pole looks around as though he's expecting someone.

We'd arrived at six in the morning. We'd come the cheapest way — the overnight bus and ferry journey from London had cost only twenty-five dollars. I can't remember how we got to the avenue de l'Opéra, but I do remember being overwhelmed by the early-morning silence, and by my tiredness and inability to find our hotel. 'Nearly there,' I lied, folding up my map. 'It's in the next street.'

'Lead on, McDuff,' Davina said.

Her languid smile annoyed me. This was not how I envisaged our arrival.

I remember waiting for her to say something more. To remark upon the exquisite beauty of Garnier's Opera House or to exclaim over the Frenchness of the Café de la Paix, but she was silent as she followed me down the sleeping avenue.

At a set of traffic lights I dropped my suitcase and held the map open with both hands. I kept repeating the name of the street we were searching for. Rue de Hanovre. It sounded efficient, even though with every repetition I knew my imagined grand entry into Paris was slipping further and further away from me.

'So,' Davina asked cheerfully, 'are we lost yet?'

'No.' More lying from me. 'We're not lost. It's just that all the streets are written in French.'

'That's a trap for young players,' she said.

I felt like crying. Why couldn't I find the street on the map? Why was our trip beginning like this? The traffic lights changed and changed again. No one was in the deserted avenue; not a single person to ask directions from. Secretly, I was glad that wasn't an option; I had no desire to be humiliated further by asking directions in mime language.

I tried to sound optimistic. 'I think I know what's happened.'

The lights changed to red again. A car edged its way towards us.

'The street doesn't run off the avenue. That's the problem.'

'Ellie.'

'Just a minute.' I kept my head in the map. I wasn't going to lose us twice. 'Ellie, there's a man ...'

Davina's voice was pulling at me. I ignored it. I didn't want to ask directions. I was trying to figure out if we should turn left or right. I also ignored the lights changing to green, and a dark car beneath my map remaining at the kerb.

'Ellie, he's ...'

'In a minute.' She sounded panicky. Things weren't that bad. We were lost in Paris, not some wilderness.

'Oh God.' Davina turned her back on the kerb and said it again. 'Oh God.'

I lifted my head from the map. She stood with her back to the road with her face screwed up and her eyes closed. Now I started to panic.

'What? What is it?'

'The car,' she said quietly.

Without opening her eyes she pointed straight ahead.

'That car.'

A dark-blue sedan was moving up the avenue. Slowly.

'What about it?'

'The man in it.' She had opened her eyes, but she was looking at the ground, 'he just …'

'What?'

' … pulled himself off.'

'What!' The map tried to envelop me. I thrashed at it, as though it was its fault.

'While he was smiling at me and …'

There was a word written on her face. I couldn't tell what it was. She shuddered into her cardigan.

'Sneering,' she said finally.

The lights changed to red again. A battered taxi brightened the kerb. I marched straight over to it, thrust the map in the driver's face, and pointed to the tiny rue de Hanovre. He looked up at me shook his head, turned, and pointed down the street. He said something I didn't understand — something that took a long time to say. Probably directions. I couldn't follow them. I didn't have one word of French then. I remember looking at the taxi driver and thinking, why is this happening to me. Why would Paris want to do this to me? To us? It's not fair. Paris isn't dangerous. Moscow is dangerous, and nothing like this happened to us there.

'How much?' I asked when he finished talking and pointing.

He looked at us and at our luggage, shrugged his shoulders, and managed to tell us 'twenty francs'.

'Hop in,' I said to Davina.

'Twenty francs,' he repeated.

I gave him the money. He did a U-turn across the intersection, turned left, and stopped outside a narrow, faded building.

'C'est ici,' he said somewhat apologetically.

We'd been three minutes away; I suppose that's what he was trying to tell us. He helped wrestle our bags onto the footpath, and we stood on the deserted street staring up at the tiny hotel.

'Bon courage, mesdemoiselles,' he said. Then he, too, was silently gone.

After some sleep and lunch and one or two glasses of wine, we decided to take the taxi driver's advice. We hit the streets of Paris armed with kangaroo pins and lazy smiles. We left the map at our hotel and let the streets take us by the hand. Our otherness was fussed over in shops, feted in cafés, and flirted with on the métro. The story of our arrival inflamed passions and prompted promises of revenge and protection. We danced from one 'je t'aime' to another, slipping in and around impossibly romantic scenarios, pretending they were real life. On our final night a married waiter pressed Davina against his starched white apron and pleaded with her to stay. It was raining lightly, just like it ought to have been. I was dazzled, spellbound by the breathlessness of haste — words spoken in haste, kisses given in haste, and the haste with which you could fall, for better and worse, completely under the thrall of a city.

Passengers begin to drift towards the door. The French Davina is standing, waiting for the next stop. A canal comes into view, and boats, too. Bastille. We're there. I leap to my feet and stand behind her, ready. The man on the pole readies himself behind me. I grip my bag tightly against my chest. I can't wait to be free of this carriage, to be breathing outside air, to be meeting Jack and Ellery on the steps of the Bastille opera house. The doors spring open, and together we knot out of the train and onto the platform. The train's warning bell sounds, and the girl who looks like Davina and the man who looks like trouble and the train all disappear together.

Out on the street, the winged genie on top of the Bastille column waves down to me. I squint up into the bright evening sun that encircles it. Then I spot Jack and Ellery waving, too, and I dash across the busy intersection to meet them outside the opera house. Ellery dances up and down the steps, telling me all about his adventures with the prehistoric animals at the Natural History Museum. He promises to take me there when I've finished buying an apartment. I squeeze his hand in mine. I feel as though I've been gone for days rather than just an afternoon. I tell him that I've had adventures today, too. He looks up at me, disappointed. I reassure him. Mine were small adventures, about people and apartments — nothing compared with mammoths and lions. He looks happy again as he jumps up a step to whisper into my ear.

'That's alright, Mum,' he says. 'That's a big adventure for you.'

Fourteen

I'm not surprised when Josephine telephones at ten in the morning. Claude always does what she says she's going to do. Hurriedly swallowing the last of my pain au chocolat, I congratulate myself on remembering to use the vous form with her. *Comment allez-vous?* Josephine is fine. She gets straight to the point. I note down the time and address of our rendezvous and, too shy to ask her to repeat them, I pray I got them right. Quai des Grands Augustins, at three this afternoon. How wonderful does that sound? I fling open the apartment windows on the sunny morning and tell Jack how pleasant Josephine was. How things are falling into place. How I have a feeling about today. Jack has a feeling, too. He feels that anything on the banks of the Seine will be too expensive.

'Ça dépend,' I say, smiling, chewing on the end of my pen. 'Ça dépend.'

I'm refusing to be put off. It's Monday, after all. My grandpa Les always said Monday was the day to start afresh.

'Did you tell Claude what our budget is?'

A tiny breeze brings the leaves on the courtyard trees to life.
'Of course I did.'

'What did she say?'

She took no notice. That's not the answer Jack's looking for.

'She thinks we can probably find an apartment for half a million.'

I try to sound unconcerned. That's not quite it. Breezy. This morning is breezy; I'll try and match that.

'Half a million what?'

I walk across the room and turn the radio on. 'Euros. What number is Radio Bleu?' I'm willing my favourite song to come on. The one by Pink Martini about ignoring difficulties. *Je veux seulement oublier* ...

'Half a million euros,' Jack throws a hand in the air, 'and then they go ballistic if you don't like it.'

'Friends of Claude's don't go ballistic, and now we have Josephine on board I'm sure things will change.'

'That,' says Jack draining the last of his coffee, 'is exactly what I'm worried about.'

We arrive at the Quai des Grands Augustins ten minutes early. We stand between two bouquinistes, and look out across the Seine. Its vigorous beauty silences us.

'God knows what we're doing here,' says Jack good-humouredly. 'We can't even afford to live by the Yarra.'

A tall, elegant woman is standing outside an antique shop smoking a cigarette. She is draped in long, flowing pieces of pale cotton and silk. Framed by the gilt and crystal that fill the window of the shop, she is the incarnation of Gatsby's Daisy.

'That's her,' I whisper to Jack.

'That woman doesn't look anything like a real estate agent.'

'Exactly,' I say, checking my watch.

The woman exhales a last puff of smoke onto the shop window, throws her cigarette butt to the ground, turns, and walks languidly towards our rendezvous.

We shake hands and introduce ourselves. Josephine is polite, gracious, and a little ethereal. She tells us that she saw us across the street looking at the river. She knew it was us straight away. She knew this because she could tell I was not French. It was Jack who confused her. He looks French. Très Français, en fait. Perhaps he has French blood. People often think that, even though I'm the one with the blood, with the ancestors. But my scant command of language always makes it impossible to explain my heredity, my tenuous claim to any Frenchness. I can't tell her that my great great great grandfather's death certificate reads: born Paris, died Buninyong. That perhaps my passion for France began with that early migration to the Ballarat goldrush. Ernest Jules La Cravino lived out the remainder of his life there. His only son married a local girl and became a successful draper. It's impossible to explain the sadness that I felt when I learned that the draper had only one son, too, my great uncle, who died fighting with the Australian infantry in a battle at the Somme. He died a day before his nineteenth birthday, five days before the war ended.

Instead I tell Josephine that, yes, everyone thinks Jack is French, even though he's not. Everywhere — in Paris, in the provinces, and once in Italy, too — he is stopped by French tourists and asked for directions. Josephine nods. When you look French this always happens. C'est normal. She presses the worn brass numbers on the door's code panel. It springs open at her touch.

We follow her floating figure down a long, cream-carpeted corridor. We pass two staircases and a heavy, glass security-door. The paintwork, the woodwork, the carpet — everything is immaculate. We alight from the unusually spacious rear lift onto the second floor. We walk down more spotless cream carpet until we are at the very back of the building. Again. You'd think that half a million euros would get you a bit closer to the front than this. It's taken nearly five minutes to get to the apartment door. With key poised, Josephine confides that she knows the owner. This, and the fact that we are friends of Claude's, gives us permission to view the apartment in the owner's absence. We are very lucky. It's difficult to find an apartment on the Seine, particularly one as lovely as this.

'J'imagine,' I say, trying to remember that that is, in fact, where we are.

A plump ginger cat is too slow to make his escape as Josephine shepherds us through the door. We tiptoe down the long hallway, past a series of stream-lined built-in cupboards, to the living room. Here everything is pale blonde wood, white leather, and cool marble. The clotted-cream paint on the walls and ceiling finishes the colour scheme perfectly. We stop and stare in admiration. What a difference furniture and decoration make.

'It's beautiful, isn't it?' says Josephine, helping us out of our speechlessness.

We stare around us. The living room is decorated in a cool minimalist style. A long, white leather sofa sits opposite an oval glass coffee table. A large bowl of white and grey stones sits on top of the table. A slender floor lamp made of paper stands next to two narrow wooden wall-mounted shelves that hold small, expensive-looking sound equipment. The all-white L-shaped kitchen is tucked in along the far wall. Together they make for a comfortably proportioned room. A generous bedroom opens off the living room via a Japanese paper sliding-door, and a luxuriously appointed bathroom and laundry run off the bedroom. It's all symmetry and understatement. I wonder if anyone really lives here.

Josephine takes us back into the hallway. We must see 'le dressing'. The 'dressing room' turns out to be the long cupboards we passed on the way in. The doors concertina open to reveal a uniform row of men's suits. It's très pratique, of course. We smile enthusiastically. We don't want to offend anything. We follow Josephine back to the kitchen, where we stand around looking past each other. The ginger cat slinks across the white floor tiles and curls in and out of a chair leg. On the white marble benchtop two lemon gerberas languish over the edge of a clear crystal vase. The whole apartment is bathed in an ethereal glow. The effect is something like moonlight.

'It has everything,' says Jack as the cat jumps onto the only chair, 'except space and windows.'

'There is one window,' says Josephine pointing behind us. We turn and stare at it. She strolls across and pulls back the curtain. The small, white window faces a white painted wall.

'Eh voilà,' she says. 'Unfortunately, there are no views of the Seine for five hundred thousand euros.'

'Five hundred thousand euros,' repeats Jack.

'It is a very good area, the sixth.' Josephine returns to us, opens her briefcase, and pulls out some papers and a slender silver pen. She lays the papers on top of the small fridge.

'It is really five hundred and forty-five thousand euros, but I think he will accept five hundred and twenty-five.'

We don't reply. She asks if we would prefer her to continue in English. In any language, this is more than we can afford. In lieu of a real response we crowd the small kitchen and watch Josephine noting down our answers to the usual real estate questions.

She drapes herself, like Claude, across the top of the small fridge. We tell her that the apartment is lovely but too small. Much too small. There's only one bedroom and nowhere to sit and eat. Josephine wonders if we have forgotten 'le dressing'. It is impossible to find an apartment with a built-in wardrobe like that. But we don't need a large wardrobe. We're not going to live here all the time. You will have luggage, Josephine tells us. We will have toys for our son. She can see that an extra bedroom could be an advantage, but a dressing room together with a large bathroom and laundry is much better. Unique. Oh-Oh. Jack's losing patience with unique. He tells Josephine that this apartment is too small and too expensive. It is not the apartment for us.

'It is not really expensive,' says Josephine sweetly. 'It is opposite the Seine.'

'We don't want an apartment opposite the Seine,' says Jack.

Josephine looks across the fridge at us. 'You don't want an apartment opposite the Seine?'

'Of course, we'd like one. But I'm afraid we don't have that sort of money. And besides. I don't know what's worse — not being near the river or being right next door without even a tiny glimpse of it.'

Josephine clicks her pen shut and smiles at me.

'Perhaps,' she says quietly, 'this apartment is not right for you.'

She traces her index finger around the edge of one of the pieces of paper. 'Claude, she is a good friend of mine. I admire her very much. Of course, I want to find something nice for you.'

'We really appreciate that,' I say. 'We're sorry.'

We stand in silence listening to the hum of the small fridge.

'Ce n'est pas grave. Grégoire, the cat, he gets lonely. It's not far for me to make a visit.'

We all look down at Grégoire. No wonder he gets lonely, living here imprisoned in this windowless wealth.

'Claude,' says Jack finally, 'told Ellie you would explain exactly how offers work.'

Josephine nods. 'It is not complicated. You make an offer to the vendor and it can be considered for seven days.'

'And after that?' Now it's Jack's turn to take a pen and paper from his pack and make notes.

'You can make other offers within the seven days, but the offer must be finished at the end of this period. When the property is under offer no one else can buy it.'

'How do you know how much to offer?'

'The agent will help you, but it is usually a little bit less. It is up to the owner whether he accepts or not. Then you must pay a deposit and then the rest of the money when everything is finished.'

'Sounds pretty much the same as the system we have in Australia,' says Jack.

Josephine picks up her fawn calf's skin briefcase and holds it in front of her chest.

'It may be similar or it may be the same, but I think we thought of it first,' she says, smiling.

When Josephine leaves us we go in search of a café. We walk along the quay lost in our thoughts. I read somewhere that Rudolph Nureyev lived on this street. That memory makes me smile. Of course, this is not real. Although we'd like to, we can't really imagine ourselves living here. It's not just the high prices of the real estate. It's the shops. All the art shops and antique shops and those tiny shops filled with half-upholstered chairs and untouchable fabric piled high on top of each other on tables and shelves and floors, they prevent us from imagining ourselves living here, too. An ancient door opens electronically onto the street. We stop to let the expensive car whisk past us.

'Let's go back to the Marais,' I say, 'to La Belle Hortense.'

'What's wrong with finding a café here?'

'It's a bit daunting here. It's a bit too ... Parisian.'

Jack laughs. 'What about tomorrow? The seventh is pretty Parisian, too.'

'It'd be impolite not to look at another of Josephine's apartments.

I won't be holding my breath, though; she was adamant that today's apartment was her best.'

'You never know,' says Jack. 'She might be keeping something up her sleeve.'

He takes my hand. I doubt that, but with only a week to go I'm definitely not brave enough to say so.

Fifteen

'You're coming with us today,' I say brightly, passing a plate of sliced apricots and peaches to Ellery.

'Where are we going?'

'To look at another apartment.'

'Why can't Jules look after me?'

'Julia has a gig, on a boat on the Seine.'

'Why can't I go? I like boats.'

'It's not for little ones.'

'In the day time.' He spits specks of peach across the dining table and looks at me as if I'm an idiot.

'Well, anyway. We'd like you to come with us. To tell us what you think.'

'About the apartment?'

'Yes.'

He squashes another piece of fruit into his mouth. 'You know what, Mum? I'll be good at that.'

'I know you will. This one's a bit further away. We'll have to take the métro.'

'I love the métro.'

'I know that, too.'

We walk along, looking up at the high walls that line the leafy street.

'It's flash around here,' says Jack appreciatively. 'Lots of trees. Lots of embassies.'

'Hmmm,' I say trying to match his enthusiasm. I'm not mad on high walls and embassies. I prefer to be in the midst of things. I want our apartment to look out on people and buses and butcher's shops. 'Don't you think we might be a bit out of our league here, too?'

'I wouldn't say that. An apartment opposite an embassy is bound to be less expensive than one opposite the Seine.'

'I'm going to live in an embassy when I grow up,' says Ellery.

We stop and look at him. He smiles broadly, pleased at having diverted our attention.

'What is an embassy, Dad?'

'That's an embassy,' says Jack, pointing at the rooftop of a large white building set back off the street.

'It's gynormous.'

'Yes. It's the opposite of what were're going to see this morning. Okay. We're nearly at Josephine's office. Please remember what I told you.'

'I know, Mum. No running around and no talking.'

'Unless someone asks you a question.'

'In English.'

'Pardon?'

'Unless someone asks me a question in English. I can't answer if someone asks me a question in French. Can I?'

Jack and I link eyes. 'No,' I say slowly, 'not unless you really wanted to.'

Ellery takes my hand and skips along beside me. I can tell by the bounce in his step that he's happy with his small win over the French language.

A long lemon trench coat hangs over the chair in front of Josephine's desk. She moves it to a coat hook when we arrive.

'I do not think there is rain today,' she says after all the bonjours and ça vas are out of the way. We introduce Ellery, who beams a blue-eyed smile around the room. It's the kind of smile that's guaranteed to produce a chocolate or a bonbon or some sort of treat. This morning is no exception. A young woman with long black hair, tied back in a ponytail, leaps up from behind her desk brandishing a box of chocolates as big as a small serving tray. She whisks the lid from the box and we stare at the contents. 'It's for you,' she says in a gorgeous, breathy accent. Ellery examines the chocolates carefully. We stand around fidgeting in the ensuing silence, willing him to make a choice. The French, conversely, indulge him all the time he wants. While they enjoy discernment, it just makes us uncomfortable.

After the selection of something long and narrow in gold paper, we are introduced to Jean-Louis, the third and final member of the team at Immobilier Rive-Gauche. In clear, economical English he gives us a brief description of this morning's apartment. I try not to look too impressed at the thought of a building from the belle epoch or flowerboxes or original parquetry. An elegant composure — that's what's needed here. That's what Jean-Louis' clear economy invites; but the harder I try for a casual stance, the more it eludes me. When his monologue is finished, he gestures towards Josephine's desk and we sit, also at attention. I shoot a look over my shoulder at Ellery and wish it was me spinning around on Mademoiselle's spare chair and playing games on Jack's mobile phone.

'I saw Claude yesterday,' says Josephine unexpectedly. 'We have the same butcher.'

'The same butcher,' I repeat lamely.

'Yes. She is very well.'

'Good. I mean très bien.' I chew at an involuntary smile. I know she doesn't mean the butcher.

'She was disappointed that you didn't like the apartment. The sixth it is very nice.'

'Oui. C'est très joli.'

Silence settles over the bureau. I try to steal a look at my watch.

'We leave in five minutes. The apartment is very close to here.'

'Ah bon,' says Jack, bringing the bureau back to life.

We step through the modest door of a small, graceful apartment building whose balconies are festooned with boxes of bright red geraniums. We drift along, noting the eggshell hue that washes the walls and the ornate cathedral window, and how together they bathe the hallway in soft sunlight. The thick Monet-blue floor carpet assists our progress. Jack and I exchange a quick smile. This is the sort of hallway we've been dreaming about. You could live in a hall like this. Forget buses and butcher's shops. This is the place to be — here in the chic seventh, living amongst Le Bon Marché, Le Lutetia, and the Pâtisserie Dalloyau. Josephine notes our delight.

'C'est très beau. Non?'

'Oui. C'est très, très beau.' I'm suddenly as sunlit as the building, completely entranced by our first real *beau bâtiment*.

In the lift, Josephine whispers that Madame is very keen to sell. This is très bien for us. Très bien, too, that the building has just been refurbished. *Tout va bien ce matin*. The lift stops, but Josephine makes no attempt to open the door. Ellery squeezes my hand, afraid there's some malfunction. There isn't — Josephine just wants us to know that we can make an offer as soon as we like. There's no point wasting time. Of course there isn't. Parisians understand the power of a beautiful hallway, of a soaring window, of possession. They have a way of getting to the heart of what you're only imagining. We glide out of the lift onto the third floor and follow our Parisian down the hall. Our footfall is silent. I wonder if the building has been sound proofed. We stop outside a carved walnut door at the very end of the hall. The right end. This time we're at the front. I cross my fingers. Oh please, please let it have a view of the street. I reach out and squeeze Jack's arm just as Josephine cautions us.

'It is best not to make Madame an offer inside. You can wait until we return to the bureau.'

'Madame will be here?' I ask, surprised.

'Yes. It is normal,' says Josephine.

'We haven't really struck an owner before,' says Jack, his voice hardly sotto voce.

Josephine eyes wash over us.

'Oui. It is better for the security,' she says, adjusting her gossamer scarf and ringing the doorbell.

'What's security?' asks Ellery

'I'll tell you later,' says Jack as the door opens to reveal Madame.

Ellery grabs my hand in fright. Madame and Josephine greet each other curtly. There's no kissing. No hand shaking. We are introduced as Monsieur and Madame who would inspect the apartment. We swallow our tiny bonjours and fall over each other stepping through the doorway. Madame says something. I recognise the words *beaucoup de choses*. Josephine turns to me and says gently, 'Madame is worried that your son will touch something.' I assure Josephine that Ellery is not a touching-things kind of child. Neither is he a standing-in-the-wings kind of child. A dreadful scenario of screaming tears, I don't want tos, and I hate Paris plays out in my mind. I look down at him. He senses his precarious status. He doesn't want to wait in the hall or at the door.

He lifts his eyes, looks up at Madame, and smiles nervously. Her reserve shifts a little. She steps aside and allows us to move the couple of steps down the hallway and into her salon.

The living room is classically French. The parquetry floor of crisscrossing triangles and squares boasts a beautiful patina. The faded pink-marble fireplace harmonises gracious curves with finely etched geometrical shapes. But, best of all, two sets of double French windows, divided by a long panel of honey bevelled wood, overlook the street. They overlook a wide, leafy street just like a Parisian apartment ought to.

'C'est très joli,' says Josephine. 'Très élégant, très classique.'

'Oh yes,' we answer in unison.

'And the view,' Josephine walks us across the room to the windows, 'c'est très lumineux.'

We stare at the fourth-floor balcony of the mansion opposite and at the tops of the plane trees.

'Mum?'

I tighten my grip on Ellery's hand and bend down close to his ear. 'Not yet,' I whisper. I know exactly what he's going to ask. Josephine turns us back into the room. Madame is no longer standing in the doorway. Perhaps it is her absence that emboldens him. 'Mum?'

'In a minute.'

Jack knows what's coming, too. 'Madame is a collector?' he asks mischievously.

'Oui,' says Josephine tightly. 'Madame est une collectionneuse.'

We walk past the windows in single file to the other end of the salon. The enormous glass display cabinets leave no space to cross the middle of the floor.

'She must have been collecting for a very long time,' says Jack, warming to his subject.

I throw him what I hope is a don't-you-dare look. The trouble with these looks is they usually incite Jack to do exactly that.

'I suppose so,' says Josephine doubtfully.

We stand at the far end of the room looking at the cabinets. Thousands of tiny China ornaments look back at us.

'Mum.'

Ellery stands his ground, refusing to be led away.

'Yes,' I sigh, 'they're ornaments.'

'That's not what I was going to say,' he says indignantly. 'I was going to say, why are the walls black?'

With the exception of the wooden panel between the windows, all the walls are covered in a thick, glossy black material. It's some sort of satin with a gold fleur du lys pattern either drawn or sewn onto it.

'Wallpaper.' I finally manage to get the word out. 'It's some kind of wallpaper.'

'What's it for?'

'Decoration.'

Ellery looks up at me amazed. 'Do you like it, Mum?'

'Um. Well.'

'It goes with the ornaments,' says Jack.

I stifle a nervous laugh.

'It is not difficult to remove,' says Josephine. 'The salon would be much bigger without it and the objets d'art.'

Objets d'art. Now, that's a brilliant description. Nobody could be offended by that. Les objets d'art sont très jolis. I don't say that, though. 'Oui. Je vois,' I say instead, feeling like I'm back in last week.

I wonder if Madame is listening to all this. After all, we're here as prospective buyers, not arbiters of taste.

'It's in the hallway, too, Mum.'

'Is it? I don't think I noticed that.' Of course I didn't. With the exception of Madame, I didn't notice anything in particular as we stepped through the front door. I was still thinking about geraniums and sunlit walls.

'Oui. It is there, too, but that also can be removed.' Josephine ignores Madame as we cross the hallway. 'Come. I will show you the other rooms.'

We follow obediently, passing Madame's stiff shadowed figure as we do so.

The other rooms, a kitchen, bathroom, bedroom, and separate toilet, are small and quaint. They in no way match the scale of the salon. The kitchen is a long strip of a room with worn wooden benches and open wooden shelving that reaches to the ceiling. It has a small central window that overlooks a pretty courtyard. The bathroom is wedged in between the walls at the top end of the hall. It has a child-size bath that runs across the room. A tiny handbasin is pinned in behind the door that opens out onto the hall. There is no window and no natural light. The bedroom is only marginally bigger. It has a three-quarter-width bed built in along one wall and a small dressing table on the other. The walls are plastered with pastel floral wallpaper, a busy contrast to the sombre black satin in the hall and salon.

'There's only one bedroom,' I say, disappointed.

'But there are two salons,' counters Josephine. 'If you want, you can make a second bedroom.'

We return to the salon. Madame follows us. Her face is impassive, but Josephine consults her watch and assures her we'll be leaving soon. We stand looking over the salon again.

'I sold an apartment last week, quite near to here. It was 120 square metres, more than double this apartment, and it was only one room,' says Josephine proudly.

I blink around the salon. My imagination has really been letting me down lately. Try as I might, I just can't imagine this room without its crammed glass cabinets, without the cloying satin wallpaper, with a new wall in the middle and a bed up one end. Seems like 'completely entranced' has completely disappeared. The more apartments I see, the more difficultly I have imagining myself living in one. I walk over to the open window and look out. I can't see myself there either, not now or tomorrow, nor in a few weeks from now, hurrying down the street towards this room and calling this apartment home.

'Does the fireplace work?' Jack stands before it and, as I turn from the window, he bobs down and peers up into the chimney as though the answer to his question lies buried in the blackened bricks.

Sixteen

On the short walk back to Immobilier Rive-Gauche, Ellery and I trail the talkative Jack and Josephine in silence.

'Are you sad, Mum?'

'No.'

'You look sad.'

'Shh.' I say taking his hand, hoping Josephine didn't hear him. 'I'm not sad. I'm just …'

Ellery tightens his grip on my hand and waits. I don't want to disappoint him by telling him I feel disappointed. I struggle to find another word.

'Let down,' I say finally. 'That's a bit like sad but not as big.'

Ellery nods knowingly. 'Like that little girl on the métro.'

'What little girl?'

'You know, that one that didn't get on with that man, probably her dad or it might have been her teacher, and all the other kids

and the train went and she was left on the platform. By herself.'
He looks up at me, his eyes wide with concern.

'I think you might feel a bit more than let down if that
happened to you.'

'What would you feel, Mum?'

'Oh, I don't know,' I say, failing to find a lighter tone. 'Worried.
You would probably be worried.'

'I think it would be bigger than worried, Mum. I think you
would be frightened.'

The late-morning sun shimmers on our faces. Of course he's
right. I hadn't thought of frightened.

At the bureau, Josephine gives Jack a plan of the apartment. It looks
better on paper. She draws a few lines here and there. There's not
really much work needed. We won't find perfect. Every apartment
needs something doing to it. N'est-ce pas? I watch as Jack bends
to Josephine's reasonableness. Is this the same man who just two
nights ago swore he would never buy an apartment that needed as
much as a coat of paint? Now, as he sits here beside me, I can tell
by the way he's listening that something has changed. It's written
there on the side of his head — a desire to make an offer, to test
the rules.

Mademoiselle sits at her desk writing. She looks up at me
and smiles reassuringly. Am I missing something? Is this it? The
apartment we've dreamed of? Well, if it is, I'd better show a bit
more enthusiasm.

'C'est toujours comme ça,' I say.

Jack and Josephine stare at me. I think I'm a bit behind in the
conversation. I try again.

'So do we know what the asking price is?'

That question stops the flow of things.

'It is four hundred and sixty-seven thousand euros,' says Josephine calmly.

She examines our faces for ... what? Shock? Relief?

'Two days ago I sold an apartment near to here for seven hundred and twenty thousand euros.'

Now we register shock.

'It was a little bit bigger, but en général ...' Her hands give a shrug.

'Do you have any other apartments you could show us?' I ask.

'Of course, I have many more apartments, but not at this price. This is a very good price. It is difficult to find a good apartment for under seven or eight hundred thousand euros.'

'Not in the fourth,' I say half under my breath.

'The fourth is very noisy,' she says.

'We've been looking in the fifth, too,' Jack says.

'Ah. The fifth is nice. Not as expensive as the seventh. Perhaps you would be better to look there.'

'Do you have any apartments in the fifth?'

'I have apartments in the sixth and seventh only. I think if you were to offer Madame four hundred and fifty-two thousand euros, she would take it.'

Jack turns to me and says, 'What do you think?'

About what? Buying it or the price?

Jean-Louis walks through the door. 'Ça va?' he asks.

'Oui, oui, ça va,' sings Josephine. 'We are about to make an offer, I think.'

'Très bien.'

Zut alors! Is that all it takes? A nod, a quick flourish of ink on paper, and the apartment cum museum is ours?

'Are we going to buy that apartment with the black walls?' Ellery looks up from the pen and paper that Mademoiselle has given him.

'No,' I say. 'Not yet. We're not sure.'

'If we make an offer,' says Jack, 'it's valid for seven days?'

'Oui. And if you make another higher offer then that is valid for seven days, too.'

'And at the end of seven days that's it. The offer is finished. We don't have to pay anything. Not a deposit or something like that.'

'No. You don't pay anything.' Josephine looks to Jean-Louis.

'No.' Jean-Louis confirms this with a smile and a frown — a curious combination.

'No. If at the end of seven days you don't want the apartment, then …' his hands cut through the air in a gesture of finality, 'it is finished.'

'Bon,' says Jack, satisfied. 'Okay then. We will make an offer for four hundred and twenty-five thousand euros.'

My heart leaps, but I can't tell whether it's from excitement or panic.

'I don't think Madame will accept such a low offer,' says Josephine.

'Well, you can put it to her and find out.'

Jack has moved into lawyer mode. Josephine and Jean-Louis begin to look a little wan.

'If she doesn't accept the offer then she doesn't accept it.'

Jean-Louis moves closer to us. 'It is important …' he says. His sentence trails away. He looks to Josephine for help. She doesn't offer any.

'It is important not to … what is the word? Not to … in French it is *vexer*. We do not want to vexer the owner. You know what it is — vexer?'

Vexer? To vex? To seriously piss someone off. Zut. I can't say that.

'It's the same in English,' I say instead, 'when you upset or offend someone.'

'Voilà.'

At last, everyone agrees on something.

'If Madame becomes vexé at your offer then it's difficult, because perhaps she will not want to consider you.'

Josephine and Jean-Louis look gravely across at us.

'I know what you mean. The same thing happened to me in Cairo once.'

Jack waves his eyes at me in warning. I pretend not to notice.

'I was bargaining for a galabiya.'

At their puzzled looks I begin explaining galabiyas. Mademoiselle helps out with a comme ça, comme ça, demonstration of the cut and length of these ubiquitous Egyptian garments. Oui, ouis all round. An interruption from Jack about my interruption, but I continue on regardless.

'It was beautifully made — all hand sewn and cut on the cross. It was the best one I'd ever seen, but I made an offer that was too low, and the tailor got so angry and upset that he closed his shop and refused to sell it to me.'

'Exactement,' says Josephine, looking at me with a new respect. 'That is exactly the problem.'

'If you don't want to put the offer to Madame then you don't have to,' says Jack.

He's losing patience just as I'm beginning to enjoy myself.

'That is our offer — four hundred and twenty-five thousand euros — and you can also tell her that the money is in the bank.'

Josephine picks up her pen and holds it between her fingers like a cigarette. 'You do not need to find a loan from the bank?'

'No.'

'That makes a difference.'

'I thought it would,' says Jack as a victory smile tugs at the left side of his mouth.

Josephine produces a printed A4 sheet of paper. She explains that we must fill out this form in order to make an offer. We read through it. It seems fairly straightforward. Josephine solemnly fills in the blanks: the address, the amount of the offer, and the date. She explains that there are two dates: today's date (the fifth of July) and the date that the offer expires (the twelfth of July). She makes sure we understand. Oui oui, nous comprenons. Ellery wants to go. He's hungry. I'm light-headed. A voice inside me keeps shouting, Oh my God, in this small moment everything could change. This is it. We're buying an apartment in Paris. And then I remember the actual apartment, and my light-headedness wrestles with sharp pangs of anxiety.

'Now you must write, "I have read and approved of the above" and then sign your name.'

Josephine hands me her pen and the declaration she has written for us to copy. I transcribe her small even script onto the form, sign and date it, and hand the pen to Jack for him to do the same.

'They don't leave anything to chance, do they?' says Jack, copying out Josephine's sentence and signing his name with a flourish I have never noticed before. His observation falls on deaf ears.

'C'mon,' says Jack as we zigzag down rue du Bac towards Sèvres Babylone, 'I'm taking us all to lunch at the Lutetia.'

'At the Lutetia? Are you sure?'

'Yep. What we need after all that is good food and champagne.'

'Can I have champagne, too, Dad?'

'No,' we say in unison. Ellery smiles broadly. He loves to have us in agreement, even if it is to dismiss one of his ambit claims.

'Are we celebrating already?' I ask.

'Yes. Our victory over the system.'

'You don't really want to buy that apartment, do you?'

'We'll talk about it over lunch. If Madame accepts our offer it might not be such a bad buy. But from what Josephine said, it's pretty clear she wants more than that. Whatever happens, we've gone through the process, and that's the best way to see how the system works.'

'It's not just a legal exercise,' I say, disappointed again.

'And it's not an exercise in signing our lives away either. We have to know what we're doing, what all the hidden costs are. We haven't even found out how much stamp duty is yet.'

I sigh in response to this and look longingly down the street to the Lutetia.

A crispy chicken rôti with pommes frites and champagne revives us. The bistro at the Lutetia is always busy at lunchtime but big enough, too, that a table somewhere can usually be found. The menu is classic bistro style with steak, fish, and chicken. It's a sort of variation on the kinds of food they serve in Victorian country pubs. Good staples cooked plainly. Food that people recognise. The main difference is that the Lutetia doesn't bother to complicate the vegetables. It's pommes frites, salade verte, or something in season. Our table is near the window. Outside, Parisian life flashes past. Inside the hurly burly of lunchtime calms down, and so do we. Every mouthful of food, every sip of champagne, consoles us through our post-mortem on the morning's events.

The apartment, when you consider it without the ornaments and the wallpaper and Madame (adds Ellery), is lovely. It's charming. It's easily the best one we've seen, because with or without these this apartment is so Parisian. It still has windows and parquetry and a fireplace and soaring walls and wood panelling and views of the street. All it really needs is a good clean-out and some paint and a bedroom for Ellery. C'est pas grave. The first two are easily done. Yoann will know a painter. I twirl my half-full champagne flute around the table-top and gaze dreamily out of the window.

I know it won't really come to that. We've probably already overplayed our hand. Jean-Louis knows what's going on. Madame looks as though she was born to play *vexer*.

Seventeen

I pace around our living room. Paris hasn't started yet, and neither have I. It's too early for both of us, even though the day is already waking. The air is dry. The sun is sliding across zinc rooftops. I'm impatient for the crash and clang of metal, for the sound of others. The rubbishmen. Monsieur le Painter. Anyone except the teeming Chinese dragons that sabotaged my dreams. I can still see them sitting in real estate offices, wearing galabiyas and waving documents at me.

I sit down next to the phone, and stack and restack my neatly labelled files. Immobilier Marais. Agence de Saint-Paul. Immobilier Catherine. I make a note to buy *Le Monde* for the classifieds. I doodle around the page, thinking about yesterday and the days before yesterday. I think about returning to Melbourne without an apartment. I think about returning to Melbourne with the wrong apartment. I write the word 'madame' in capitals, and underline it. If our offer is accepted, that's it. I'm cross with myself for not feeling happy and grateful, but *Are we doing the right thing?* hammers at my brain instead.

A word as sharp as a stone comes hurtling through the window. He's there. Monsieur le Painter says good morning. I jump up and strain out of the window to the street below. 'Bonjour monsieur,' I yell. I shouldn't have. Everything goes silent after that.

At twelve past ten the phone rings. I look at Jack, straighten up, and ready myself. Three rings. That should be enough. I answer with my best allô. Someone says something in French. I hang up.

'What happened?'

'I didn't answer properly. I should have said hello in English.'

Jack shakes his head and asks if I would like another coffee. The phone rings again. This time I answer in my normal voice. My heart is racing so loudly that it takes me a few seconds to realise that it's not Josephine on the line, but another woman who sounds a lot like Josephine and who is also talking about an apartment.

'It's Véronique,' I yell in a whisper with my hand over the mouthpiece. I listen as she tells me that the Americans had something unexpected come up. It was very disappointing because they had made an offer on the wedge and everything was looking good. But now … The sound of a Gallic shrug comes over the phone line. Donc. So would we still be interested? Would we? I don't know. I equivocate with a few ums and ahs. Véronique is an excellent people-person; even on the phone she knows we could be within reach.

'Four hundred thousand euros,' she says.

She is confident that Madame Martin will accept that amount. This is a once-in-a-lifetime opportunity. That worries me. That's exactly the sort of opportunity I'm after. I try to remember the original price. My files are out of reach and the phone is not hands-free. I'm waving at Jack to pass me her file when the 'mon mari' defence springs to mind. Malheureusement, my husband is not here at the moment. We have to consider this together. Such a decision is très important. N'est-ce pas? Of course, Véronique agrees. Decorum dictates a deference to reasonableness. I promise to ring her back. The second I hang up the phone rings again. It's Claude.

The switch into French takes me by surprise. I jump to my

feet and knock a file full of real estate brochures flying to the floor. What is she saying? Something about Josephine. The word Josephine is clear enough. Ellery comes skipping down the stairs.

'Mum. Mum. I made …'

Jack emerges from the kitchen. 'Mummy's on the phone.'

'I want to tell her about the rocket I made.'

'When she's off the phone.'

'Mum.'

'Pardon, Claude?' I hold my hand over my free ear to block out the noise. I think she's saying something about our offer. She sounds pleased. Josephine is pleased, too. I breathe a sigh of relief. Everything is going well. Josephine is très gentille, très charmante. Claude cuts my effusiveness. Josephine is très professionnelle. Oui. Oui. Je sais. Of course she is. Everyone here is professional at something. Ellery turns the television on. Jack yells at him to turn it off. Claude wants details. Très joli, très calme, très lumineux. All my practised real estate words come tumbling out of my mouth. Claude is going to Burgundy for a few days. She will ring again when she returns. She has every confidence in Josephine. The apartment will be perfect for us. She hangs up and leaves me staring into the dead receiver.

Ellery pops his head up out of the grotto and screams across the park to me. I wave back and as Jack emerges, too, I take their picture. Buttes-Chaumont is Jack's favourite Paris park. He says it reminds him of Central Park in New York. I can't imagine anywhere in New York being as calm as it is here.

A garden policewoman rides past on her bicycle talking into a walkie-talkie. I wonder what sort of training you need to become a garden policewoman. She looks like Véronique. Maybe we should have another look at the wedge. I wonder if you can make offers on two apartments at once. I pull *Le Monde* from my bag. The apartments for sale are arranged similarly to those in *De Particulier à Particulier*, in order of arrondissement. I turn to the fourth; there are only two, and they're both wildly expensive. I move on to the fifth. Fifty square metres, in a charming street, close to the Panthéon. That sounds promising. I circle it in red. Now it looks even more promising.

I am nearly asleep, stretched out on the warm springy grass, when my mobile phone rings. It's Josephine. Madame has not accepted our offer, but the good news is she is not vexé. That is très bien for everyone. So now it is up to us to make another offer. Perhaps four hundred and forty-five thousand. Maybe we could go as low as four hundred and forty, seeing how Madame has retained her good humour. I promise to call back as soon as I have spoken to Jack. I snap my phone closed, and sit up hugging my legs and staring across to the grotto on top of the tiny island in front of me.

Tearing through our picnic lunch of camembert-filled baguettes, I tell Jack about Josephine's call, and show him the advertisement for the apartment in the fifth. He's not impressed by either. Four hundred and forty is too much, and fifty square metres is too small.

Josephine rings again. She's leaving Paris for a long weekend and wants to finalise things before she goes. I take a deep breath. She knows what I'm about to say. She says that if we make another offer, she thinks Madame will accept it. I tell her that I'm desolée, but mon mari will not make a higher offer. Our original bid of four hundred and twenty-five thousand euros stands. There is such a long silence that Ellery looks up from his lunch, suspicious. Perhaps I have started playing games on my mobile phone. Finally, Josephine says that if we want the apartment we will have to offer another ten thousand. Madame will not accept anything less. Then she tells me matter-of-factly that Madame's mother is dying. She must sell and move to look after her. 'Oh,' I say. 'I'm sorry.'

I feel wretched now. I try to fix Madame in my mind's eye, hidden in the hallway of her own apartment — an apartment she must have owned for twenty or thirty years. How many years would it take to collect all those ornaments? Is she going to take them with her to wherever she's going? Some of them are old. All of them are fragile. I ask if it would be better to withdraw, but that's not how it's done. If Madame does not accept our offer within seven days it will lapse. It cannot be withdrawn. Josephine has another call coming in. She tells me politely that she will acquaint Madame with the situation and call me again tomorrow. À bientôt — and now there's another dead phone in my hand.

'Josephine wants us to make another offer, but I told her we couldn't,' I say quietly.

'Good,' says Jack cheerfully. 'You're right. This apartment doesn't sound too bad. It's got two bedrooms and a bath. I don't know how the hell they fit all that into fifty square metres.'

'The French are brilliant at design.' There is no enthusiasm in my remark. I drain the last of my mineral water.

'What's the matter?' Jack props himself up on his elbow.

'Madame's mother is very ill.'

'Which Madame?'

'The one who owns the apartment.'

'Is she going to die?' asks Ellery his mouth full of Haribo sugar jubes.

'Of course not.' I fiddle with my mobile. 'Josephine's expecting us to make a counter-offer.'

'Well, when we don't she'll see that that's our best price, and that will be the end of it.'

'You were the one who wanted to make the offer.'

'We had to make an offer on one of them.'

'We don't have to buy all the ornaments as well, though, do we?' asks Ellery.

'No.'

'We're going to get nowhere if you're going to worry yourself to death over every owner you meet.'

'It's difficult when you know them. It's hard not to put yourself in their shoes.'

'We don't know her. She barely said hello to us.'

'You know what I mean.'

Back at our apartment, I phone Véronique. She's disappointed when I tell her we're finished with the wedge. I was expecting vexé, but she graciously accepts the news that we've made an offer on another apartment. She sniffs a little, though, when I tell her that it's in the seventh. Véronique thinks we're better suited to the fourth. Do I realise that in the fourth the price per square metre is about five thousand euros, but in the seventh it is closer to eight? She doesn't wait for an answer. She has to go. She promises to ring if she finds us anything else. She has some new Americans. She wishes us luck. I like Véronique.

Yoann rings. He's been to see the wedge. He was taking a visiting Estonian actor to dine at a Moroccan restaurant in the third and they walked right past it. He says the building is très exceptionnel. Zut. It's too late now. We've made an offer on a normal building in the seventh. I decide not to mention the ornaments and the black-satin wallpaper. Yoann thinks we can make an offer on two apartments at the same time. He promises to find out. I tell him about the apartment in the newspaper. That it's in rue Saint-Jacques. That I've made a rendezvous to see the agent tomorrow. I know he'll be interested. His oboe teacher lives in that street.

I am still thinking about taking up the oboe when Josephine rings again. We have moved on to speaking in Franglais. Paradoxically, this mutation of French and English collapses both languages into comprehension. No, we haven't changed our minds. Our original offer still stands. Bien. Bien. She sounds a bit rushed. She's leaving soon. Jean-Louis will be handling things now. We can speak to him any time. Is there anything else we need to know? I can't think of anything. Très bien. The weather is supposed to be nice. No rain from now on. She promises there are no other apartments that would suit us. She has every faith in Jean-Louis. He is très professionnel. She wishes us bonne chance. Bon courage. I thank her for everything and wait on the empty line. Two real estate goodbyes in one day. That doesn't augur well.

Julia rings. Does Ellery want to go and see *Ice Age*? Jack bursts through the front door. The bank has eaten his credit card. The dry cleaners aren't open. What day is it? Wednesday. The dry cleaners doesn't open on Wednesday. Ellery spills a glass of orange juice on the floor. He doesn't want to see *Ice Age*. He wants to me to buy him a Game Boy.

I'm still mopping up the orange juice when Jean-Louis phones. Do I realise tomorrow is Thursday? We should know one way or the other by then. If we could find another ten thousand euros … He promises to call as soon as he hears from Madame.

'Il fait beau,' I say impulsively, but it doesn't assuage the sorrow I feel at letting everyone down.

'The weather?' asks Jean-Louis. 'You are speaking about the weather?'

'Oui,' I say, regretting I mentioned it. Of course, he thinks I mean the apartment.

Eighteen

The number 38 is my favourite bus. It picks us up at Châtelet, crosses the Seine, and lurches along boulevard Saint-Michel. You can catch it to the Panthéon, the Sorbonne, the Jardin du Luxembourg, or all the way to Montparnasse. This morning it's taking us to rue Saint-Jacques.

The number 69 is my second favourite. It goes to La Tour Eiffel. It's the cheapest guide bus in Paris. For the price of a métro ticket you can creep along from rue du Bac to avenue Rapp, passing dozens of exquisite boutiques along the way. I'm also fond of the open-back bus that goes down rue des Francs-Bourgeois. Unfortunately, they're retiring it soon. I'm unhappy about that. That bus reminds me of Melbourne's trams — not the new French ones — the old ones with their wooden running rails and open middle section you could jump onto. If you're fast enough you can jump onto the back of this bus. That's probably why they're getting rid of it — jumping onto moving trams and buses is not the sport it used to be.

The Sorbonne is on rue Saint-Jacques. I ventured in there once to make inquiries about learning French. They told me I would have to take a test to determine what level I was. The test would be in French. I told them I didn't have a level. How could I take a test in French if I hadn't any French? Monsieur smiled down at me. I have no idea why he seemed so tall. Maybe because the office was all enormous dark wood. It reminded me of the time I had to report to the Supreme Court in Melbourne and tell them that I couldn't do jury duty because I was about to start a role in the television series *Prisoner*. Pas de problème. Nothing to worry about. If I didn't write one word of French in the test, the Sorbonne would know that I knew nothing. It was that simple. Humiliating but simple. I thanked Monsieur and walked out into the arcaded courtyard and pressed my hands against the soft ancient stones and promised I would return.

'This is it,' says Jack, leaping to his feet. An electronic voice announces our stop. We swing out of the door and onto the street. We amble along, squinting up at the buildings, speculating on which one houses *our* apartment. I've given up trying not to think like this.

At L'Agence Saint-Jacques, Monsieur sits at an oversized chair squashed in between two desks. As the door heralds our arrival, he swivels round to greet us.

'Bonjour, messieurs-dames,' he says cheerfully.

'Bonjour, monsieur,' we chorus.

'The English, they are always on time,' he declares, moving around from behind his desk towards us.

'We're Australian,' I say, more hopefully than I thought I was going to.

'Ah,' he says. 'I have a cousin who is married to an Australian. He lives in Sydney. Do you live in Sydney?'

'No. We live in Melbourne,' says Jack.

'Melbourne. I know Melbourne,' he says proudly. 'It is smaller than Sydney.'

'Just a bit,' I say, trying not to sound miffed.

'But my favourite place,' Monsieur continues as though I hadn't spoken, 'is Kangaroo Island. Kangaroo Island is wonderful. You have been there?'

We shake our heads and manage oblique smiles. I'm not even sure where it is.

'You must go. There are kangaroos everywhere. It is very interesting.'

Now we nod. 'Everyone says that.'

'Then everyone is correct. Now,' says Monsieur, clapping his hands together, 'you are wanting to buy an apartment?'

'Yes,' says Jack cautiously, 'we're thinking about it.'

'Of course you are. Everyone wants to buy an apartment in Paris. C'est normal. Please,' he says, 'sit down.'

He leads the way to the chairs as though they are on the other side of dangerous waters. We introduce ourselves. He is Monsieur Rolland. He seats himself and takes up a pen. He is warm and open. I have a sudden urge to tell him all that's happened, to ask his advice, but I can tell that Jack feels the opposite. He doesn't like to be second guessed.

'Eh, voilà,' says Monsieur when he has finished noting our details. 'Unfortunately, I have nothing for you at the moment.'

How can he be so certain? We haven't even told him what type of apartment we're looking for.

'The good apartments sell quickly. Even with the prices going up, even with the euro, still they sell.'

'What about the one in the paper,' says Jack, 'the one we phoned about yesterday?'

I whisk the newspaper from my bag and hold up the circled advertisement for Monsieur to see. He purses his lips together, raises his eyebrows, and nods. 'Ah, oui. Now I remember.'

I knew it. Of course he has an apartment for us. It says so in the newspaper.

'Mais, it is very small,' says Monsieur, 'I think perhaps you are looking for something bigger.'

'Is it big enough for two people?' asks Jack. Then, without waiting for an answer, he turns to me and says, 'Darling, there's no point looking at it if it's not big enough for two people.'

'I do not think,' says Monsieur smilingly, 'that that is the question. There is at the moment a mother with three or four children living there. The husband has gone now and so she has to find somewhere else.'

What does he mean, 'gone'?

'Is it renovated?' asks Jack.

'Oh, it is a lovely apartment and in excellent condition even with …' he waves a hand at the ceiling. 'It is a pity you did not come earlier. I sold two other apartments in the same building last week. Two apartments. Both of them would have been much better for you.' He shrugs and gives us an apologetic look.

'How much is it?' Jack asks.

'How much?'

'What is the cost?'

'Ah. Yes. It is four hundred and thirty thousand euros.'

'And it is 50 square metres?'

'It is 53.5. I have the certificate.' Monsieur walks over to the other desk, rummages through a file, extracts a piece of paper, and hands it to Jack with the usual 'voilà'.

We pore over the plan and its measurements. Monsieur explains that the apartment looks bigger than it is because it has a lot of space you can't measure. A law called *la loi Carrez* guarantees the habitable square-metre measurement of apartments. Since this law has come into effect, all apartments have to be certified with their exact measurement of 'surfaces habitables' before they can be sold. It is forbidden, completely forbidden, to include uninhabitable surfaces in the measurements.

Vous voyez? Not really. Monsieur Rolland is thrilled. He retrieves the plan, throws it down on the desk and, using his pen as a pointer, begins to guide us through the rooms of the apartment. Par exemple: in the living room there is a fireplace; the space for the hearth cannot be measured. There is a cupboard in the bedroom; you cannot live in a cupboard, so this space cannot be measured. You cannot live on the window-sills, so that space … Oh, yes. Now we understand the rules. We bend closer trying to beat Monsieur to the next example. Jack pounces on the space under the kitchen sink. Voilà. Monsieur concedes the sink. The bathroom basin. Oui. Ça c'est la même chose. He pays that one, too. Jack is a good competitor, but he's not up to Monsieur's standard. He can't see any others, but there must be one because Monsieur stands to one side looking at us expectantly.

'No,' says Jack finally. 'I give up.'

'Bon,' says Monsieur, 'you will not see it. Here ...' He taps the end of his pen at a space just inside the front door. 'Here is a small cupboard. It is not very interesting. It is for the electricity and things like that. That is the last piece of space where you cannot live.' He straightens up and looks at us. 'It is good to buy an apartment with this system.'

'Oui, je comprends maintenant. C'est très intéressant.'

'Je vous en prie, madame.'

'Mais, maintenant, nous voudrions vraiment voir l'appartement. C'est possible?'

Monsieur regards me suspiciously. 'You speak French very well,' he says.

'Un petit peu.'

I don't know why I bother to continue with this line. No Parisian ever believes me. I think they prefer you to answer yes or no. You do or you don't. Un petit peu is inconclusive, vague. It's an answer that's treated with disbelief, disdain, or both.

'No,' Monsieur says firmly, 'you speak well.'

I affect a modest look and a bit of a shrug.

'If you wish, I can show you the apartment, but it is not right for you.'

'Well, if it is possible, monsieur,' says Jack, coming to my rescue, 'we would like to see it; even if it's small, it will help us make a comparison.'

'A comparison?'

Monsieur clearly does not think this is a reason to look at an apartment. Nonetheless he defers to our wishes, picks up the phone, makes a call and, voilà, we can see it in two hours. He gives us the name of another real estate agency we can visit in the meantime. He assures us that this is a very good agency, large and reputable. He impresses upon us the importance of large. We do not have time to waste on small agencies. Big agencies have lots of apartments. They are used to dealing with foreigners. Some of them have people who speak English or even Spanish.

He produces a copy of *De Particulier à Particulier*. Do we know this publication? It's also a good place to find apartments. These are for private sale. There are no agents' fees. Agents' fees are très très chers — as much as 5 or 6 per cent. We nod gravely. Why is he telling us this? Doesn't he want to make money? He reads out a couple of descriptions from the paper and insists that we take his copy with us. He ushers us to the door. We shake hands.

'How much per square metre is an apartment in Melbourne?' he asks suddenly.

'I'm not sure,' says Jack. 'We don't sell property by the square metre.'

'But you have the same system of measurement, n'est-ce pas?'

'Yes, but we don't use it like you do to sell property.'

'Then how do you know if the apartment is a good price or not?'

'Because … ' Jack looks to me for help, but I don't offer any. 'Well,' he continues, 'it's complicated, because most properties, in Melbourne at least, are sold by auction. They do not have a fixed sale price.'

'What is an … what was the word?'

'Auction. It's a system where people bid against each other to buy a property, and the person who makes the highest bid is the one who buys it,' says Jack.

Monsieur Rolland looks surprised. 'That is very complicated, non?'

'Not really,' I say. 'It can be quite exciting.'

Monsieur looks philosophical.

'Ah well,' he says. 'En fait, you are very lucky that the system in France is not exciting. C'est très, très simple. You see an apartment, you make an offer, and you buy it. Voilà.'

Nineteen

It is just after midday as we walk down the boulevard Saint-Germain searching for the agency recommended by Monsieur Rolland. There are people everywhere, bustling around in the hot afternoon sun. It's hard not to be distracted by them and the elegant shops with their sale signs. Absolutely everything is 'en soldes'.

'I haven't even had time to set foot into a shop,' I say, coveting all the adorable little dresses in the window of Baby Dior as we sail past. 'I'm missing all the sales.'

'Well, you can't go to the sales and buy apartments,' says Jack, relieved.

Agence Immobilière Qualité is a large, confident-looking establishment. We scan the photographs in the window for possibilities.

'They're spending a bit on presentation here,' says Jack. 'I don't know if that's good or bad.'

'Well, at least we know what to do now,' I say. 'Just choose a photograph, make an offer, and voilà.'

'It's all very well for him,' says, Jack moving onto the second window. 'Here we are, have a look at this.'

We read through the specifications of an apartment near the Jardin des Plantes. The photograph shows high ceilings, an impressive stone fireplace, and long windows flooded with sunlight. It's 95 square metres with two bedrooms, two bathrooms, a leafy courtyard, and costs four hundred and ten thousand euros. Excitement quickens through us.

'That looks alright,' says Jack.

'It's gorgeous.' I read through the details again. 'How come it isn't sold? There must be something wrong with it.'

'You'd better go in and find out.'

'Now? Do we have time?'

I look past the photographs to my reflection.

'You look fine. We've got ten minutes or so. Just keep calm and don't get side-tracked.'

'Why do I always look fine?'

'Okay. You look lovely.'

'You're just saying that.'

'You're only going into a real estate agent's office.'

'Even so.' I straighten my dress and sashay through the door.

'Hello,' I say, surprising myself and the young woman who sits at the reception desk, 'I'm Australian and I want to buy an apartment in Paris.'

I beam at her so optimistically that her surprise gives way to astonishment.

'Oui. Yes, madame.' She looks around the spacious reception. 'Je, I will …' She points in the direction of an adjacent office. 'I'm sorry. I have no English.'

She walks hurriedly across to the door, knocks, and disappears inside. I stand in the empty room congratulating myself. That wasn't difficult. Just say who you are and why you're here — that's the way to get things moving.

Mademoiselle steps cautiously back into the reception followed by a tall, attractive man who smiles and introduces himself.

'Bonjour, madame. My name is Delemer. Henri Delemer.'

He sounds like a painter. He looks a bit like one, too, with his unruly hair and intense gaze.

'Enchantée, Monsieur Delemer. Je suis Ellie Nielsen.'

'Vous parlez français?'

'I try to, but it's difficult.'

He smiles at me. 'I am the same. English, it is difficult, too.'

Monsieur Henri Delemer is très intéressant. He reminds me of the actor Daniel Auteuil. Not that I actually know Daniel Auteuil — not yet anyway.

'Fruit and vegetables are the easiest,' I say. 'I'm very good at les fruits et les légumes, except for salad.'

His brow knots a little and softens his face. 'Les fruits and les légumes?'

'Yes. I spend a lot of time going to the markets. That's why I can speak fruit and vegetable quite well. It doesn't help much with apartment buying, though.'

Henri Delemer laughs gently and lowers his eyes to steal a look at Mademoiselle. She's not laughing.

'Please,' he says, pointing towards his office door, 'come and I will see if I can help you.'

'Vous êtes très gentil, monsieur.' And he is, too. Très très gentil.

Monsieur Delemer's office is small and neat without anything particularly French to recommend it. Except for Monsieur himself, of course. I sit opposite him and he asks me what I'm searching for. I swallow an urge to tell him I don't know. I just want to find an apartment I love. The thought surprises me. It's not even on the list. It ought to be number one: an apartment we love. He waits patiently for me to answer. He has blue eyes. Can you be French and have blue eyes? He seems to favour blue. There's a bluish painting on the wall behind him and a small blue paperweight on a pile of papers to my left. On top of the filing cabinet a deep-blue vase holds three blown white flowers. Oh, yes. The Jardin des Plantes.

'Monsieur,' I say, breaking abruptly from my reverie and startling him. 'I am interested in the apartment near the Jardin des Plantes. I saw it in the window.'

'Les Jardin des Plantes,' he repeats thoughtfully. 'Ah oui. Je sais. The one with 95 square metres and very high ceilings?'

'Yes. Yes,' I say enthusiastically. 'That's the one.'

'Oh dear.'

Oh dear? Where did he get that from? Daniel Auteuil would never say that.

'Desolé.'

He looks it, too.

'Je suis très desolé, madame.'

Why? I try not to panic. His face practises a sentence.

'Unfortunately …'

I hate sentences that begin with unfortunately.

'… I have sold this apartment already.'

'Sold it!' My affability slides from my face. 'You've sold it?'

'Yes. I am sorry, but I have sold it tomorrow, or is it yesterday?'

'Yesterday?'

'It is strange. I had this apartment for weeks and months, and nobody wanted it, and now there are two people in one week.'

I make a super-human effort not to throw my head in my hands and wail. Don't! Don't tell me the details. Don't tell me that if I'd come just last week, last Monday, yesterday — if I had come yesterday, that glorious, beautiful apartment would be ours. If I hadn't spent so much time looking at derelict buildings or the wedge or apartments with no windows, then this apartment … this apartment. I can't go on. It's agonising.

'Oui, it is strange,' says Monsieur again.

I force myself to look at him. He doesn't look quite as 'desolé' as he did a minute ago.

'Why on earth doesn't it have a sold sign on it?'

'A sold sign?' He looks back at me, puzzled. 'What is a sold sign?'

'It's a sign. With "sold" written on it.'

How could a real estate agent not know what a sold sign is? Don't they have sold signs in Paris? Of course they must, but it doesn't matter now. Whether they do or they don't, there's no way I'm going to get the apartment unsold on a technicality.

'Ah. Of course. I know what it is,' says Monsieur, a look of relief smoothing his face. 'A sold sign. Yes. No. It does not have a sign. Je ne sais pas pourquoi. It is … par inadvertance. You know what it is?'

'Yes. Yes. It's an oversight.'

'Exactement!'

He looks pleased now.

His phone rings and as he answers it my mobile rings, too. Its ringing is incredibly loud. I stare at my bag in horror. Monsieur looks at me looking at my bag, and nods for me to take the call. Zut. It's Jean-Louis. How am I going? Ça va. Ça va. What should I tell him? That I'm in a meeting? That could make him suspicious. Of what? Of two-timing him with another real estate agent? I could tell him I'm at lunch. No. He might ask where. Or what I'm eating. I throw a look at Monsieur Delemer. He's still on the phone. He's saying something about an owner and times of the day. Après-midi. Quatorze heures et demie. Seize heures peut-être.

That's one I'm familiar with. He has a very charming manner, has Monsieur.

'Madame Nielsen?' Jean-Louis is checking to see if I'm still on the line.

'Oui, oui, bien sûr, je suis là.'

Monsieur Delemer glances at me. Now what's on his face? Curiosity? Amusement? Hmmm. Well, I can do charming, too. Fire with fire. That's the way to handle the situation.

'Thank you so much for calling, Jean-Louis.'

If Jean-Louis is surprised at my effusiveness he doesn't show it. He continues on, oblivious to the way his name now fills the small bureau.

'Madame will not accept four hundred and twenty-five thousand euros.'

'Ça va. I didn't think she would,' I say blithely.

'But,' continues Jean-Louis, 'she will accept four hundred and thirty-two thousand.'

'Really?' I forget blithe and charming, and gape into my mobile phone.

That's thirty-five thousand less than she asked for. That's a lot. A slight flutter of panic tickles the edges of my skin. Suppose the system is not quite as we understand it to be? Suppose Madame accepts our offer and we're forced to buy her apartment?

'C'est incroyable.'

'So, you want to agree to four hundred and thirty-two thousand?' prompts Jean-Louis.

'Je ne sais pas,' I say, raising my eyebrows in apology to Monsieur Delemer. 'Je vais y réfléchir and call you back soon. À bientôt.'

The line is dead. I pretend that it isn't.

'À demain, Jean-Louis. Je t'embrasse.' I close the phone and turn to face Monsieur Delemer. 'I'm so sorry. A friend. He wants us to have dinner tomorrow night.'

'You have a lot of friends in Paris?' Monsieur asks.

Not as many as I'd like to leaps into my head, and I have to struggle with myself to make it stay there.

'A few,' I say coyly, 'just a few.'

Monsieur Delemer smiles. 'That is why you are searching for a very big apartment.'

I blush. 'Not really.'

'But the apartment near to the Jardin des Plantes, it was very big.'

'I know. I mean, it can't be too small, but it doesn't have to be big either.'

Monsieur nods, but I can tell he doesn't understand. Well, I don't understand either. Why am I so afraid to say what it is that I'm looking for?

'Monsieur,' I begin, 'we, that's me and my husband and our son, are looking for a modest, two-bedroomed apartment, somewhere in central Paris. It must be above the first floor and generally renovated. We are able to do some small things like painting, but not much more. Our budget is around four hundred and fifty thousand euros. Do you have anything at all that sounds like that?'

'En fait,' says Monsieur Delemer, 'I do have an apartment I think you will like. It is close to Maubert Mutualité, and four hundred and thirty-five thousand euros.'

I wait for him to tell me that this is a very good price, but he says nothing else. He leans back in his chair waiting for me to respond. Perhaps all of Paris is divided up into manageable sections each costing four hundred and thirty-five thousand euros.

'When can we see it?'

'Tomorrow, if you want.' He consults a dark-blue leather-bound diary that lies balanced on the edge of his desk. 'I have someone already at midday. Are you free to come after them at half past twelve?'

'Parfait, monsieur.'

'It is number 5, rue Dante.'

Now that's a promising address. I give him one of my best smiles. He takes up a card from a pile near the paperweight and writes the details on the back and hands it to me.

'Voilà.'

'Merci beaucoup, monsieur.' I move towards the door.

'It is a pretty apartment. I'm sure you will like it.'

I linger in the doorway. It's the first time I've heard an apartment described as pretty.

'À demain, Monsieur Delemer.'

'À demain, Madame Nielsen.'

The cordiality of the whole scene thrills me. I love cordiality. I sing an au revoir to Mademoiselle and skip out onto the street.

I'm Australian, and I want to buy an apartment in Paris. The sentence keeps going around and around in my head. I tell Jack there were no raised eyebrows or exchanged looks.

'He didn't try to sell me an apartment that I couldn't afford or give me a French lesson.'

'He probably thought it wasn't worth it since you only spoke in English.'

'That had nothing to do with it. They treated me like an equal.'

Of course they did, I think. That's what the French are supposed to do. Égalitaire and all that.

'I suppose you're going to pretend to be an Australian all the time now,' says Jack.

'What do you mean, pretend? I am an Australian.'

'Then why are you always telling me you don't know who you are?'

'That's different. I don't mean I don't know where I come from.'

'Oh,' says Jack, throwing the *De Particulier à Particulier* into a bin on the street. 'I thought it did mean that.'

I take his arm and look up at him. The sun plays with his face so I can't tell whether he's joking or not.

Twenty

I pour Perrier into a glass filled with ice and slices of fresh lemon, and gulp down a couple of mouthfuls. 'The last time I ordered one of these I got a beer,' I say.

'Things are improving then,' says Jack, opening his menu.

He takes hold of my left arm and turns it over to read my watch.

'C'mon, we'd better order something quickly if we're going to get back to Monsieur Rolland by two.'

I try to read the menu, but I'm not really concentrating. I'm thinking about rue Dante and Henri Delemer and how thrilling the left bank is. I don't want to eat quickly. I want to have a long lunch. Like we used to.

'Are there any chops?'

'Chops?' Jack looks up from his menu. 'What sort of chops?'

'Like the ones we had on our first visit to La Tour Eiffel. Remember?'

'Of course I remember. You made us walk up the stairs. It nearly killed me,' he says happily.

Our first visit to the Eiffel Tower is still vivid. I suppose that's true for everyone. It's not the sort of place you could ever forget having been to. We didn't want our visit to end. After taking the lift to the top and back again we decided to see if the restaurant on the second floor had a table for lunch. The odds were against us. It was the height of summer and there were tourists everywhere. Perhaps that's why I thought it would be a good idea to take the stairs. We arrived so breathless we could barely speak, but the waiter was impressed by our audacity (or perhaps it was our naivety) and led us across the length of the restaurant to the best table in the place. To celebrate, we ordered lamb chops and a bottle of Sancerre rouge.

We think now that the view down the Champ de Mars must have hypnotised us, because when we'd finished our meal we ordered another bottle of wine and then another. Our lunch was long and languid. We talked about how wonderful the world was and how lucky we were to have each other and long, summer days to spend in Paris. We made a list of the things we loved. Those things that made the days unique. Zinc. Gargoyles. Nutella crêpes. Wrought iron. Coffee chocolates. Sky. What fun we'd had leaping from the wrong métro, ordering the wrong meal, cashing travellers' cheques in the wrong bank, and walking — always walking — the wrong way to somewhere fabulous.

We talked and drank and dreamed until the dinner crowd arrived. Even at seven o'oclock the sun was still high in the sky. We walked unsteadily along the banks of the Seine, draped ourselves on the cool grass, and fell into a wine-induced slumber. When we woke, the air was warm and the sky was starry dark. Our things! But everything was just where we'd left them. My bag was sprawled on the ground near my head. Our cameras were somewhere near our feet. I remember we walked off arm-in-arm along the Champ de Mars, still hypnotised, trying to remember the name of our hotel, thinking we might get something to eat.

'Côtelette d'agneau,' says Jack. 'The plat du jour. I think that's what we had.'

Côtelette d'agneau. Sancerre rouge. All the time in the world. That's what I'd like. Instead we have Monsieur Rolland at two, and an apartment with space you can't live in.

'I hope that she has left,' says Monsieur Rolland, pressing the code into the door on rue Saint-Jacques.

I presume he is talking about the owner and her children. I say that I thought owners preferred to be present when someone looked through their apartment.

'That is true,' Monsieur says. 'But in this case, Madame is not the owner. She is the renter.'

I meet Jack's raised eyebrow as we follow Monsieur through the door and down a long hallway. The hall has a warm, terracotta-tiled floor. There are lots of exposed pipes and woodwork painted sea blue. The building has a fresh, optimistic feel.

At the end of a narrow staircase we find a metal-covered door. It has a brass doorbell in its middle and an ancient door-handle that sits next to a modern one. Monsieur rings the bell. When no one answers he turns his key solemnly in the lock and ushers us into the room.

The apartment is flooded with light, but we get our bearings as though we're adjusting to the dark.

'Je n'y crois pas,' mutters Monsieur Rolland. He throws his arms in the air. 'C'est terrible.'

'Pas du tout, monsieur.' I try to sound reassuring, but the lack of sea-blue optimism and warm terracotta makes it difficult to sound convincing.

Monsieur cannot bring himself to look at us. He seems genuinely upset. I glance around the kitchen. The mess is not that bad. It's not really a mess at all when you have a closer look at it. It's just things. Normal baby and kids' things. A highchair and another small plastic one. There's something that looks like a bassinette on the kitchen bench and dishes piled high on the sink, but they're all sparkling clean.

Monsieur opens a small door squashed at the end of the sink's draining board. We step around the highchair and peer in. It's a child's bedroom — a room so small it could be a pantry. A set of bunk beds, prettily made up with Barbie doona covers, takes up all the available space. There is a small frosted window that lets in some light, and a fluffy pink rug on the floor.

'The second bedroom is over there,' says Monsieur, pointing in the direction of what appears to be a curtained-off kitchen cupboard. He picks his way across the room and pulls back the curtain. Tucked into a cordoned-off niche is a small double bed. 'Cosy' is Monsieur's description. We manage half-hearted agreement, even though 'forlorn' is the word that springs into my mind.

Monsieur guides us around the table and into the adjoining living room. It's small but pretty, too, with its tiny marble fireplace and narrow windows that overlook the street. A cot faces one window and a single mattress lies on the hearth facing the other. A smiling, long-eared rabbit sits on the mattress looking out. I look out, too, willing the street beyond to do something, to change things, to find this family an apartment that better suits their needs.

We take a last look around. Monsieur Rolland attempts a parting sentence, but his words fail him. I know how that feels.

'Bon,' says Jack, his eyes following the parting figure of Monsieur down the street. 'Well, that's that. It's rue Dante tomorrow or nothing.'

I suppose that's right, but I'm still thinking about Madame and her children and wondering what happened to her husband.

'Cheer up,' says Jack. 'You never know, maybe Jean-Louis will come good.'

'Jean-Louis!' I rummage inside my bag for my phone. 'He called while I was with Henri.'

'Whose Henry?'

'Monsieur Delemer. Madame will accept four hundred and thirty-two.'

'Quelle surprise,' Jack says. 'We're getting closer.'

'What do you mean? I thought ...'

'Only joking.' He shakes his head at me. 'Don't worry. He'll call back.'

We walk towards the Seine heading for home. There are buskers on the Pont Saint-Louis and people watching, taking photos and videos, throwing coins into hats. We watch, too, as a young man dressed as a tramp juggles batons and invites a giggling young woman to kiss him on the cheek. Everyone is having fun. Of course they are. That's what you do when you're a tourist.

'Let's go to the Eiffel Tower,' I say impulsively.

'You're not still thinking about those chops?'

I laugh too loudly, and divert some attention from the busker. After a moment's pause, I lean into Jack and whisper, 'It's us I'm thinking about. Let's go and be tourists again.'

Twenty-one

Ellery has decided to he will go and see *Ice Age*. He decided that when Jack told him rue Dante had something to do with hell.

Still feeling touristy, we decide to rendezvous with Julia at Virgin Megastore on the Champs-Élysées and take a taxi to see our last apartment.

With the practised eye of real estate agents, we take in the streetscape. As well as apartment buildings, rue Dante houses a small Franprix supermarket and a post office. Number five is small, ancient, and two minutes' walk from the nearest métro stop and less than five minutes' walk to the Seine. It's in the midst of everything and quiet, too. Claude would definitely approve. But where is Monsieur Henri Delemer?

Jack suggests that perhaps the twelve o'clock person has already made an offer. Has snapped up the perfect apartment right out from under our very noses. I worry that maybe we are supposed to meet at Monsieur's bureau. Maybe something got lost in translation. I stop feeling touristy. I thrust my watch under Jack's nose. I tell him that it's nearly twenty to one. No one could be looking at an apartment for that long. Not from twelve o'clock until twenty to one. That's forty minutes. You don't get forty minutes. Ten. Fifteen at the most. But you don't get forty. Something has gone wrong.

Jack looks infuriatingly calm. Like the street. He and the street look the same. He thinks it will be helpful to tell me that maybe you do get forty minutes (nearly forty-five now) if you have decided to buy. If you are, for example, discussing exactly what offer you will make, forty-five minutes could go past quite quickly. That must be it. That's the only explanation that makes sense. Oh no. Not again. Don't tell me the perfect apartment has been sold out from under us again. Everything's too quick. I can't keep up with it. I'm never going to be in the right place at the right time. Timing. That's it. It's all a question of timing. I should know that. That's what I forgot to concentrate on. Timing. How could I forget that?

Jack thinks I'm exaggerating. There hasn't been a whole raft of apartments sold out from under us. There hasn't been one. Not technically speaking. But that's not the point. The point is … Jack thinks my watch has stopped. That's ridiculous. If my watch had stopped it wouldn't be nearly ten to one. Ten to one!

Monsieur Delemer ambles through the door of the apartment building. A petite blonde woman follows him. We pose as Madame et Monsieur Invisible, and wait for Monsieur to finish talking to the woman. I strain to piece their conversation together. She has to discuss it with her husband. Isn't that line a ruse? I look at her a little more closely. She looks very left bank. The collar of her rose-coloured shirt dress is turned up to meet her hair. A silver chain bracelet dangles from her right arm. She flicks her hair behind an ear as she talks. She wears no make-up and no other jewellery. I press my sunglasses against my face. That's funny. Madame reminds me of someone.

Jack is pulling at my arm. He is the loudest whisperer I have ever heard. He tells me to stop staring at Madame. He says I always stare at people who look like me. Look like me? Monsieur Delemer au revoirs Madame and turns to us with a thousand desolés. That must be his favourite word. I assure him that I love standing around the street in the morning sun and the afternoon sun — it's the luxury of being a tourist. We have all the time in the world.

The L-shaped living room on the third floor of number five rue Dante is beautifully cluttered. A low wall of books faces two long windows. Sheer white curtains flank the windows and billow in the breeze. Paintings of all shapes and sizes adorn the pale walls. Small round, painted, wooden tables hold rough-hewn pottery lamps. A knotted cream rug sits on the old pine floorboards, and a two-person, linen-upholstered sofa sits on top of it. Monsieur

Delemer is still apologising for keeping us waiting as I go into a state of rapture.

I stand in the window and gaze out at the splendour of newly cleaned zinc guttering. Imagine looking at that everyday. You could never tire of zinc guttering. Henri Delemer clearly agrees with me. He leaves Jack to examine the ladder that doubles as a staircase to the mezzanine, and sits down on the blue sofa. He motions for me to sit beside him. And then he points upwards out through the open window. Sky, he tells me.

In this apartment you can sit down and look at sky. Your own piece of sky. That's such a rarity in Paris. And the piece that comes with this apartment is achingly blue and soft, just like the sofa I'm sitting on.

Where is the form? Give me a pen — I'm ready to sign anything. Jack calls out something about the ladder being dangerous. But I'm off the sofa and running my hands along the books. There must be hundreds and hundreds of books. A library. This apartment has its own library. That wasn't mentioned. Henri is not sure why not. The shelves are attached. It seems likely that they come with the apartment. Jack wants to know where I think we are going to get five hundred books from to fill the shelves. Henri agrees that the ladder has seen better days, but he says that it is a very simple matter to insert a small staircase. He suggests one of those circular ones. He thinks you can buy them at Ikea. Jack throws me an exasperated look and starts waving at the kitchen. Well, I can see that it's small, but it has everything you need. Henri turns on the light, but the windowless room doesn't brighten much. I'm not planning to spend all my time in the kitchen anyway.

Henri is holding the ladder and inviting us to climb up to the mezzanine level. The tranquility of the master bedroom helps us forget the ordeal of the ladder. The white linen-covered bed stretches the length of the room to us. It's surrounded by long white drops of cotton which shroud it off from the living room below. Tangles of potted ivy sit in terracotta pots on a long table that runs behind the bright orange bedhead. An ornate iron chair completes the room. Jack is saying that there are no cupboards when Henri reveals a whole corridor of cupboards built into a gap in the wall between the master bedroom and the second bedroom.

The second bedroom is spacious and bright and furnished with a baby's cot and a pale-green dressing table on which sit four Paddington bears. Jack mumbles that at least this room has walls. This observation causes him to embark on a monologue about the necessity of walls for a good night's sleep. It would be impossible, completely impossible, for him to sleep in a room without walls. Henri mentions the curtains: with curtains, privacy is not a problem. No, but noise is: Jack explains that noise is the problem, not privacy. Henri looks at me sympathetically. It would be easy to swap rooms. The baby could sleep in the first bedroom and we could sleep in the room with walls. Voilà.

How do you get the furniture in? That's the next thing Jack wants to know. How do you get a double bed and a dressing table and, now that we're in the bathroom (which has a laundry!), a washing machine and a dryer up a ladder? Henri points at the skylight in the bathroom by way of an answer. We are both so astonished by the bathroom that we forget to pursue this question. The bathroom has a bath and a shower and space for the washing machine and dryer. It is six months old. It is the bathroom to end all bathrooms. I can barely contain my excitement. This is it. We've found it. With only one day to go — we've found our piece of Paris.

I stand in the living room with my back to the ladder. I can't bear to watch Jack climbing down it again. He will have an absolutely-not look on his face that I don't want to see. I decide to return to the sofa and look up again at the beautiful slice of sky. I invite Jack to join me, but he's asking Monsieur Henri questions. Lots of questions — about when would the apartment be vacant, how long would settlement take, the amount of deposit needed, does he have a notaire, and what sort of offer should we make. I can hardly bare to contemplate the half-space between me and the sky. Its closeness makes me giddy. He likes it, too. Jack likes the apartment, too. It's so warm I can hardly breathe. Now I see why you need only five or ten minutes to inspect an apartment. Of course you only need five or ten minutes. That's all it takes to spot perfection.

Soon we are back in the cool white corridor. I am floating down the stairs, feeling the curve of wooden railing under my fingertips as my eyes follow the ancient, worn wooden beams that support the ceiling. Everywhere you turn there's something lovely here.

Out on the street the breeze does nothing to cool my ardour. I want to steal the key that Henri cradles in his palm and dance away with it — but I don't. For some reason, dancing around in front of a real estate agent seems inappropriate. So I stand regarding Henri with what I hope he will read as a grateful expression on my face, trying to think of a circumstance when it would be appropriate to dance in the street with a real estate agent.

Of course, Jack can tell I'm delirious, so he bids Monsieur au revoir and promises to phone tomorrow morning with his decision on the offer. I keep nodding and smiling. Henri warns us that Madame before us is entranced with the apartment, too. It is just a question of the husband. She may phone this afternoon with an offer and then ... voilà. That would be it. Done. Finished. The gentle breeze starts lashing at my hair. I can't see properly. Henri looks at me with concern. Perhaps I need some water.

'Goes very badly in the heat,' says Jack, making me sound like a racehorse.

'My cat, she is also the same,' says Henri. 'I think it is the fur.'

They both look at me intently. I push my hair from my eyes and try to look as human as I can.

Twenty-two

We slide into the first café chairs we see and order coffee. I look across at Jack. He doesn't return my gaze. He stares into his coffee. I knew it. He doesn't like it. He doesn't like the best apartment in Paris. That's probably a bit of an exaggeration. The best apartment in Paris is bound to have sky you can see standing up. But this one comes close. So close.

The Beatles' 'Michelle Ma Belle' plays on the radio. It competes easily with the drone from the coffee machine. The small, round table we sit at is made from cheap, brown wood. Most of the dark-metal window frames are held together by gaffer tape. I shift my gaze to the partially clean brown plastic ashtray, and realise that some things here are not quite as I imagined them. Some things you can't ignore.

'I'm not saying I don't like it,' says Jack at last. 'It's just that it's got some problems.'

I sip my coffee. I should have ordered something effervescent.

'It's really a flat for two people.'

'Well, that's an improvement on the apartment we've already made an offer on. It's an apartment for one person.'

'You know what I mean, darling,' he says quietly. 'It's not just a question of the wall. I suppose you could put a wall in, but it would make that bedroom very dark. It didn't have any windows — did you notice that? Just a minute. That means you couldn't put a wall in.'

I throw him a make-up-your-mind look and fiddle with my sunglasses.

'You could, of course, replace the ladder. I don't think a circular staircase would be much better than a ladder, but you could put in a small, normal staircase.'

I meet his remarks with silence. What on earth's a normal staircase? I don't know why I'm cross with him. He didn't design the apartment.

'And there's another thing.'

I knew there would be. I stare past him. Métro Maubert Mutualité is straight ahead. All those lovely 'M's. I can feel their hum on my lips. Its sign is one of those gorgeous art nouveau designs. I imagine myself giving directions to visitors. Take the number 10 line in the direction of Gare d'Austerlitz to Maubert Mutualité, exit right on boulevard Saint-Germain, and rue Dante is the second on your right. Jack pushes his sliver of chocolate towards me.

'Do you want mine, too?' he asks.

I smile down at the little square offering. I unwrap it and let it melt slowly on the tip of my tongue. 'Okay. What's the other thing?'

'The bathroom.'

'The bathroom? I thought that was the best room in the place.'

'Well, it would be if it wasn't for the toilet.'

I squeeze my chocolate-stained lips together.

'What's wrong with the toilet?'

'Well, at the moment, every time you want to use it you have to climb up the ladder.'

'Right.' I sip my coffee and nod. He's got a point. 'You mean if Ellery was in a hurry, for instance.'

'Yes, there's that and any visitors. They would have to walk straight through our bedroom to get to the toilet.'

'Yes. I suppose that's a bit tricky.'

'I'm not saying it's insurmountable, but it is a problem.'

It's always worrying when Jack adopts a reasonable tone.

I spin the ashtray around. 'It's a lovely apartment, though.'

Jack nods. 'I agree with that. But …'

My phone rings. It's Jean-Louis. Damn. I knew I should have called him back. I can't hear what he's saying. He's no match for the coffee machine–Beatles combination. I dash out onto the street. It sounds like Madame has agreed to accept our offer. *Zut alors!* Now what? He says it again. Madame will accept our offer of four hundred and twenty-five thousand euros. That's forty-two thousand less than her asking price. That's nearly eighty-five thousand Australian dollars. Should I ask Jack? The 'mon mari' defence springs to mind. No. I'm sick of that line. Malheureusement. That's a better way to go.

'Unfortunately …'

There is a short silence on the line. Maybe he hates that word, too.

' … we have decided to buy another apartment.'

'Another apartment?'

'Oui. Nous sommes très, très desolé, but it's bigger, with two bedrooms.'

Another silence.

'Madame will be very disappointed.'

Please don't tell me that. I feel bad enough as it is. Jean-Louis keeps his composure. I wish he wouldn't. He explains that if we withdraw, now that Madame has accepted our offer, the process will come to an end. It will not be possible to make any offers on this apartment again. It will be finished. Do I understand? I rub the space between my eyes.

'Oui, Jean-Louis. Je comprends. We do not want to buy Madame's apartment. C'est fini.'

Josephine was right. Jean-Louis is très professionnel. He tells me he is sorry. He bids me goodbye and bonne chance. He continues to be cordial, even though deep down he is très très vexé.

'Well that's that problem solved.' I swallow the last of my cold coffee. 'Rue Dante is the only apartment we have left now.'

'Darling …'

Jack reaches for my hand. I pull it away. I'm letting everybody down. I can't hold hands when I feel like I'm letting people down.

There are hues of blue in the plume on Joan of Arc's helmet that are the same colour as rue Dante's patch of sky. The painting, even though it's a very bad one, is out of place in this café. Joan is defeated by the dull surroundings. Her zeal is no match for a half-clean ashtray. I stare wistfully into my empty cup. Maybe it's always like that. Maybe I ought to give up. I remember playing Olive in Ray Lawler's *Summer of the Seventeenth Doll*. I remember the heartbreak of clinging to a dream that no one else shared.

'I'm sorry,' I say. 'But we did try. Didn't we?'

Twenty-three

Yoann shrugs. His dark-green shrugging shoulder complements the burnt-orange walls of L'Amuse Bouche perfectly. There are some great restaurants in the fourteenth (I think I forgot to factor that in when I was listing its merits), and this is one of my favourites.

'You know, Jack, it is perfectly easy to put in a wall.'

Yoann's broad shoulders settle at the end of his sentence. Jack replaces his knife and fork onto his goat's-cheese salad.

'What do you mean, easy?'

'Well, it is much better to put in a wall than to take one down,' says Yoann, examining his water glass. 'To put in a wall is not expensive. To take out a wall, now that is expensive.'

'How much to put in a staircase?'

I raise an eyebrow at Jack across the table.

'What?' he says. 'I only asked how much a staircase would cost.'

Both Athina and Yoann look at me quizzically. I blush.

'Jack doesn't want to put in any walls or staircases.'

'It would, of course, depend on the type of staircase,' continues Yoann, undeterred.

'Perhaps, if you could arrange for another viewing of the apartment, we could come, too. Then we would have a better idea about what needs to be done,' suggests Athina.

'That's not a bad idea,' says Jack, attacking the remainder of his salad.

I burn my mouth on the hot creamy sauce my scallops swim in. It has the paradoxical effect of reminding me how good they are. As my tongue nurses my scalded palate I feel guilty for paying them scant attention. But I can't concentrate on my food and on what Jack's saying all at the same time. What is he saying? We've talked all afternoon about it. We've decided not to make an offer on rue Dante. But now he makes it sound as if there's just a couple of things that need clearing up, and voilà! Well, I wish he'd make up his mind. Athina leans towards me and asks if everything's okay. I look back at her dejectedly. I assure her that everything's fine and then I make a liar out of myself by telling her about everything that's not fine.

'A couple of nights ago I dreamt that all my teeth fell out. Do you know what that means?'

Madame places a parmentier de carnard in front of me as Athina shakes her head in answer.

'I love this dish,' I say, drawing my plate a little closer to bask in its warmth. Jack and Yoann interrupt their conversation, which has moved from walls and stairs to organic food and the state of the Green party in France, to accept their main courses of red mullet and cod fish. Athina's lamb pie arrives last as we raise our glasses with an enthusiastic 'santé'. Uncharacteristically, I remember to look everyone in the eye as we toast. Athina holds my gaze as we lower our glasses.

'What does it mean?' she asks.

'Fear. If you dream that your teeth have fallen out, it means you are afraid.'

I sample my parmentier, and nod my satisfaction with the dish and my assertion about dreamed-of teeth.

'Afraid? What is there to be afraid of? You're not afraid of anything.' Athina shakes her head and tries unsuccessfully to impale small, golden flakes of pastry onto her fork.

'It wasn't just one tooth. It was all my teeth. At least all the ones on the top. I think I had one left, sort of just past the middle. It had gone all pointy.'

I swallow some wine.

'And then tonight, when I was getting ready to come out to dinner, it suddenly occurred to me. Fear. That was what the dream was all about.'

I lower my voice and add, 'The holes were big and black. I've been running my tongue across my teeth ever since — just to make sure they're still there.'

Athina balances her cutlery on either side of her plate. 'If you don't find an apartment, it's not the end of the world.'

'That's what I tell myself. But other times it feels like the search for the Golden Fleece. Isn't that terrible?'

'I think it's marvellous. Everyone should have a Golden Fleece. And I'm not saying that just because I'm Greek.'

I laugh down at my dinner plate. 'We leave the day after tomorrow, you know. I think it's impossible now.'

'You can continue looking when you come back.'

'I know. But I'm worried that when we get home everything will fade away. There won't be another time. That this is our only chance. That's what I'm afraid of. I'm afraid my energy will run out or my brain will stop working or Jack will change his mind.' I grab my wine glass and hold it at my lips and manage a weak smile. 'It's pathetic isn't it?'

'It's not pathetic to be afraid. Some secret part of me is afraid every day living here in a country that is not my own. Living through winter after winter. Missing the light, my family, and Twisties. I envy you returning in two days.'

We neglect our meals and look sadly into each other's eyes.

'It's funny, isn't it?' I say.

'Yes,' Athina agrees. 'It's funny.'

'Come on, you two,' says Jack. 'Don't start getting morbid.'

'It's not morbid to discuss life,' I say.

'It usually is if you're involved.'

Athina looks scandalised.

'I'm only joking. I'm getting sick of talking about apartments.'

'We weren't talking about apartments. We were talking about dentistry.'

'Dentistry?'

'The two are very similar,' says Yoann, a warm smile lighting his face.

Athina and I walk arm in arm, behind Jack and Yoann, along the dark street to Yoann's car. Yoann takes his usual route along avenue du Général Leclerc, past the newly restored lion, down avenue Denfert-Rochereau, past the Observatoire de Paris, and into boulevard Saint-Michel. As the boulevard crosses Saint-Germain, he points to the right.

'Your apartment is just down there. Maubert Mutualité. There you would be very close to the Musée de Cluny.'

'Don't start,' says Jack.

'Don't start?'

Athina translates. 'It means commence pas.'

'I was not starting anything.' Yoann feigns innocence. 'It is just that museum, which is my favourite, is very close to here, and it would be good to have an apartment so close to it.'

'That's very helpful,' says Jack.

Yoann shrugs and smiles as he drives away from the Musée de Cluny and crosses the Seine.

We drive on through the glittering night. It's gone so fast. Our time in Paris has flashed past even though, as we crawl down rue des Francs-Bourgeois and turn right into rue Vieille du Temple, it feels like we've been here forever. When we cross over rue des Blancs Manteaux, I see myself on day one of our search trailing along behind Monsieur Impeccable. I wonder why I was so certain of success. No one could seriously expect to buy a piece of Paris in only two weeks. Our progress down the narrow one-way street is slow. There are people everywhere weaving in and around each other's lives, and for two wonderful weeks I was one of them.

'What will you do tomorrow?' asks Athina brightly.

'I can tell you what we're not doing,' says Jack.

'I want to buy a few things for Ellery and some presents. I haven't bought a thing yet. Imagine coming to Paris and not buying anything.'

'Imagine,' says Jack.

'You'll be back next year,' whispers Athina, 'and now you know what you're looking for, it'll be easier to find it.'

I smile at her and then turn and look out of the car window. I close my eyes against all the bright lights in case they make my eyes water. We arrive at our door. Two young men stand in front of it, so deep in conversation that they don't even look up as our car comes to a halt next to them. A few metres away Monsieur le Painter works vigorously at a canvas. The night shimmers with activity and purpose. I unfasten my seatbelt and press myself awkwardly through the gap in the front seat to kiss Athina and Yoann goodnight.

Jack takes my hand as we stand on the footpath and watch their car crawl away. 'We're lucky to have friends like that,' he says, kissing the side of my head.

'That's why it's always sad when it's time to leave.'

'What if I shout you a mojito?'

Mon mari always comes to my rescue. I squeeze his hand and shake my head.

'We should get back. It's been a long day, and what about Julia?'

'I rang her earlier and asked if she could stay the night.'

'Did you? Is she?'

He inclines his head to mine and kisses me softly.

'I know you,' he says tenderly, and he does, too.

Twenty-four

'So,' says Julia, bouncing into our bedroom with a freshly brewed coffee in her hand, 'big night last night?'

I sit up in bed grimacing at the sunny morning. 'What time is it?'

'Nine-ish. Jack's taken Ellery out for breakfast. How was yesterday? With the apartment. Is it the one?'

I hold the hot coffee close to my face to try and wake myself up.

'Nearly. But not quite.'

Julia plonks herself down on the bed.

'What happened?'

I ruffle my free hand through my hair. I've got the sort of hair that never looks like bed-hair even when I'm actually in bed.

'It didn't have any walls.'

'None?'

'None to speak of.'

'Apart from that?'

'It was perfect.'

Julia turns and looks out of the open window.

'Well, at least you tried,' she says. 'What are you doing today?'

'Ellery's going downstairs to play with Remi and his Game Boy. We're going shopping and then to lunch. We've finished with apartments. Or they've finished with us. Either way — you want to come?'

'Sounds more like a policy speech than an invitation. Are you sure? Don't you and Jack want to, you know …'

'That's okay,' I say, 'we did all that last night.'

'Oh, là, là.' Julia laughs and leaps up off the bed. 'Where are we going?'

'The Jules Verne.'

'No! We're not!'

'You're right. We're not.'

We travel along the tiny street in single file. Bonjours to madames et monsieurs bounce out of the shops and cafés as we pass. Bright sunshine plays with the buildings and adds drama to the oranges, greens, pinks, and yellows of the produce that we flash past. I pass several real estate agents' offices without a sideways glance. For the first time in nearly two weeks I'm walking at the same pace as the rest of Paris. Jack turns around to check directions. I nod and point straight ahead. I have only a vague idea of where we're going, but the more we walk the lighter I feel. The more we walk the more I think I would be perfectly happy to just keep walking because today Paris is wooing me. At least five 'bonjour madames' in one morning. I'm sure that's a record. Jack turns around to check directions again.

'What are you beaming at?' he asks.

'Nothing,' I say, smiling even more. 'Where's Julia?'

'She's gone across to that newsstand. Something she had to read about *Sex and The City*. Can you remember where the shop is?'

'Not really. It's a labyrinth around here. All these little streets leading from one to another.'

'Well, we know it's somewhere near the first apartment we stayed in. If we head that way we'll probably find it. Julia!'

Julia darts gracefully around a car as it mounts the footpath seemingly in her pursuit.

'It's okay — they're going to do another series.'

'Thank God for that. We're going over to rue des Lombards.'

'What for?'

'We think we can find the shop from there, if we retrace our steps.'

Julia dances beside me on the footpath.

'That's not the real reason,' she says.

I look at her mystified. 'Real reason? Why would I need a real reason to walk down rue des Lombards?'

'Because it gives you an excuse to see your butcher's shop again.'

'N'importe quoi,' I say surprising myself.

'There's our door,' says Jack. And so it is — the door of the first apartment we rented in Paris. It stands on the busy pedestrian street as it always did, squashed between two frenzied cafés. We stand opposite and stare up at the building. Our windows are open. I almost expect to see myself leaning out of one, holding Ellery aloft. I can still feel the joy I felt then as I held his tiny body and watched him watching Paris. A motor bike dodges us.

'I thought this was supposed to be a pedestrian street,' says Jack as we jump out of the way.

'I think it's both,' I say.

'What? Pedestrian and non-pedestrian?'

'That's right.'

Jack shakes his head. He loves logic that is contrary to his own.

'I remember now. The kid's clothing shop is just down there.' I point to where rue Nicolas Flamel intersects with rue des Lombards.

'Then where's the butcher's shop?' asks Julia.

'Over there,' I say, pointing in the direction of boulevard de Sébastopol, 'on the next corner.'

My arm is still stretched out pointing across the street when I realise that it isn't.

'It's gone.'

Jack is the first one to say what I cannot even bring myself to think.

'It can't be gone. It must be on another corner.'

'It has to be that corner,' says Julia. 'There's the jeweller's shop next door.'

We stare at the building. Flimsy tables and chairs spill out of the corner door and down along the street. A large plastic awning protects the patrons from the sun and forms a sort of terrace. The interior is painted in garish oranges and reds. Hushed techno-music throbs onto the street.

'It's a gay bar! My butcher's shop has turned into a gay bar.'

'Well, why wouldn't it? This is a gay area.'

Jack looks at me as though he was expecting this all along.

'I know that.' I spit the words out. 'That's not the point. I just can't believe it's gone. My butcher's shop is gone.'

'A lot of gays are vegetarian,' says Julia authoritatively.

'And how would you know that?'

I throw her a withering look, but my anger is losing the battle against my tears.

'Because I have a cousin who's gay.'

'Oh, brilliant. And he's a vegetarian, I suppose.'

'No. I don't think so.'

'The problem is that nobody cooks anymore. Not even the French.'

Now it's Jack's turn to become an authority on something he knows nothing about.

'Of course they do. Look at all the markets everywhere — packed with people buying food to cook.'

'Hmmm.'

Jack and Julia muse together. I turn away from them confused. Of course the French still cook. Perhaps they don't eat as much meat as they used to. Frozen, pre-packaged, take-home, microwave friendly Picard pops into my head. Oh my God. Perhaps they're right. There's no fur, no heads, no eyes anymore. I stand on the street, defeated. My butcher's shop has been twenty-first centuried. How could they let this happen? I thought the French were supposed to have laws to protect against this sort of thing.

'There's no point standing around here moping,' says Jack. 'Anyway, I thought we were going shopping.'

'C'mon Elles,' says Julia, taking my arm.

'There's no point,' continues Jack, 'getting all worked up about it. It was only a butcher's shop.'

I try to look proud and defiant like Joan of Arc, but instead tears well in my eyes, and my voice catches. Ray Lawler's play comes spinning into my mind. I can hear Roo telling Olive there are no more eagles. No more flying out of the sun. I can see now why she tore them all to bits. Why she ripped apart seventeen tulled and tinselled cupie dolls. I, too, want to shout out, 'You give it back to me — give me back what you've taken,' but I lack Olive's passion. Instead I swallow my anguish and say, 'Well, that's where you're wrong. In France there is no such thing as *only* a butcher's shop.'

Jack throws me a pitying look, turns, and marches off down rue Nicolas Flamel.

'Elles,' says Julia soothingly, 'we're using up valuable shopping time.'

I drag up a half-smile and slowly follow her down the street.

As we round the corner we see Jack waving madly, walking quickly back towards us. He arrives at our side bursting to tell us something. Now what? He's only been gone two minutes.

Twenty-five

Immo Flamel is only a few metres around the corner from the butcher's shop (or what was the butcher's shop), but this is the first time I've ever noticed it. Jack positions us in front of a photograph in the agency's window. We stare at it as he translates.

'Près de l'Hôtel de Ville,' he says proudly, as though he personally is responsible for the text. He turns from the window to his audience.

'Close to the Town Hall.'

'The town hall,' we echo.

Of course, Julia and I both know that. The ad is easy to translate, but as it's Jack's discovery we defer to his method of disclosure.

'Eighty square metres. Two bedrooms. Separate kitchen. In very good condition. On the fourth floor. With a lift.'

He turns back to gauge our reaction. Space. Bedrooms. Lifts. *Zut alors!* What are we supposed to do now?

'You'd better go in and ask them about it,' says Jack.

'Me?'

'Of course you.'

'Couldn't you do it? Just this once.'

'Why?'

'Because, well, I wasn't expecting to. I'm still in shock.'

'That's ridiculous. Anyway, it's up to you — but this looks pretty promising.'

We turn and look again. He's right. It does look promising. It's big, with proper walls and windows and a fireplace. It even has sky. What's wrong with me? I peer through the window. The office is small and open-plan. A young woman, in her mid-twenties, occupies one of the two desks. My go-on voice battles with my what's-the-point voice. We're leaving tomorrow. This could be our last opportunity; but even if it's perfect, how on earth are we going manage to buy it before tomorrow? It's futile. Impossible. Even the butcher's shop knew when to quit.

'If you like, Elles, I'll go in with you.'

Julia's voice halts the war in my head.

'No,' I say, 'that's it. None of us wants to stand around here for hours while I fill out another file with another real estate agent. No. We're going shopping and to lunch like we planned.'

I turn away from the window and start off down the street. Jack and Julia follow. There is no dissension. There are sad faces. I attempt rational.

'I mean, how could we do it? Even if it's perfect it's too late now.'

'They might let us see it today,' Jack says hopefully.

'And what good would that do?'

What am I saying? Whose side am I on?

'Well, if we really, really like it, well, something will sort itself out.'

I can't believe my ears. I'm the 'something will sort itself out' person. Not Jack. The wedge and the diamond and the apartment crammed with ornaments swirl around in my head. Those apartments looked great in the ads, too. If only we'd walked down this street earlier. Then again, what led us here today? Chance? Destiny? The word 'destiny' fills me with a heart-racing lightness that I always associate with hope or hunger. On this occasion, it's both.

'Alright,' I say to Julia. 'Lead on, McDuff.'

'What?'

'Let's do it. One more real estate agent won't kill me.'

'I'll wait here,' says Jack, 'just in case.'

I throw him a smile, and grab Julia by the arm.

'Okay. Come and watch me confuse the French.'

The young woman at the desk doesn't bother to stop what she's doing as we enter her office. When she does look up in response to our collective 'bonjour', her manner is efficient rather than friendly. She raises an eyebrow, a gesture that cues us to get to the point of our interruption. The office is disconcertingly quiet. No phones ring. No one occupies the small office at the back of the room. No noise from the street intrudes. We all wait for me to begin.

'L'appartement près de l'Hôtel de Ville...'

That's as far as I get before Mademoiselle interrupts me.

'Comment?'

Well, of course she doesn't understand what I said. I haven't said anything yet.

'Dans la fenêtre,' says Julia.

Mademoiselle's briskness softens a little at the sound of Julia's perfect accent. 'Oui.'

'Il y a une affiche d'un appartement près de l'Hôtel de Ville.'

'Dans la fenêtre?' Mademoiselle looks confused.

'La vitrine,' I volunteer.

Mademoiselle nods her chin curtly at my assistance, rises from her desk, and walks towards the window. She peers at the backs of the advertisements, shakes her head, and walks out onto the street. A couple of moments later she returns to the back of the window and pulls the ad in question out of the display. She holds it up to us.

'This?' she asks.

Julia and I nod at her enthusiastically.

'Oui, mademoiselle. C'est ça.'

Mademoiselle places the photograph and its accompanying description in front of us.

'I have more photos on ...' she stares at her computer, but the word won't come, 'l'ordinateur,' she says finally with a small, resigned pout of her lips. 'Et en Anglais?'

Julia graciously leaves the English to me.

'Computer.'

'Computer.' Mademoiselle repeats the word and shakes her head slightly as though this is the craziest word she has ever heard.

'Alors. I have more photos on the computer.'

Photos on the computer. This is a first. I exchange a 'not bad' look with Julia. Mademoiselle, relaxing into the world of her 'ordinateur', gestures us to sit down. I cast my eyes over the advertisement's photograph of the living room as we wait. It does look lovely. The fact that there are more photos to be seen fuels my optimism. Mademoiselle is clicking buttons and her tongue.

'Attendez. Attendez.'

Julia and I exchange a smile. Things are going well. We have seats and Mademoiselle on the computer and not a single other person in attendance to monitor my performance.

'Et voilà.'

We jump to attention as Mademoiselle swings her screen around to face us.

'Voici les photos.'

We look at the small screen with rapt attention. Mademoiselle describes what we are looking at. First there's the living room, the same as the photo in the advertisement, but clearer. With its yellow walls and long windows, the room is warm and elegant. The master bedroom is a dramatic dark blue with a small white fireplace.

'En marbre,' I say almost under my breath — my optimism fast becoming dazzling possibility.

'Oui, oui,' says Mademoiselle pausing to look at the photograph, too. 'C'est en marbre.'

Our interest interests her. She looks at us from one to the other.

'Avec un dressing aussi. Vous êtes Anglaise?'

'Non, nous sommes Australiennes,' I say with perfect pronunciation.

'Ah! Australienne. Très bien.'

She allows herself a smile. No teeth showing, but a smile all the same.

'Vous voulez acheter un appartement à Paris?'

She speaks rapidly, her eyes darting around us nervously, and there's something else ... it's difficult to say, curiosity, watchfulness?

'Oui, mademoiselle. My friend,' Julia indicates me, 'would like to buy an apartment in Paris.'

I avoid Mademoiselle's eyes. After two weeks of dragging this sentence all over Paris it's beginning to sound, even in a real estate agent's office, excruciatingly embarrassing.

'Dans le quatrième?'

'Oui. Dans le quatrième.' I knew there'd be an interrogation. Can't we please just continue with the photographs? But Mademoiselle is intrigued now. She slows down a bit and concentrates on a real smile.

'Vous parlez français?' she asks.

'Oui. Bien sûr.'

Julia starts to say something, but Mademoiselle stops her with a wave of her hand.

'Vous, mademoiselle,' she says pointedly, 'parlez très bien français. Très, très bien.'

Julia throws me one of her quivering smiles.

'Vous avez appris le français en Australie?'

'Oui,' says Julia. 'Lots of Australians learn French.'

'Vraiment?' Mademoiselle folds across her desk and looks at me as though I'm living proof that this is a lie. I nod apologetically. It's a cue to move on. The second bedroom is large enough for a double bed and an armoire. It's the largest second bedroom I've ever seen. As crisp white cotton, pale-pastel jaquards, and bold geometric linens float around in my head, I forget momentarily the mathematical precision that selecting such bedding requires.

'Madame.'

Mademoiselle startles me back into the room.

'La cuisine.'

I snap to attention and look at the kitchen. It's new and fresh looking, with a tiny white table for two set against a lemon wall. Madame says something to Julia and waits while I smile and look pleased that the kitchen also has a dishwasher, which the owners are prepared to leave in the apartment, and a brand new oven. From the kitchen we glimpse the entrance hall, where a long, filmy curtain covers the window. Everywhere we look it's gorgeous, but Mademoiselle keeps the best for last — the bureau.

The study, a triangular-shaped room in mauve, boasts a spectacular view straight down a spectacular Parisian street. The shock of this room and its view leave us gaping at the photo until Mademoiselle's 'it's nice' sends us into spasms of laughter. Nice! It's extraordinary. The blurb under the photograph in la vitrine mentions a view from the bureau window, but it says nothing that prepares us for this. Oh yes! This is it. This is most definitely it. This is the view you imagine looking out on when you stand on a street and stare up at an apartment window. This is what you see — vigorous beauty and sky you can touch. Window boxes and chimney pots and balconies competing with hurrying people, surging traffic, and flashing lights. The whole of Paris is stretching out before you and there you stand, at your window, stretching out to embrace it. Views like this are priceless, but this one is for sale. I want to hug Mademoiselle. I want to invite her to our house-warming party; but while I'm moving in, Mademoiselle has moved on to what looks like a photograph of some bathroom tiles.

'Tiles. These are the bathroom tiles.'

I laugh a little hysterically.

'Oh! I must get my husband.'

A puzzled Mademoiselle looks to Julia for an explanation. Julia tells her that Madame's husband is waiting outside. I leap up from my chair and confuse things further by launching into a monologue about the rooms, the colours, the view. I forget my English-for-foreigners pace. Everything comes tumbling out of my mouth at once. Is that the real price? Is that the real size? Is that the real view? Oui. Oui. Oui. All the way home. Everything is as it seems. It's all real. It's all happening. My excitement and my sudden exit astonish Mademoiselle.

'Why,' she asks as I get to the door, 'is your husband outside?'

'Because,' I say in a calmer voice, 'he is very afraid of real estate agents.'

I dash out of the door, leaving poor Julia to translate.

Jack is as impressed as I am with the photos of the apartment. 'Do we know where it is?' he asks.

'Only that it's somewhere around here.'

Mademoiselle is vague about the apartment's exact location. As usual, the name and number of the street are withheld for security reasons until the correct procedures are gone through. Only after a file has been opened and a rendezvous for viewing agreed upon is the address disclosed. Mademoiselle can only confirm that the apartment is near the Hôtel de Ville. Jack presses her for the name of the street. She registers our disappointment at not knowing, but Mademoiselle is a professional and she sticks to the rules.

'Ce n'est pas possible.'

She compensates by drawing our attention back to the bureau.

'This room here,' she says, 'is on a corner.'

We peer at the photograph. So. It's on a corner. Now we're narrowing it down.

'Je vois,' I say. 'C'est un bâtiment unique.'

Mademoiselle looks impressed. So do Jack and Julia. In the time it takes to realise we're looking at a genuinely unique building, the energy in the room moves up a degree or two.

'Oui,' says Mademoiselle, 'tout à fait.'

As evidence, she launches into a complicated speech about street corners, little streets, big streets, the Hôtel de Ville, the view, the light, and the quiet. Or the lack thereof? I turn to Julia for help. She easily turns fifteen sentences into one. The apartment is on the corner of a small, quiet, big street. D'accord. That sounds good.

'C'est près d'ici?' I ask.

'Oui, oui, oui.'

Mademoiselle answers me with a grave look that enhances her emphatic repetition.

'Oui. C'est par là.'

She waves her arm in the direction of the window. We follow it all the way down to her finger tips, but we're too late. The shops that were on the opposite side of rue Nicolas Flamel when we came in are still out there. They have not been replaced by a magical *bâtiment unique*.

'Par là?' I repeat.

'Oui,' says Mademoiselle without gesturing, without even looking up this time. 'Oui, par là.'

Oh well, even the most scintillating of conversations must come to an end. Still, I'm overjoyed that the apartment, this perfect Parisian apartment with room and light and corner windows, is just there somewhere, just across the street, just around the corner. This is the Paris we know. The right bank. The Marais. It's where we want to be. All those other apartments were just practice. I cross my legs and my fingers in readiness for my next question.

'Mademoiselle,' I pause, and let the soft, upward inflection hang in the air. Mademoiselle lifts her head to me. 'Oui,' she says.

'Mademoiselle …'

I've got everyone's attention now. I'm beginning to see how useful repetition can be.

'C'est possible de voir l'appartement aujourd'hui?'

'Aujourd'hui?'

'Oui.'

I try to look calm and serious. I try to look as though the answer to this question is of no consequence. Mademoiselle sucks in her cheeks. I hold my breath. She flicks her eyes across her computer screen.

'Aujourd'hui. Aujourd'hui. Peut-être.'

Peut-être. What a wonderful, wonderful word. Perhaps we can see the apartment today. I turn and beam at Jack. He returns my smile, and I realise for the first time that we are sitting together, in an agence immobilière, smiling at each other openly.

Mademoiselle does not know what has happened, but she knows that something has — something other than people wandering in and asking lots of time-wasting questions. Her mouth softens. Her long black ponytail creeps up her back and decorates her shoulder. She taps keys at her keyboard with renewed concentration. Today. Perhaps today is the day. We tell her that tomorrow we return to Oz. Australia! Tomorrow! Now it's her turn to look amazed. Now it's Julia's turn to embark on a monologue about our travels. She mentions Gasgony and Provence, Languedoc and Normandy. Mademoiselle looks at us unbelievingly. Such a long time to spend in la belle France. C'est incroyable. C'est fantastique. Les Australiens ont beaucoup d'esprit. Yes. She will let us see the apartment today. Her eyes are smiling with ours. Things could not be going better. Then suddenly they're not.

'Zut!'

Mademoiselle makes no attempt to hide her annoyance. She dismisses her computer keyboard as if it's at fault.

'Ce n'est pas possible.'

She wrestles the disappointment from her face and looks up at us.

'Ce n'est pas possible parce que …'

Obviously, the owners are busy today. It's Saturday. Lots of Parisians work on Saturdays. Pas de problème. We can see it tomorrow. Our flight is not until midnight. Tomorrow will be fine. We don't have much to do. Just pack. That's all. We can wait one more day.

I smile reassuringly and say, 'C'est bien. We have time tomorrow, too.'

'Ce n'est pas possible de voir l'appartement pour quatre ou cinq semaines.'

I nearly throw myself at Julia. Four or five weeks! Please tell me she didn't say four or five weeks!

'Jules?'

Julia nods.

'That's what she said. It's not possible to see the apartment for four or five weeks.'

Mademoiselle nods, and confirms Julia's translation.

'Oui. C'est vrai.'

Ahhh. It can't be true. Why would that be true? I want to collapse over the desk or onto something lower. Why on earth …? Why is there always something?

'Why is that?' asks Jack flatly. 'Why can't we see the apartment for four or five weeks?'

'Les propriétaires,' Mademoiselle looks to Julia for help, 'ils sont en Provence.'

In Provence. The sentence flies around and around in my head. The owners are in Provence. And? There's no point asking that. I know what the 'and' is. And … it is not possible to see the apartment without the owners being present.

'Ils sont en vacances,' says Mademoiselle apologetically. 'C'est normal en juillet.'

'The owners are on holiday in Provence. It's normal to take holidays in …'

'Thank you, Julia. I understood that.'

I don't know why I'm snapping at Julia. It's not her fault. Jack moves away from the desk.

'Ah well,' he says. 'That's that, then.'

What? He can't be giving up. Just like that. I feel like crumbling and kicking the desk. I don't know which is harder to control.

'Mais,' says Mademoiselle, looking up at us brightly, 'mais on peut voir l'appartement quand ils reviennent.'

She's trying hard to quell our disappointment, but what's the point? We won't be here to look at the apartment when the owners get back. This is our last day. That was our last chance. Despite everything, I didn't really think we'd fail. I was prepared for little failures, the usual ups and downs, but ultimately I always imagined we'd succeed. The problem is that grand ideas are always subject to the vagaries of detail. Why shouldn't the owners of this apartment be on holiday? Why shouldn't the butcher's shop become a gay bar? Why shouldn't I stand in the window of a Paris apartment and squeeze lemons into the morning light?

'Ce n'est pas la peine.'

There's no point. The finality in my voice fills the room.

Jack puts his hand on my arm and asks if there's a plan of the apartment. Mademoiselle searches the dossier. No. There is nothing. No picture. No plan. Nothing we can take with us. I sigh, and fiddle with the strap on my bag.

'We're going to buy our son some clothes.'

Mademoiselle looks up at me. I can't tell whether she understood me or not.

'I email you,' she says hopefully.

'Email?'

'Oui. Les photos.'

'Merci, mademoiselle. That would be nice.'

She pushes a piece of paper towards me and holds out a pen. Wearily, I oblige her. She picks up my address, reads it and then places it with the photo of the apartment. She takes a card from a pile on her desk and hands it to me.

'C'est mon email.'

'Merci.'

Immo Flamel. Mademoiselle Madeleine Lafleur. I smile at the abbreviation of immobilère. Immo. It sounds like a combustible chemical.

'I will email you when the owners return,' says Madeleine.

'I'll be in Australia. I don't think …'

But Mademoiselle Madeleine is not easily defeated. She turns her attention from me to Julia. She unveils a new plan for viewing the apartment. When the owners return from Provence she will email me and then I can come back and see it. Ça va. The absurdity of this idea cheers everyone up. Julia explains that Australia is a very long way away, but Madeleine shrugs at our distance. If you like the apartment, she argues, distance is no impediment. It seems churlish to argue otherwise. We stand around trying to look as though this idea could somehow be put into practice.

'Julia will still be here,' says Jack, tapping her on the shoulder. 'She could look at the apartment for us.'

'Bien sûr,' says Madeleine.

'And Yoann and Athina,' says Julia. 'You could ask them to look at it, too.'

'Yes,' says Jack, 'and maybe Claude and that builder friend of Yoann's, what's his name? Bernard?'

'Benoît, and he lives in Brittany.'

'Well, that's a damn side closer than Melbourne.'

Madeleine stands and shakes hands with us. She seems happy with the way things have ended up. She finishes with another monologue about holidays in Provence and friends looking at the apartment and something about a courtyard. A courtyard! All that and a courtyard, too. It's unbearable. We leave in a flurry of madames, monsieurs, and à bientôts. À bientôt. J'espère. Of course this apartment is not possible, but out on the street in the mid-morning sun we start to pretend that it is.

Twenty-six

'Okay,' says Jack. 'As far as I can see, we've got three choices.'

Choices? He has our attention.

'We can either go shopping or go to lunch or ...'

I can tell from the look on his face that his third choice is pretty good.

'... we can open a bank account.'

Never before has the prospect of opening a bank account seemed so sensational. It's an inspired idea. Why didn't we think of it earlier? How would you buy an apartment anywhere without a bank account? We attack the problem logically. First, we'll need to return to our apartment and get our passports, and then we'll need to find a bank. That shouldn't be too difficult. There are hundreds of banks in Paris.

I take Jack's arm. I really want to hug him, but this sort of impetuosity is at odds with the professionalism demanded of a bank-account holder. I can so easily imagine myself whisking my chequebook from my handbag and signing for groceries, for tickets to the cinema, for a scarf at Hermès. That's going a bit far. I'm much too terrified to set foot into any shop that displays its wares without a price tag. Even so, a Paris chequebook is a licence to buy anything. It will give me a million marvellous opportunities to demonstrate publicly that I am part of this city. I haven't just galloped in to gaze up at the Tour Eiffel or queue up for Sainte Chapelle or sigh into the Seine. I'm going to be where the real Parisians are — inside. My chequebook and I are going to be making all those small, crucial, everyday decisions that make up real Parisian life. That perfect lamp. Those wine glasses. A snowy pair of white cotton pillow cases. (I hope I'm not developing a linen fetish.) I look up into the cloudless sky. Just over there. Our apartment is somewhere just over there.

'Look!' I startle Jack and Julia by pointing to a tiny street that snakes its way in between two buildings.

'That must be it.'

'What?'

'The apartment. It must be down there.'

We rush down the little street. Of course it must be down here. This is near the Hôtel de Ville and …

'What about the trees? The ones we could see from the study window?' asks Julia.

Were there trees? I can't remember trees.

'Well, maybe it's off a street down that street,' says Jack.

He wants to go and have a look. He's worse than me.

'We'll recognise it when we see it,' he says.

'From the outside,' says Julia doubtfully, but she follows us nonetheless.

The first corner apartment building we come across is narrow and freshly painted. It has cute dormer windows that spring out of its roof. We try to make it 'our' apartment, but all its windows face directly onto other buildings. We find another possibility a block further down, but all its corner windows face the BHV department store. We turn around and walk back towards the Hôtel de Ville. How could it be just over there? The only thing over there is the BHV. It's enormous. It takes up about three blocks. There's not an apartment building in sight. We retrace our steps to Immo Flamel. It can't be that hard to find a long, narrow window with the right view.

We take a new route and discover a secluded corner separated from the street by three or four steps. These ancient steps lead to a small terrace on which sits an ailing apartment building. The building juts out at a dramatic angle onto the terrace. It leaves only the tiniest gap for pedestrians to squeeze past into a passage that leads away to another street. A middle-aged man and his dog are sprawled across the apartment's doorway. We keep our voices down so as not to wake them.

'This must be it,' whispers Jack confidently.

We stare up at the fourth floor. Yes. There is a corner window, and it faces out across to the Hôtel de Ville and its square, which is crisscrossed with plane trees.

'This has to be it,' I say, satisfied. 'There are no other buildings along here that face the town hall or have views of trees.'

'It's in serious need of a paint job,' says Julia.

'That's probably why it's so cheap,' says Jack and then adds hastily, 'relatively speaking.'

'Didn't Mademoiselle Madeleine say something about a courtyard?' Julia asks. 'This building couldn't possibly have one.'

'She didn't have any photos of a courtyard,' I say.

'That's hardly proof,' says Jack.

'Maybe she meant this terrace we're standing on. It sort of doubles as a courtyard.'

Monsieur's dog stirs and cocks an ear towards us.

'She also said the building had just been cleaned,' says Julia.

'Are you sure? Maybe she said it was going to be cleaned.'

There's no point being logical. I'm not interested in logic. Intuition — that's what's needed here.

'Well,' says Jack, 'we know it's completely renovated inside, so it doesn't really matter that the outside is such a wreck. The building's small. It won't take much to clean it up, and in the meantime it will keep the rates down.'

'Complètement fous,' says Julia. 'Both of you.'

Monsieur's dog gets to its feet.

'I hope he's just visiting. He doesn't look very friendly,' I say, backing away. 'Let's go and find a bank.'

'Where are you going to look?' asks Julia.

'On the rue de Rivoli. We ought to try and find a local one.'

'Maybe we'd better ring Yoann or Athina and see which one they recommend,' says Jack.

'We don't have time for that. They close early on Saturdays.'

'Why don't you just take whichever one is crazy enough to give you an account.'

'That's very helpful, Julia,' says Jack. 'But I think that will depend on you.'

'On me? Why?'

'You're the one with a degree in French and commerce. You can translate.'

'Oh, great. What about lunch?'

'Don't worry. Jack will shout us Nutella crêpes on the way,' I say, hurrying down the steps.

Twenty-seven

The banks on the rue de Rivoli don't look well disposed to issue anyone with a chequebook. They're not at all like real banks. They lack people and tellers and places to queue. After a hot, disappointing hour traipsing up the street to the Bastille and back again, we wonder if there are better banks on the other side of the river. We cross the Seine and begin our search anew on boulevard Saint-Germain. We head in the direction of the Odéon. It would be nice to have a bank close to the theatre.

'There's one,' yells Jack, pointing across the street.

'Crédit Agricole. Is that a bank?'

'Yes. They had one on the rue de Rivoli, too.'

We cross the boulevard and stand outside it.

'It doesn't look very friendly.'

'Friendly?' says Jack, peering through the frosted window. 'Why would you expect a bank to be friendly?'

'Is one of you going in?' asks Julia. 'Security's checking you out.'

'Not me. I don't like the look of it.'

'Neither do I,' says Jack.

'Hopeless.'

Julia tosses us a smile and marches further up the street. She stops outside the Banque de Paris.

'Well? Anything wrong with this one?'

We stand on the footpath examining the building.

'I'm not mad on it. It's a bit big.'

Jack agrees. We move on.

'CCF across the street.'

Julia is a great bank scout. I suppose that comes of having a degree in commerce. We shake our heads.

'No.'

'Banque Société Générale.'

'Looks a bit flash,' says Jack.

'Banque Populaire.'

'Looks okay. Let's just go on a bit further.'

'Good idea,' says Julia, flicking her long brown curls about her shoulders. 'We wouldn't want to miss any.'

'What about that one with the pig in the window?' asks Jack.

'That's a phone shop,' says Julia.

'Why would a phone shop have an enormous pig in the window?'

'Look,' I point across the street, 'there's another CCF.'

'I'm not crossing over again, it's too hot on that side,' says Jack.

We press along the boulevard, ignoring our increasing hunger and thirst.

'There's another one.' I point to a small building a few doors ahead.

'They're certainly popular,' says Jack as we line up at the CCF's door. 'What do you think?'

'It looks okay. I mean, it looks sort of like a bank. Have you ever heard of it?'

'Not really.'

'It's close to the FNAC,' says Julia. 'You can do your banking and your CD shopping all at the same time.'

'That's a good point. Okay. Let's do it.'

We examine the bank's security door dubiously.

'Maybe we'd better work out what we're going to say before we go in.'

'Right. Has anyone got any money?' asks Jack.

'Money?'

'They'll want money. They're a bank.'

He searches his pockets.

'Ten, twelve. There might be some in this pocket. Yes. I've got fourteen euros.'

'You must have more than that.'

'We're going home tomorrow. I'm letting myself run out.'

I rummage around in my bag for my wallet.

'I'm in the same boat.'

'How much money have you got, Julia?' asks Jack.

'Me?'

'Are there any other Julias here?'

'Okay. I took one hundred euros out of an ATM earlier this morning. It's my rent money.'

'Good. We'll borrow that. We'll need a hundred at least. Especially if we tell them we're opening an account to buy an apartment.'

'Is that what we're going to tell them?'

'We have to tell them something. Why not the truth?'

'What if they don't believe us?'

'What if I won't give you the money?'

We fix Julia with a don't-even-think-about-it look.

'Seriously. Do I have to do all the talking and give you all my money as well?'

As usual, her quivering top lip undermines her attempt at indignation.

'Stop whingeing and hand it over,' says Jack. 'I'm not walking around for miles trying to find an ATM that'll take my card.'

Julia slides a small red notebook out of her bag and passes Jack the two fifty-euro notes that are folded inside it. I look up nervously at the bank's blinking security cameras. They make me feel criminal.

The glass door opens automatically at the touch of a button. We step through the doorway in single file. A second glass door does not open. We stand imprisoned between one door and the next, waiting while whirring security cameras vet us. I stifle a laugh. It would be funny if this was as far as we managed to get. A green light connected to a buzzer flashes and shrills. A scraping mechanical voice invites us to step out of the chamber and into the bank. We tumble out into the foyer, grateful for our release into the quiet, cream room. The walls are flanked by a series of blonde wooden doors. A pale, curved receptionist makes handwritten notes at a pale, curved reception desk. She looks up at us apprehensively and asks for our account number. We waver.

'Bonjour, mademoiselle,' I say doubtfully.

She puts her pen down and says something else about an account. We shake our heads and stand bravely in front of her desk. Her apprehension turns to concern.

'Nous,' I say, gesturing inanely, 'nous voudrions ouvrir une …'

What is the word for bank account? I forgot to think of that. Maybe cheque account is better. I think cheque is the same in French and English. I smile at Mademoiselle, whose pale features are now darkened by a frown. Prodded by Jack, Julia steps up to the desk and takes over.

'Madame et Monsieur voudraient ouvrir un compte bancaire,' she says confidently.

Mademoiselle looks grateful for Julia's flawless French. She straightens the papers on her desk and tells us that that will be fine. She can make an appointment for us early next week. Next week! There is no next week. We need an account today. Now. Jack throws me a don't-panic look. Julia is explaining politely that next week is too late. She is telling Mademoiselle that tomorrow we return to Australia and today we have found an apartment. C'est incroyable. We were en route to buy some clothes for Madame and Monsieur's little son when, voilà, we found the perfect apartment and now we need a bank to match. Curiosity creeps across Mademoiselle's face. I try to look like an Australian trapped by French circumstance.

'Vous êtes Australienne?' she asks Julia.

'Oui,' says Julia. 'Nous sommes tous Australiens.'

'You speak French very well,' says Mademoiselle. 'I will go and ask one of my colleagues.'

She disappears behind one of the blonde doors. We move away from the reception desk for a whispered emergency meeting.

'Okay,' says Jack, assuming the role of coach. 'You're doing a great job, Jules. Keep at it.'

'Do you think so?'

'Absolutely. The bit about the little son,' I touch her lightly on the arm, 'that was brilliant.'

'Keep at her, Jules. We might steal it in the last quarter.'

Mademoiselle returns, leaving the door to her colleague's office wide open.

'Bien. Madame Perraud will see you soon,' she says. Her eyes sweep the floor. 'You have your passports?'

We rush them to her desk and wave them in the air like flags.

'Bien.'

She doesn't look at them or us. They sit on the top of her desk, closed and disappointed. She hands Julia a form, and we settle ourselves in the cream bucket chairs to fill it out. Name, date of birth, address, passport number. No trick questions there. Madame Perraud is talking loudly on the telephone. We complete our form and return it to Mademoiselle. Then we wait. Madame Perraud continues on the phone. She is animated and giggly. We wait five minutes, then ten, then longer. Jack reckons she's talking to a girlfriend about last night's date. I remind him that Madame is a married banker. He looks at me as if this is evidence.

One of the other doors opens and a man walks across the foyer to the reception desk. He looks briefly in our direction. We smile weakly. He asks Mademoiselle for an explanation. She says something inaudible and points at Madame Perraud's open door. He marches into her office and silences a loud peel of laughter. Muffled voices follow. Monsieur reappears and walks briskly back to his office. Another five minutes crawls past. Jack is entertaining us with an absurd interpretation of a bank brochure when Madame Perraud, a small, blonde, and exceptionally pretty young woman in her late twenties, walks into the foyer, shakes our hands, and offers us a dozen désolés.

We sit in Madame Perraud's office. It is small and neat, with a floor-to-ceiling window that looks out onto boulevard Saint-Germain. I'm glad I don't work here. I'd get nothing done staring out at the boulevard all day long. We exchange greetings and give our first names. Madame leaves her desk to close the door. When she comes back she is Amandine. She smiles. I notice that her cheeks are a little flushed. She says something I don't understand. Julia responds with lively agreement. We wait in the wings. Amandine has heard that in Australia things are very relaxed. Australians use first names, even in banks. They never worry. They are easygoing and cheerful. They smile a lot. In the confines of the small bank office we concur with this view and widen our smiles as proof. It seems to be a positive basis from which to get down to business. Happy, carefree Australians are just the sort of clients this bank wants.

Amandine produces a form and adopts a solemnity commensurate with bank business. We defer to her tone. Who speaks French? An easy first question. Julia explains that we all do but, since opening a bank account is a serious affair, we have sought her assistance because, living in Paris, she is more confident in the language than we are. Amandine imagines that we must be very modest. We try modest, but it's elusive. Next she moves into a series of complicated apologies about her lack of English, the amount of questions she must ask, and her interest in Australia. She and her husband, of only five weeks, are going to Kangaroo Island and Port Douglas for their honeymoon at Christmas time. Très bien. Ça va. That's a good place to start. We have the whole afternoon ahead of us.

Yes, Kangaroo Island is groaning with kangaroos. Yes. Lots of French people go there. No. We haven't been. Malheureusement. Australia is a very big country. It's très difficile to see everything. Yes. We've been to Port Douglas and the Great Barrier Reef. Très bien. Très intéressant. In December? Does anyone go to Port Douglas in December? What about the jellyfish and the humidity and the rain? What we need here is a bit of lip pursing or shoulder shrugging. I try for an Australian equivalent. An eyebrow shrug? A blank stare? I manage a sort of wide-eyed grimace. It doesn't do the trick. As impromptu ambassadors, we're hopeless.

Amandine looks worried. Isn't Port Douglas nice? Oh, yes. We took some Parisian friends there just last year. They thought it was paradise. And they loved the crocodiles. Amandine's face lights up again. That's the reason they chose Australia — for the adventure. Hunger grips my stomach. It rumbles loudly. Yes. There is plenty of adventure to be had in Australia. You can eat kangaroo one day and crocodile the next. Amandine covers her mouth with her hands.

Donc. The banks in France are not easygoing and carefree. They have forms and rules and questions. Amandine starts with our passports. We have different names. A married couple with different names? C'est normal en Australie? Well, it's not uncommon, but I wouldn't say it's normal either. Un petit peu. Finally this phrase comes in handy. It's a little bit normal. Ah. Très bien. Amandine pulls a form from a pile behind her and copies our names onto it. She returns to us with an approving nod. So what we want is a chequebook in both our names? Exactly. Nothing could be simpler. Just a few more questions. Votre travail?

'Barrister,' says Jack.

Amandine looks mystified. 'Qu'est ce que c'est un …?'

'It's like an advocat,' says Jack.

Julia interjects. 'Monsieur is a queen's counsel,' she says importantly. She knows a thing or two about how banks work.

'Counsel?' says Amandine. 'That is like conseil?'

Julia and I nod soberly.

'So,' she says, looking at Jack, amazed. 'You give advice to the Queen?'

'Exactly,' says Jack, and Amandine makes a satisfied note.

'And Madame?'

Panic pricks at my eyes. What am I going to say? I don't have a profession. I don't think I've ever had one. Of course, I've been meaning to get one, but I've been busy. I'm a mother, but I don't think that counts. In a bank you have to be something else. Amandine is waiting. Who am I?

'Ellie est comédienne,' says Julia.

A comedian? Is that a profession? The bank seems to think it is.

'Ah,' says Amandine, 'une comédienne. Très bien.'

'En anglaise, c'est actress,' continues Julia.

'Actress.' Amandine tests out the word, rolling the esses into zeds. She flashes me a smile and adds 'comédienne' to the form. She writes slowly. I blush scarlet. She confides in Julia that my modesty does not fool her. She can tell that I am an actress. I have an actress' face: loud and animated. She asks me if I'm famous. I laugh a little hysterically and blush even redder. I used to be an actress, that's true, but the small forays I made into the worlds of theatre and television could hardly be classed as a career. I shake my head at her. Amandine nods at me knowingly. She picks up my passport and studies my photo.

'I think, in Australie, you are famous,' she says.

It seems to be a bank imperative. I lower my eyes with my voice. 'Peut-être un petit peu.'

I steal a look out of the window, half expecting a lightning bolt to strike me where I sit.

Amandine finishes with our passports and our professions, and looks up at us encouragingly. *Le livret de famille.* Next she would like our family book. The livret de famille is a personal record of all births, deaths, and marriages. It's the road map of a French family's life. It explains who you are. Without one you're a non-person.

There are no family books in Australia. Amandine looks at us disbelievingly. Attendez. Now she understands. Pas de problème. She will be happy to look at the Australian equivalent of a French family book.

'Ça n'existe pas en Australie,' I say again cheerfully.

Amandine turns her doubting face to Julia.

'C'est vrai,' says Julia apologetically.

Amandine looks down at the form and then back at us. She needs more convincing. She tells Julia that we must have something like it. How could a country operate without a family book?

'I'm certain ...' begins Julia, but her voice trails off. Amandine has planted seeds of doubt.

'Australia is a very young country,' I say reassuringly. 'We don't even have an identity card yet.'

Amandine hollows her cheeks at Julia's translation. She begins to be persuaded. She tells Julia that in France there is no identity card either. France is a free country. Australia is a free country, too. France and Australia: liberty, equality, fraternity. Amandine will just make a note about the family book. It shouldn't be a problem. And if it is a problem we can just get a letter from the Australian government saying that family books do not exist there. Or we could type the letter and get the government to stamp it. That would be fine, too. Of course, we are only too happy to do any or all of those things. The Australian government is very accommodating. Happy and carefree like its citizens. Or are Australians subjects? Amandine questions Jack. Of course he'll know. He gives advice to the queen of England. Julia and I join an expectant Amandine to await the counsel's counsel.

Amandine swivels her chair around and types all the information into her computer. Donc. We want to open a cheque account. Why? Because we are buying an apartment in Paris. Très bien. She taps away and asks for the address. We shift uncomfortably in our chairs and exchange furtive glances. The address. We all want to know the address. Amandine stops typing and looks to Julia. I look at Jack. I'm sure I said 'buying' not 'bought'. J'achète. J'ai acheté. Zut! Now we're going to look like liars. There is absolutely no way a bank is ever going to give a chequebook to liars. Especially not to foreign liars. Again, heat runs from my neck up to my face. Julia comes wonderfully, inspirationally, to the rescue.

'L'appartement est près de l'Hôtel de Ville.'

Amandine leans over her desk.

'Près de l'Hôtel de Ville,' she repeats. 'C'est la rue de Rivoli?'

Expectation hangs in the air. Now what? We can't go around saying we own an apartment when we don't, and on the rue de Rivoli of all places. I've never even imagined owning an apartment on the rue de Rivoli — the same way as I've never imagined owning an apartment on Sydney Harbour or the Strand or Nevsky Prospekt. There's an address. Nevsky Prospekt, Saint Petersburg. An apartment there would be worth a fortune now. The rue de Rivoli, Paris. Fifth Avenue, New York. The world is full of the most fabulous addresses.

'Oui et non.' Julia's voice fills the room. I make an effort to concentrate. She is saying there are offers pending. That we are deciding between two apartments. It is a difficult decision to make. Très difficile. One apartment is on rue Vieille du Temple and the other is on rue Nicolas Flamel. Both streets run off the rue de Rivoli. Amandine struggles to contain her delight. She used to live, until her marriage, on rue de Rivoli, near the Place du Marché Sainte Catherine. Oh, yes, we all know the Place du Marché Sainte Catherine. She launches into a description of the square's beauty and its cafés and salon du thés. How fortunate we are to be buying an apartment near there. 'Fortunate' is an understatement. It's a miracle. Amandine's warm and friendly manner, the elegant bustle on boulevard Saint-Germain, fourteen days that seem to go on and on: they are all miracles. Two Saturdays ago I could not imagine discussing a neighbourhood in Paris as though it were my own. I couldn't have imagined sitting in a bank (on a weekend!) opening a cheque account. My dream was never radical enough to cast the mundane as sublime. But donc. It is settled. Of course we need a cheque book. It's très nécessaire. Pas de problème. I could kiss Julia. And Amandine, too.

There are only a couple more questions. These are the personal ones. Amandine looks out onto the boulevard. She apologises that the bank must ask such personal questions. She shifts uncomfortably in her seat, preparing herself. We snap to attention. What could she possibly want to know? What could be more difficult than guessing the address of an apartment we are yet to see? Money. The personal question is about money. Amandine looks at Jack. She is sorry, but she has to ask how much he earns. How does she know just by looking at him that he's the one with the money? I'm the one who's supposed to be famous.

Jack fiddles with his shirt cuff. Of course, he doesn't blame Mademoiselle. Sorry, Madame. Banks must ask all manner of silly questions; everybody knows that. It is the same the world over. Jack explains this in Franglais to a sympathetic Amandine. He finishes with the melodramatic assertion that information about his earnings is strictly confidential and that his privacy must be completely protected. Amandine assures him that the bank would never breach such a confidence. Never, never. Jack fixes her with an intense look and says, 'I'll write it down'.

Amandine hands him some paper and a pen. Like a child in an exam, he bends over the desk and shields the paper from our eyes. Nobody speaks. This is a serious matter. That's why it's so hard to keep a straight face. Jack folds the paper in half and pushes it across the desk to Amandine, who unfolds it in slow motion. She examines it, refolds it, and then looks across at Jack. The suspense is impressive. Our banker is something of an actress, too.

'Très bien,' she says finally, pushing her combed fringe from her forehead. 'C'est parfait.'

What's perfect? What on earth did he write? And why is he still holding the very pretty Amandine's gaze in such an infuriatingly self-satisfied way? I wrestle with an urge to give him a good shove.

'Et les autres questions?' asks Julia sweetly.

Amandine assures us that there is absolutely no need for any further questions. No need at all. Everything is in order. She will finish typing the information and then she will organise the chequebook. She is sorry to keep us so long, but bank business ... she waves a perfectly manicured hand at us.

'Pas du tout.'

Jack jumps in with this. I can't believe it. That's one of my favourites.

'Melbourne,' says Amandine unexpectedly as she continues at her computer. 'The bank has an office in Melbourne.'

'Really?'

'Oui. It is in Bourke Street. Do you know Bourke Street?'

'I work just around the corner from there,' says Jack. 'A branch in Bourke Street? You wouldn't credit it.'

Amandine returns to her task with renewed vigour. Busy boulevard Saint-Germain pulses along outside. We, in contrast, are cocooned in a calm, comfortable, by-appointment-only bank, feeling pretty pleased with ourselves. I risk a tiny wink at Jack. Our instincts were right. If you want things to work out, go to the boulevard Saint-Germain: it's that kind of street.

'Voilà.' Amandine spins around in her chair to face us. 'Now,' she says, 'do you want a chequebook that goes comme çi ou comme ça?'

She gives an elaborate demonstration. Chequebooks can open like this (to the left-hand side, as is usual) or like that (with the cover opening up and away from the cheque). We mime opening our imaginary chequebooks. It's comme çi or comme ça. Never have I had so much fun in a bank.

'We don't have chequebook choice in Australia,' I say.

Amandine tries to look sympathetic, but fails to conceal her delight in this lack.

'Il y a beaucoup de choix en France.'

Well, that's the beauty of it. She modifies her tone and congratulates us for finding an apartment. It is not easy to choose the right apartment. How long did we search? She is incredulous at two weeks.

'C'est incroyable.'

'Oui. Je sais.'

Jack's frowning at me. I suppose I am getting a little carried away. There is no apartment yet. Sometimes it's hard to remember that. So the choice for the chequebook? Again I put an imaginary chequebook through the comme-çi, comme-ça test.

'Which one is the most French?' I ask.

Amandine looks a little confused.

'Do Parisians open their chequebooks this way or that way?'

Amandine considers my question and then, with a perfect lip-pout, half-shoulder-shrug combination, she answers, 'Les deux'.

'Both?'

I don't mean to say this out loud, but I can't really believe that Amandine (a banker, after all) could have failed to notice that nearly all Parisians open their chequebooks up and away from the cheque. They do not use the Australian method. I suppose ours is the Anglo-Saxon method, but it could just as easily be American. I've no idea who invented the chequebook or when, but I do know that Amandine is being coy. Is it modesty or an attempt to protect French-opening chequebooks from being usurped by foreigners? I bite my lip into a sort of a pout and choose the upward-opening version.

'Finally,' says Jack.

'It's an important choice,' I say. 'I haven't waited all this time for a French chequebook to end up getting the wrong one.'

My stomach rumbles like thunder. Amandine looks alarmed. She consults her watch. Haven't we had lunch yet? Oh là là là là. She flicks her fingers across her keyboard. Voilà. The chequebook has been commanded. How much money would we like to deposit?

'Is there a limit?' asks Jack.

'A limite?'

Amandine looks to Julia.

'Is there a certain amount they must deposit?'

'No,' says Amandine. 'C'est comme vous voulez.'

'Whatever you want,' says Julia

'What are the fees then?' asks Jack.

'Fees?'

Julia asks the same question about five different ways, but Amandine assures us there are no fees. Cheques are free? That can't be right. The question of bank fees or our failure to grasp the lack of them keeps us going around in circles. Amandine produces a brochure that is supposed to explain everything about fee structure. She marks the relevant paragraphs with a pen. We peer at them. They're incomprehensible. Bon. It would be ungracious to say we still don't have a clue. We move on to the deposit.

One hundred euros is fine. Parfait. There is no reason to have money sitting in a cheque account for no reason. That's perfectly clear. Jack turns to Julia and asks her for the money. Julia says that she's already given it to him. I make a close examination of the floor while my talking-about-money phobia makes a comeback. Jack searches his pockets and eventually — voilà! — Julia's money is in his hand and on the desk.

'I've spent all my euros,' he says, 'so now I have to borrow money from Julia.'

Amandine laughs out loud at this and says something about Australian humour and openness. She doesn't say anything about showing off. She helps Jack fill out a deposit slip and then asks if we need a credit card. A French credit card — what a bonus. The ignominy of having my Australian card turned upside-down and inside-out and wrestled into a machine will be a thing of the past. Chequebooks, credit cards — what next? Maybe I'll get a driving licence or a mobile phone or an email address. Ellie. Jack is asking me something. (There's never enough time for thinking.) He doesn't think we need a French credit card. He tells Amandine it would only confuse things. She looks a bit disappointed, but she understands. I don't. I'm quite fond of a bit of confusion.

Et voilà. That's everything. Amandine pushes all the paperwork into a pile and places it inside a smooth, white manila folder. She hands Jack a receipt for Julia's one hundred euros, and tells him that our chequebook will arrive in Australia in around seven to ten days. She gives us her card: Amandine Perraud, banquière. As of today she is our personal banker. We are to telephone if we have any problems. She is here at the CCF to help us. There are handshakes and smiles all round. We tell Amandine that she is the best banker in the whole of Paris. We hope she and her husband have a wonderful time at Port Douglas and Kangaroo Island.

'Vous êtes vraiment charmants.'

Amandine says this twice. She cannot stop thanking us. She cannot stop thinking about how much she will love Australia. In this tiny light-filled office, it seems none of us can reach the door. The blonde door handle is nearly within grasp when she thinks of one last question.

'Comment avez-vous choisi le CCF?'

'How?'

We repeat the word in unison. It hangs in the air, buying time.

Amandine thinks language is the problem. She gives us a couple of possibilities. Perhaps it was recommended to us. Perhaps we heard that it was the best bank in France and all of Asia, too.

Hmmm. Perhaps if any of us had asked any questions about a bank at all …

'We chose it because it looked nice,' I say. 'It was fate.'

Amandine stares at me. Her wide blue eyes move from happy to puzzled.

'Fate. Qu'est ce que c'est, fate?'

'C'est le destin,' says Julia.

'That's right. We walked down the rue de Rivoli and then up the boulevard Saint-Germain until we found a bank that looked …'

Amandine is concentrating hard on what I'm saying. Of course, this is not the way to find a bank. There are proper protocols for everything in Paris. Suddenly I can't disappoint her. I can't hurt her feelings.

'Professional.'

The right word arrives at last.

'Until we found a bank that looked professional and friendly — that's a difficult combination to find.'

Amandine's eyes flash at us. She pulls the door open.

'Vous êtes très gentils.'

She extends her hand. We take turns at taking it. I wonder how long it takes to be on kissing terms with your banker.

'Bon voyage,' she remembers when we are nearly at the door to the street.

I turn from the thick, glass security door and wave, 'Et vous Amandine, bon voyage.'

The receptionist looks up from her desk disapprovingly. Amandine's hands flutter from her side to catch the smile on her lips.

'What I want to know,' says Julia as we skip down boulevard Saint-Germain, 'is — what did you write on that paper?'

'If I wanted you to know that, Julia,' says Jack, turning to her as he links his arm in mine, 'I wouldn't have written it down.'

'Merde!'

We walk towards the Odéon and find a café table on the street near the theatre. We order three glasses of Sancerre blanc and three baguettes fromage. The waiter looks uncertain at the uniform order. I worry him even more by stretching my arms up and out towards the afternoon sun. It's happened. I can feel it. Paris wants me to stay.

Twenty-eight

I'm sitting on the floor surrounded by clothes and shoes and books and toys and a million things that are not going to fit into three small suitcases. Why does this always happen? No matter how carefully I pack, I always end up with excess baggage.

Every departure-morning is the same. I work myself into a frenzy worrying about weight and cost and offending the airline. Apart from the expense, paying twice for something robs it of that exotic I-bought-it-overseas quality. And then you never know exactly which item caused the surplus. Maybe it's those last-minute shoes at only 30 euros a pair. Obviously it's bad economic management to buy only one pair at that price, but three pairs may have been overdoing it. Perhaps it's the perfume. It's scandalous to charge excess baggage on gifts, and why am I travelling with three pairs of jeans? In summer? I justify one pair by putting it into my clothes-to-wear-on-the-plane pile. Books should be exempt, too. I always buy too many books. There are two dresses, a cardigan and two shirts that came for a holiday, and at least 3 kilos of things to make my hair look as though I haven't touched it.

I'm defeated before I even begin to sort out Jack's and Ellery's things. Jack always brings stuff that never makes it out of his suitcase. And now there's just as much stuff that won't go in: a box of olive-scented soaps, two boxes of chocolates, a painting, a pot of mustard, a market basket, two bottles of wine and, at last count, twelve soft toys.

'I blame Jack for this,' I say, getting up off the floor and standing in the middle of the luggage chaos.

Yoann looks up from his drawing. He is sitting at our dining table, helping Ellery draw a picture of Barbar the elephant.

'It's not his fault he has a birthday in July.'

'I know, but just look at this stuff. How on earth am I going to fit it all in?'

'I'll help, Mum.' Ellery jumps down from his chair and stands next to me.

'Help! I suppose you think hiding all those toys in everybody's luggage was being helpful.'

'No. That was being smart,' he says grinning wickedly, 'Jules thinks ...'

'Julia thinks it's hilarious. I know.'

Yoann stands up and walks towards the open window and looks out at the courtyard.

'Jack has a few presents; but you, Ellie, I think you have a lot more things.'

I look down at my suitcase. Perhaps I was a bit rash with that painting from Normandy, but really I haven't bought very much — just a few books and shoes.

'That's not true. I've hardly had any time to shop.'

'What about your fashion-victim coat?'

'Yoann, you're so unfair about that coat. It's nothing like fashion-victim.'

It lies across the back of the sofa brazenly displaying red floral stripes, two large, round silver buckles at oversized pockets, a collar big enough to land a small aircraft on, and swags of bias-cut, dark blue denim.

'It's heavy. I concede that.'

I rub my hand across my eyes. Why did I buy that coat? It seems to be mocking the whole packing process.

'I'll put it in Ellery's bag,' I say half to myself. 'He's got the lightest luggage.'

'Mum! What about all my friends?' says Ellery, alarmed.

'Don't worry. They're all coming with us,' I say, closing my eyes against the very thought. 'Even though your soft toys seem to multiply as we stand here, they don't actually weigh much.'

'I hope we can fit this in,' says Yoann, holding up the finished drawing of Barbar toasting Jack's birthday with a glass of champagne.

'Not more presents. His birthday's not for another two days.'

'Mummm. It's only little.'

'That's what you said about that dolphin you talked your father into buying at that service station on the auto route, and it's bigger than you.'

'He can't help being big,' says Ellery loyally. 'I love A13.'

'I know you do. Of course we can take the drawing. It's a work of art.'

'Oh, it is nothing,' says Yoann, but the gentle curve of his mouth betrays his pleasure at my praise.

'There is a condition, though — you have to take this bottle of wine.'

Yoann looks surprised and then shakes his head.

'It is very kind of you, but I cannot.'

'Please. You'd be doing me a favour. I can't fit two bottles in the luggage. I'm struggling to fit one in.'

'Oh, I think we can do it,' says Yoann as he bends down and helps me assemble the baggage.

In less than an hour we squash nearly all the belongings into the three suitcases. The casualties are a crushed eye shadow, a button from Jack's new Agnes B jacket, and Eyore's ear catching in a zip. At the end of this ordeal my hair is welded to my head with perspiration, my clothes are covered in grime, and three of my fingernails are missing.

'Voilà,' says Yoann, standing back and surveying our work.

Small sparkles of perspiration glitter on his forehead, too, but his trousers remain perfectly creased and his fingernails are all intact. I sigh and look around the room. The suitcases, too, are holding their own. None of them has yet threatened to burst under the strain.

'What about these?' Ellery does his best to juggle a kite, a small bucket and spade, and a soccer ball.

'Where on earth did they come from?'

'They're mine.'

He holds his things protectively against his chest. He knows I'm ruthless when it comes to other people's possessions.

Jack storms through the front door, carrying two large bottles of mineral water and a baguette.

'Bonjour, bonjour. It's getting hot out there.'

He looks around at the luggage.

'Great job. You've fitted everything in.'

'Practically. There's still a couple of things. Yoann is taking Ellery's fishing net and his Lego and that Three Little Pigs' house that Claude bought him.'

'He's just minding them, isn't he Mum?'

'That's right.'

'Until we get our own apartment. When are we getting our own apartment?'

'I don't know. Soon.'

'Ellie told me about the apartment near the Hôtel de Ville, Jack. If you want, I am happy to look at it for you.'

'Thanks, Yoann. You heard that the owners are in Provence. I wouldn't hold my breath.'

'Comment?'

'Jack doesn't think that it sounds very hopeful. Yesterday he thought it sounded hopeful. But today …'

I shrug by way of finishing.

'It is normal to be on holidays in July. You should not worry. You have an account at the CCF. This is a very good bank, one of the best; and if the apartment is what you want, you can return in the spring.'

'We can't just come and go, and come and go,' says Jack testily.

'I've asked Yoann to take one of those bottles of wine,' I say, trying to change the subject. Trying not to think too closely about what our leaving today really means. 'I can only fit one in.'

'Good idea,' says Jack.

'But,' says Yoann, 'they are presents for your birthday.'

'It's one bottle of wine,' says Jack. 'It's better for you to have it than just leave it here.'

Yoann picks up the wine bottle.

'The problem,' he says, turning it slowly in his hand, 'is that this is an excellent wine.'

'That's a problem?'

'Yes, because I cannot accept such a wine. Perhaps I can take the other one, but I cannot take this Château d'Yquem.'

'Alright. Why don't you give Yoann the other one and we'll keep this one?'

'Because the other one is from Yoann and Athina. That's why. They're not getting that back.'

'Sorry, Yoann,' says Jack looking at him sheepishly.

Yoann puts the bottle of wine on the table. 'There is,' he says, 'only one thing to do in a situation like this.' His shrug is executed with exquisite timing. 'We must drink it.'

'Drink it? But it's only …' I turn my watchband around so that I can read the time, 'it's eleven o'clock.'

Yoann moves to the open window. He has solved the problem. He will wait for us to catch up. Yoann's relationship with time is different to mine. In all the years I've known him, I've never seen him competing with it. For him, things happen in time, not on time. Conversely, I'm always under time's pressure. I always feel late. Time runs away from me. It leaves me breathless. It's time and space that confound everything.

That's what this quest was really about. Trying to find some space to put my time in Paris into. That's what I really wanted to buy: square metres of time. And then what? I would never consider making pastry at two in the morning or drinking wine at eleven. I'm not the sort of person who can weave magic out of nothing. I lift the bottle from the table and examine its label. It's a gift from a Melbourne friend who's on sabbatical at the Louis Pasteur Institute. Of course they would want us to enjoy it — regardless of the time. What rule says you can't drink wine at eleven in the morning? Monsieur le Painter floats into my mind. The bottle rests heavily in my hand. The vineyard has been producing wine for over three hundred years; it says this in tiny print at the bottom of the label. Yoann turns back into the room. His eyes smile contentedly behind his glasses. Of course we must drink this wine. It's what time can't measure that's important. I'm searching for glasses. I feel reckless. I can't see properly. There must be something in my eyes. How else could I have mistaken this extraordinary bottle of wine for an ordinary one?

I decide to spend my last afternoon walking. It's hot, and I'm a little light-headed. I want to wander. I want to bid Paris goodbye in my own time, by myself, quietly. The small shops on the île Saint-Louis stretch out before me. The full flavours of lunchtime fill the air. The aromas of pommes frites, juicy melons, and pungent cheese assail me as I meander. Every bistro, every café, is bursting with diners. Lunchtime is such a Paris time of day — everybody eating, everybody talking. The cadence of perfectly formed French rings in my ears. Perhaps I should be having lunch on my last day. Wouldn't I feel happier squashed into a tiny wooden seat, pulling bread apart, selecting a barely cooked green bean from my salade niçoise?

I couldn't bear it. That would make me feel like I was staying. That would make me feel like I do when I'm strolling through the Luxembourg Gardens or visiting one of my favourite museums: the D'Orsay, the Cluny, or the Musée Picasso. It would make me remember the thrill of climbing the Tour Eiffel or walking into Notre-Dame or down the Champs-Élysées. The toyshop interrupts my thoughts. I press my face up against the window. Shiny, wooden-headed Pinocchios, emerald-jacketed King Barbars, and white, curly-haired Milous stare back at me. What wonderful lives they lead, squashed together in the little shop on the narrow footpath of beautiful rue Saint-Louis-en-l'Île.

'Excusez-moi, madame.'

Tall-suited Monsieur walks around me. The heat and humidity do not slow him. He knows where he's going. He's not wrestling with some shaky, floating bubble of an idea that he might live another kind of life. Of course I don't know that, but it comforts me to think it all the same. I'm not going in. I can't fit another thing in our luggage. I pass the foie gras shop next door and the lingerie shop further on and the butcher's shop close to that. It's easy to pass this butcher's shop. It's crammed full of long-necked dead-eyed ducks. I pass Berthillon, where the usual queue of ice-cream lovers crushes against the tiny counter. I weave around them, cross the street, and find myself face to face with a family of elephants.

The sculpted elephants are plump and smooth with cheeky faces and trunks raised into the air for good luck. I stare at them longingly. I love elephants. The shop is empty except for Madame, who sits at a desk on the far side of the gallery. She looks across at me. I try for an expression that suggests an appreciation of sculptured baby elephants. I think she's an on-the-cusp Madame — not quite young enough to be addressed as Mademoiselle. I linger at the window. Mademoiselle or Madame? It's difficult to concentrate in the afternoon heat when the elephants are so distracting, but I must make a decision before I go in. Is that where I'm going to go? My mind wanders over to the Place des Vosges. Jack and Yoann have taken Ellery there for a last play in the sandpit. If they were here instead we'd be inside already. Yoann would be talking to Madame. Their discussion would be earnest and congenial. I move away from the window. Allez. Did I say that? It takes me a moment to translate. Allez? My go-on voice is speaking to me in French. J'y crois pas! I move towards the door of the gallery. It springs open at my touch.

After the clamour of the hot street the gallery is an oasis. Hypnotic Moroccan-style music wafts around the room. Mademoiselle/Madame looks up and smiles warmly. I smile back as our 'Bonjour, madame's collide. Yes. I made the right choice. Madame is a madame.

Her slow, broad smile continues to spread across her face. She invites me to look around. There are elephants, birds, and lots of pregnant women with full bellies and sturdy legs and arms. The work is sensual and pragmatic. I walk slowly around the glass cabinets. All the sculptures are in bronze. Madame gives me some information about the artist. Her lips move gracefully, like soundwaves, in and around her careful articulated French. The artist is African. His work is beautiful. I ignore my excess-baggage voice.

'Très intéressant,' I say.

Madame looks up from her work and asks if she can help. Yes. I would like to look at the baby. Madame takes it out of the cabinet and places it on a nearby shelf. He's small and solid, playful and exuberant. He's yet to learn that his species is in danger. I ask to look at another sculpture. It's of a woman sitting with folded legs and curled arms, reading a book. It's a study in contemplative serenity. I'm torn between the two. Madame sympathises. It's a difficult choice. The adult or the baby? Maturity or youth? We talk about the sculptor and his work — about the promise that his pieces hold. We talk about shape and space and distant continents. My adult brain stops scalding my infant tongue. Our conversation, these precious scraps of words, thrills me. Now, when I'm about to leave, I find my voice. I make mistakes, everywhere, but I plough on. I just want to keep talking. I'll talk about anything. Anything to keep me here, just a little longer.

Twenty-nine

The elephant weighs three kilos. It may even weigh four. I carry it across the Pont Louis Philippe daydreaming. I have a little piece of Paris with me fashioned by a stranger who also knows what journeying is.

A beautiful young American asks if I will take a photo of her and her mother. I oblige smilingly. They position themselves along the bridge's railing, leaning up and backwards, looking towards each other, the river, the sun, and me all at the same time. They tell me that they've just arrived. I tell them that I'm leaving.

'You've such a long way to go,' they say, looking concerned.

I smile my agreement until they are gone, until they have crossed the bridge onto l'île Saint-Louis. The bells of Notre-Dame chime overhead. It's four o'clock already. It's time to fly south.

I am barely in the door when the downstairs buzzer announces Athina's arrival. She walks into the living room carrying a basket full of olives, homemade tzatziki, and bread.

'Ça va?'

She kisses me twice on each cheek.

'Ça va.'

It's amazing how two little words can make you feel so lovely. We unload the basket in the kitchen while I tell her about today and yesterday. She listens quietly as she arranges food on a tray.

'I know it's difficult to have to leave and then come back in a few weeks, but when you buy an apartment isn't that what you'll do anyway?'

I pile six small plates together and look at her.

'I suppose so. I haven't really thought about it.'

'It's one of the problems of trying to buy in summer — people on holiday.'

'Well, you'd think they'd wait until they returned to advertise their apartments.'

'Why? If they'd done that you wouldn't have discovered it.'

For some reason, I resist the urge to give her a hug.

We take the food, plates, and glasses into the living room. From the window I can hear Ellery's high-pitched voice regaling Yoann with his exploits at the Luxembourg Gardens. I open the door and wait for them. They dribble up the stairs and into the room a tangle of buckets and spades, balls and champagne.

'So,' says Jack, walking over and kissing me on the cheek. 'How did you go?'

'Très bien. I went to the île Saint-Louis and bought an elephant.'

'Not bad for an afternoon's work. Don't we already have an elephant in amongst all those toys?'

'Not like this one.'

We stand around the dining table holding our glasses of champagne high in the air. Santé. Showered, changed, and sipping champagne, I'm enjoying our little farewell party. We go through the usual flight detail questions — when we'll get home, where we'll refuel.

'We're not going business class,' says Ellery, grinning at us, his teeth streaked with half-eaten olives.

'Aren't you?' Athina looks surprised.

'The day I start paying for kids to fly business class is the day I'll give it away,' says Jack emphatically.

'We had frequent-flyer points on the way here,' I say. 'We don't have enough to get us back.'

'So that is why you are upset at leaving,' says Yoann.

'Of course,' I say, 'the extra baggage allowance is crucial.'

I twirl my champagne glass in my hand and drain the last of its bubbles. How lucky we are. How extraordinarily lucky to be standing here with wonderful, generous friends in this beautiful ancient room on a warm midsummer's evening in Paris.

'If this was it, if it all stopped here, I think I'd be happy with that.'

Everyone looks at me in alarm. I laugh into my empty glass.

'I mean the apartment hunting. Not life.'

Jack pretends to look sad.

'I think we know what we're doing now. We can look again next year.'

Jack groans and refills everyone's glasses.

'The one near the Hôtel de Ville,' says Yoann. 'I think it might be a good one.'

'It would want to be brilliant,' says Jack, 'to make it worthwhile turning around and coming all the way back here just to look at it.'

'Are we coming back to Paris, Mummy?'

'No. Yes. Well, we are. We're just not sure when.'

'Didn't we buy an apartment?'

'No.'

'Why not?'

'It's complicated,' says Athina gently.

'Why? There are thousands and millions of apartments here,' says Ellery, pointing at the window to the street beyond.

'They're not all for sale though, peanut,' says Jack.

The downstairs buzzer sounds.

Julia's laughing voice can be heard through the open window. 'Drunk all the champagne yet?'

I press the button, open the front door, and unnecessarily announce her arrival.

Julia waltzes into the room. Her loud giggle (the one that drives Madame on the second floor crazy) precedes her. She is carrying a paper bag almost as big as she is.

'Bonsoir tout le monde. How did the packing go?'

I eye the bag suspiciously as she moves around the room kissing everyone.

'The usual struggle,' I say. 'What's in the bag?'

'Yes, Jules,' says Ellery, leaping up and down at her feet. 'What's in it?'

'Champagne first,' says Julia, gliding into a chair so that she and Ellery are at the same head height. 'Now …'

Ellery needs no more cueing. He stands in front of Julia at military-like attention.

'Now, remember when we went to Disney Land?'

'Yes.'

'And remember what you really, really wanted to buy, but I said it was much too big to fit into your suitcase?'

'Yes, Jules, yes.'

'Well, I was fibbing. Here.'

Julia hands the enormous bag to Ellery. He takes it and squeezes it against his chest as though he is breathing it in. We wait for him to open it, but he stands hugging the gift to his chest in rapture.

'Come on, we've got a plane to catch, you know. Let's see what it is.'

'I know what it is, Mum. Don't I, Jules?'

'I think you might,' she says teasingly.

Ellery squeals with delight, tears open the paper bag, and squeals again.

'It's him! It's him!'

King Louis has a huge round tummy, squat legs, and long, oversized arms. In that way he is no different to any other gorilla. But his bright-orange fuzzy body, his soft, pink face, and his enormously bright blue-eyed stare render him adorable.

'King Louis. King Louis,' Ellery screams.

He has arms that encircle you, and everyone wants a turn. It's clear he'll have to come with us. We are smitten, too.

'He is very funny,' says Yoann. 'You could put him in the market basket. I think he would like it there.'

'Brilliant,' I say. 'Qantas is going to love that.'

Jack is opening another bottle of champagne. I finish what's in my glass with unusual speed and wait for more. What am I doing? I think I'm trying to dull my complicity in the burgeoning baggage. I can hardly complain about a large, *light*, fluffy gorilla when I have another small African animal, which weighs twenty times as much, secreted in my hand luggage. The ice-cold champagne starts to make me feel hot. Yoann is describing something in earnest to Athina. Her delighted n'importe quois fill the room. It's the story of this morning's wine. She slips her hand into mine. I squeeze it and turn towards the front door.

There's the luggage, lined up, strapped up, packed, ready to go. Ready to go. I hate ready to go. Someone says fifteen minutes. The countdown to the limbo land of hemisphere-crossing has begun. We look at each other sadly but of course we're going to pretend to be happy instead. There's the last minute have-we-got-everything check. There's the effort of getting all our baggage down four flights of stairs, across the courtyard, through the door, and onto the busy street. There's the sudden arrival of the taxi station wagon — le brake. We load our bags and ourselves roughly and quickly — our taxi is blocking the one-way street. Our movement, our leaving Paris, is causing a standstill. There are hurried kisses and fat fought-back tears and good luck wishes and thank yous. Rue Vieille du Temple starts to shrink into the past. Inside the creeping taxi, the light, the noise, the gaiety of Paris is already somebody else's life.

Thirty

The young man at the Qantas desk bears an uncanny resemblance to that first young man at the Marais Immobilière. Perhaps it is him. Didn't he say something about working for an airline? He's looking at me, waiting for me to say something, do something. The internal organ design of Charles de Gaulle airport always confuses me. The tickets. He wants the tickets. I fumble around with the zip on my large document wallet. Monsieur, or Etienne, as it says on a small name-tag that is pinned above his breast pocket, watches patiently as I pluck tickets and passports from a jumble of paperwork.

Ellery is standing behind me, holding King Louis with one hand and pulling on my arm with the other. He is worried that Qantas will refuse to let the king on board. I turn to him with an impatient grimace. Didn't I just explain that, standing here at this desk, the exchange of tickets and passports and baggage is a very, very delicate negotiation? It requires tact, diplomacy, nerves of steel. Anything can go wrong. In the time it takes to say 'Bonjour, monsieur' you can be given the worst seat on the plane. You can be squashed up the back, in a dark middle aisle, near the toilets. Your hand luggage could be deemed too big; your real luggage, too heavy. I must be free to concentrate. No arm pulling. No mum, mum. Monsieur Etienne has asked me something. I don't know what, even though he's speaking English. Jack is trying to stop Ellery distracting me by lifting the first bag onto the scales. I can feel something of a minor scuffle breaking out behind me. Concentration is somewhere out of reach.

The first bag, Ellery's, registers sixteen kilos. Brilliant. Always start with the smallest suitcase. I try to look like a sophisticated, urbane traveller who barely needs any luggage. I say something and my words sound blurry. My suitcase is next. It weighs in at twenty-four kilos. Twenty-four kilos. That's not much. I want to leap around the airport shouting and high-fiveing: twenty-four kilos, twenty-four kilos. This is a personal best. I do the sums quickly in my head — sixteen and twenty-four, sixteen and twenty-four. What the hell is sixteen and twenty-four?

Jack's bag wobbles along the conveyor belt before I even get time to check its weight. Etienne is tapping away at his computer — happily! He's done the sums. He must have done the sums by now. We've made it. Another triumph over the skies. He looks up at me. His smile is open and friendly. Do I have any more bags? He wants to know if we have any more bags? The market basket sits on the trolley with our hand luggage. Should I? Shouldn't I?

'There's a market basket.'

I whisk it out of the trolley and wave it in the air.

'We don't have to take it. It's sentimental. We bought it in a tiny village not far from Toulouse. Well, not that close, but not that far. Saint-Antonin-Something-Something. There's a gorgeous restaurant there.'

Etienne leans towards me. 'Saint-Antonin-Noble-Val. Very beautiful.'

'That's it. Anyway I bought it there. I don't have to keep it. They're not very expensive but ...'

I fling the basket down onto the luggage conveyor-belt.

'It's not that it weighs anything. But those straps, they could get caught in something — it could be dangerous.'

'A dangerous market basket,' says Etienne.

'I don't want King Louis to go in the basket,' cries Ellery, pushing in front of me. 'King Louis wants to go with me.'

'I'll tell you where King Louis will be going in a minute,' says Jack.

'Of course he's not going in the basket,' I say. 'We don't even know if the basket ...'

'Is there anything else?' asks Etienne. He picks up the basket, takes up some tape with Qantas printed all over it, and fixes the long straps together.

Anything else? I don't think I can cope with anything else. Etienne smiles pleasantly. He looks as though he tapes up the straps of market baskets everyday. Jack is trying to move Ellery out from under my feet. He gets tangled up in the trolley. My hand luggage falls to the ground with a thud.

'My elephant!'

The words escape from me before I can stop them.

'We do not carry elephants,' says Etienne, 'but the basket is no problem. I am French. I cannot refuse such a basket.'

As the machine spits out our baggage tickets I bend down and rescue my bag from the floor, hiss at Ellery to please be quiet, and wink at Jack — we've made it. We're on. I am still half up and half down when Etienne leans over to look for me and says, 'How would you like to travel business class?'

What? That can't be a question. Surely it must be a statement. Does anyone ever say, 'No, I would prefer to travel economy'?

'Business class? Us? But there are three of us. We have a child.'

'Does that make four?' asks Etienne, laughing. 'I only have three seats. The gorilla will have to share.'

I want to scale the counter and hug him. Even though I'm hot and dishevelled and talking telephone numbers, he still wants to fly us business class — for free!

'Thank you,' says Jack.

'Mille fois merci,' I say at last, overdoing it even at the eleventh hour.

Etienne returns our passports, tickets, and boarding passes. He tells us which gate, what time, and which direction. He wishes us a bon voyage. And just like that, we are flying away. With our seat-belts fastened and our headphones on, immobilised blankly in limbo luxury, we roar away home.

Thirty-one

I'm delirious for the first few days. Jack makes me cups of tea and Vegemite on toast. He puts Pink Martini's *Sympathique* on the CD player. It was buried in my suitcase — a little piece of Paris put there by Athina. *Je ne veux pas déjeuner. Je veux seulement oublier.* That's it, exactly. But I can't forget. Even when I have the music blaring, my jetlagged mind still plays a cacophony of people, appointments, and apartments. I want to stop thinking about it, but Melbourne's crisp, invigorating winter won't let me. I want to jump straight to the part where my apartment-hunting journey metamorphoses into travel stories. Where the disappointments are glossed over, and the tricky bits turned into humour. That's when I'll forget that there is no apartment. That it's finished. I failed.

Ellery dances around me.

'Pinch and a punch for the first of the month.'

I nurse my wounded arm and look down at my giggling son.

'You just hit me.'

'No I didn't. That's what you do on the first of the month.'

'Who says so?'

He looks at me exasperated.

'Everyone, Mum. Everyone says that.'

He leaps around the kitchen flaying at the air with a ping pong bat. *The Age* newspaper lies in pieces on the table. I run a diffident eye across it. Saturday 1 August. Already. It's two weeks since we left. I sigh and gaze out of the window. *Je ne veux pas* ... I can see the apartment across the street and the girl with the lemon squeezer. I can see myself staring at her, debating what to wear. My copy of *De Particulier à Particulier* lies on the bed. *Je veux seulement oublier* ...

The phone rings. It's my brother Jim. He wants to know how it's going. That's what he always wants to know.

'Pas mal,' I say.

'What's that mean?' he asks. 'Speak to me in Melbourne.'

'I've got PPD,' I say. 'Post-Paris depression.'

'I get that, too,' he says, 'even when I'm there.'

He's in Melbourne to see some bloke, I mean expert, about parts for his Alfa Romeo. He'll be a couple of hours and then he's coming over.

We sit at my kitchen table turning the photos the right way up. I found them an hour ago. Four pictures of Paris, the bedrooms, the kitchen, and the living room are all waiting patiently in my laptop inbox. They'd been sitting there for three days, and now they're miraculously in my kitchen. They're all side-ways and upside-down, and so am I for seeing them. Madeleine's done what she said she was going to do. She's sent the photos. She remembered us. She remembered me. I was remembered in Paris. Jim taps at the computer while I tell him about Madeleine and Immo Flamel and the holidaying owners. I try to sound matter-of-fact, but I can't hide the excited panic that the right-way-round photos provoke.

I tell Jim it's all pretty straightforward. Our friends will look at the apartment for us. If they like it and it's still for sale, I'll jump on a plane and pop over to see it myself. The owners are away until September. We've got plenty of time to organise things. Imagine. Just when I thought it was finished, I can feel it all starting again. My PPD leaves me. I swap Pink Martini for Paris Combo's *Living Room*. And even though the title is the only lyric I can understand, it still speaks to me of apartments.

Jack downloads the photos and thrashes out the logistics. There's a lot to do. I've got to email Madeleine. Ring Athina and Julia. Ring the travel agent. He thinks we can do it. He thinks it's worth it. It's only an airfare. It's only a week. What? He wants me to go back and do everything in one week? N'importe quoi. Go to Paris, buy the apartment, fly back. Voilà. Our chequebook arrives in the mail.

The bank is ready to transfer the funds. A friend recommends a Melbourne solicitor who specialises in French conveyancing. Everything is in order. Everything is ready. My crackpot idea has gone mainstream.

Two weeks sail past. I talk the whole process over and over, but somehow I'm not ready. I don't send Madeleine an email. I don't ring Athina or Julia. I don't find out about flights. I stare at my empty computer screen. The owners are probably back by now. The apartment's probably sold by now. I stop staring at the photos. I stop listening to Paris Combo. I can't imagine myself buying an apartment that Jack hasn't seen. I can't remember my French. I can't imagine me coping. It's too big a decision. I don't want to go by myself. I can't buy an apartment in Paris alone.

It's three weeks since my missive from Madeleine. I'm staring into the phone, talking to Jim.

'I don't think I can do it. I think I need more time.'

'Well, there's your problem. Less thinking, more action,' he says. 'You only get one lifetime, so get on with it. I'd come with you if I wasn't flat out with the Alfa.'

'Oh, you'd be a great help,' I say, wishing like mad that he would come.

'Get your people to call my people,' he says.

He likes to pretend he's still living in corporate America.

He's right. One lifetime is all the time you get. It ought to be enough. I jump as the phone rings again. It's Athina. She's back from her holiday in Greece. She wants to know if we've heard from Madeleine. I surprise myself with a rush of sentences. I thought I'd forgotten all that. I thought I'd left all those French sentences in Paris. I think about obfuscating, but I always tell Athina everything.

She listens as I describe the past few weeks: the doldrums, the excitement, the panic. I tell her how the scenario spins around and around in my head until I'm talking nonsense. Je dis n'importe quoi. Athina laughs delightedly on the other end of the line. Of course I'm talking nonsense. It's all a bit premature. She and Yoann will look at the apartment and then I can decide. It might be terrible. That's true. Surprisingly, I hadn't thought of that. I catch a glimpse of my reflection in the door of the microwave. I'm standing in my Melbourne kitchen speaking in a foreign language. I'm not translating. I'm talking and listening. In French. Je parle bien français. Of course, Athina is right. Things will work out. It's just that they rarely work out in the way that you expect them to.

I think it makes sense. I check it at least ten times before I press 'send'. It's my first email in French. My desk is a clutter of dictionaries, grammar books, and verb-conjugating tables. Nine short sentences (two-and-a-half-hours' worth) and a cheery 'I hope you can understand my French!' to end with. I press the button and send my letter across the world. My bronze elephant sits on my desk. I turn him around to face me.

'Okay,' I say, 'you elephants are supposed to bring good luck. Do something.'

Jack walks into the study and turns on the light.

'Why are you sitting in the dark talking to yourself?'

'I've just sent an email to Madeleine at Immo Flamel.'

'I thought you'd gone cold on that idea.'

'I had, but that was before I remembered my French.'

'What's that got to do with it?'

'It seemed like a good omen. Athina's back.'

I push a copy of my email in front of him. He bends towards me, reads it, and then kisses me on the top of the head.

'That's excellent,' he says.

I don't think his command of French runs to such an appraisal, but I'm pleased nonetheless.

Madeleine has replied to my email.

'L'appartement que je vous ai présenté en juillet est toujours à vendre.' It's still for sale! And the most amazing news of all is that it's on the rue de Rivoli. The so, so Parisian rue de Rivoli. I dash around the house repeating the address as though it had the power to make magic.

There's so much to do. And fast. It won't stay on the market forever. I search for some paper. I've got to make a list. It ought to be pretty straightforward after that. I email back. I arrange a rendezvous for Athina and Yoann and Julia. Jack warns me about getting too excited, about all the logistics, but I'm not listening. At the end of the week, when our friends have seen it, I'm still not listening. I don't care if the bathroom is too small or the courtyard is run-down or the rue de Rivoli is too noisy. The French have brilliant double-glazing. Everyone knows that.

Why worry about minor details when everybody — Athina, Yoann, Julia, and Claude — thinks the apartment is perfect. Okay. Nearly perfect. Even so, they think I should jump on the next plane to Paris and see for myself. Madeleine agrees. She thinks we should make an offer right now. She says it's dead easy to buy an apartment by email. (She didn't exactly say that.) Just send over a power of attorney and voilà! Pas de problème. It couldn't be simpler. That worries me. I tell her we'd prefer to make an offer in person. She understands. C'est comme vous voulez. She sends me more details and *sincères salutations*. Zut alors! Salutations — coming to me from Paris.

The flight to Paris via Sydney and Singapore is long and lonely. I miss Jack listing all the movies he knows I'd like to see. I miss

Ellery's eager assistance with the vagaries of the remote control. I wonder how he'll cope without me. I wonder if the man beside me, who has battened himself down with a blanket and an eyepatch, is travelling to Paris, too. I jab restlessly at my TV screen, envious of his ability to surrender, as Jack's parting words loop around and around in my head: 'Remember, whatever you do, don't buy it unless you're certain.'

Thirty-two

I arrive at Paris Charles de Gaulle airport at 6.10am. I'm right on time. As the moving floor conveys me towards customs, I marvel at my situation. Only six weeks ago I was on this same stretch of conveyance, but moving in the opposite direction — moving towards a galaxy far, far away. At least that's what it felt like. Now it feels like I'm moving forward and backwards simultaneously.

The customs officer glances at my passport, stamps it, and returns it to me wordlessly. I squash it into my documents folder, which is close to bursting point due to the volume of stiff Powers of Attorney, Jack's thick, white business cards, and photocopies of our passports, bank statements, and marriage certificate. Armed with an arsenal of paperwork, I'm ready for a volley of questions and manila folders. I know I'm outnumbered, but I also know that I've enlisted the aid of a secret weapon — a French chequebook. My personal one sits at the front of all these papers, and will help narrow the odds. It's a testament to my right to buy a piece of Paris.

Hampered by wind and rain and some invisible force that keeps us at crawling pace, the bus from Charles de Gaulle to

Montparnasse takes more than two hours. The northern outskirts of Paris look more forlorn than usual. I hold my too-thin coat around my neck and shiver. The Paris I left such a short time ago is no longer in evidence. The further we journey, the slower we progress. That seems to be happening a bit lately.

Trapped inside the crawling bus, I'm assailed by what-ifs. What if I can't tell if I'm certain? What if I'm only a little bit certain? What if the freeway is blocked for the rest of the day and I miss my rendezvous with Madeleine? I search in my coat sleeve for my watch. Nearly nine o'clock. I ought to ring Athina and tell her of my delay. Her phone number is not in my mobile. Zut! Have I packed my Filofax? What if I haven't packed my Filofax?

I arrive at Athina's apartment close to ten-thirty. She has freshly brewed coffee and baguettes and jam waiting. I eat and drink hungrily. I wish I could finish my breakfast with a large glass of red. I've no sense of what time it is. We discuss the apartment. The courtyard is really old and crumbling (derelict, according to Julia), but it's about to undergo a major renovation. The bathroom is minuscule, even by Parisian standards, but it's brand new. The windows are all new. The plumbing and wiring are new, and the view from the study is breathtaking. We don't mention the torrential rain beating down on the street outside. Or the thick, grey, low-lying clouds.

'Does it have any sky?'

'Le ciel?'

'Yes. Does it have its own sky?'

'Elle, it's got seven or eight windows.'

'That's not the same thing.'

'It must have sky. The view down the rue de Rivoli goes almost to the Bastille.'

I stare out at the rain and steel myself to ask what I really want to know.

'So why do they want to sell it?'

Athina's deep-brown eyes look across at me. She shrugs almost imperceptibly. 'Because they're moving, I suppose.'

'Out of Paris? Or just out of the apartment?'

'They spend a lot of time working outside of Paris. The apartment has become too big. They're moving into something smaller.'

'What? Whoever heard of a Paris apartment that was too big?' I make a scoffing noise and drain my third cup of coffee. 'As if that's a real reason.'

Athina tilts her head at me with a concerned maybe-I-need-a-lie-down look on her face.

'Non. C'est normal. If you are spending a lot of time out of Paris you would need a smaller apartment.'

There's not a hint of sarcasm in her answer. I knew there wouldn't be — the why of selling is not a French concept. In Melbourne the vendor sells a house or an apartment for a specific reason — a reason that exonerates the house from all blame. The vendors are selling because they need a garden or a garage, or somewhere closer to schools or the beach or the city. In Paris, it is impolite to ask such a question. We've already discussed this on the phone. I've already offended others by asking this in the past. But it worries me. What if there's something terribly wrong with it? Some fatal flaw a foreigner would never detect? I fiddle with my documents' folder. It's hard to accept that a place that's the size of a postage stamp could become too large to continue living in. And then there's that other nagging question: why hasn't anyone else bought it?

'Well, that doesn't explain why it's so cheap.'

'Cheap?' Athina looks up from the papers I have dumped in front of her.

I feel a faint blush at the base of my neck. 'Inexpensive …'

Athina frowns and gently purses her lips. With a valiant effort, I manage not to copy her.

'I mean per square metre. It's five thousand five hundred euros per square metre. That's less expensive than the apartment on rue Dante or the wedge. Don't you think that's strange?'

Athina continues to look at my papers. 'I wouldn't say strange.' She tidies them into a neat pile. 'It's probably just good fortune.' She tilts her strong jaw towards me. 'Luck seems to follow you around.'

'Me?' I stare at her, astonished.

We arrive on the rue de Rivoli a little before four in the afternoon. Our appointment is not until four-thirty, but I want to look at the building without the real estate agent being there. I want to stand on the street and look up at the windows and lose myself in possibility. We dash out of the métro at the Hôtel de Ville and, voilà, we're face to face with a sturdy Marais-blue door. My eyes move up the length of the building. It is as Madeleine described — élégant and in bon état. It's a real Parisian building on a famous Parisian street. I want to claim our apartment immediately. I want to push the door open, take the stairs two at a time, arrive pen in hand, and say, 'Where do I sign?' I don't, though. That's the kind of behaviour that even expatriates find alarming.

We cross the street for another perspective. Hundreds of people bustle past. Outside the BHV department store, loud street-vendors demonstrate the latest citrus-juicers, vegetable-peelers, and home dry-cleaning kits. Cars and buses and motorbikes and bicycles scream past. The palace-like Town Hall, l'Hôtel de Ville, sits solemnly across the street. The leaves on the plane trees in the Town Hall square shimmer with clinging raindrops. The juxtaposition between its quiet grandeur and the unpretentious clamour of the street fills me with optimism. A fine film of rain blurs the scene. It blurs the boundaries. I look up to the fourth floor, to the long windows, to the graceful tangled curves of the iron lacework, to the smooth slant of the zinc roofing tiles and the symmetry of tiny, jutting chimney pots. I don't feel incompetent, inadequate, or excluded. I feel vital: a microscopic part of Paris' swirling, luminous life. A clock somewhere chimes four, and for some reason I give in to the urge to give Athina a hug.

Madeleine arrives on time. She greets us warmly, and leads us through the blue door past the tiny collection of ordinary metal letterboxes to a modern glass security-door. This door opens onto an elegant wooden staircase. This staircase is for building A. We walk past it and into the courtyard that leads us to the doorway of building B. I don't dwell on the appearance of the courtyard, even though it's exactly as Julia described it — derelict. I'm chastising myself for wishing that *our* apartment was in the salubrious building A. It is impossible to tell from the street, but the apartment houses three discrete but conjoined buildings — A, B, and C. The entrances to buildings B and C are dark and dingy. No one mentioned that.

The lift is too small for the three of us, so we climb the stairs. They are narrow and worn, and creak sadly under our footfall. The walls, too, are lifeless and neglected. Paint flakes from them like dry skin. On the dark and musty fourth-floor landing we ring the bell on a dark-brown door. I stand in the gloom, feeling numb. I wasn't actually prepared to believe 'derelict'. I just like the drama of the word. But that's not quite the right description. Dilapidated is closer. There's something miserable about dilapidated.

The door takes forever to open. Athina and Madeleine stare straight ahead. Expectantly? In the gloom, it's hard to tell. I catalogue all the foyers, entrances, staircases I've seen so far. Even that dreadful diamond-shaped one had a better entrance than this.

The door opens slowly. A slight, dark-haired man with earnest eyes and a cautious smile stands aside to let us enter.

He greets Madeleine and Athina cordially — with firm handshakes — but with no kisses. He greets me nervously in halting English. His name is Luc. The first boy I ever fell in love with was named Luke. With or without a K, I've had a soft spot for Lukes ever since. Another dark-haired, attractive man bounces through a doorway and stands shaking our hands in the foyer. Foyer? As I repeat Sébastien's name, trying to commit it to memory, trying not to get the two of them mixed up, I'm surprised that this room, l'entrée, is so large and bleak. It's dark-green walls and sombre antiques fill me with dread.

There are some questions about my flight, and apologies for the bad weather, and gracious compliments about Australia. Luc points out of the window to the courtyard below, and says something about the restoration and the cost involved. I manage to steer a course through all this, but I'm not really concentrating. I want to move. I want to see the living room and the bedrooms and the kitchen. I want to see it all right away. I want to get it over and done with.

It's Madeleine who finally opens the door to the salon and ushers us through it. It's a shock. It's spacious and cosy (a combination that Parisians manage with artful effortlessness), and wonderfully bright. It's a robust mixture of yellow walls, red soft furnishings, and dark, wooden furniture. Luc and Sébastien position themselves, almost apologetically, in front of the fireplace. Athina lingers in the doorway and leaves it to Madeleine to march about the room listing the features.

She points out beaucoup de space, beaucoup de light, and beaucoup de charm. It's all there. It's all true. I wait for her to finish. There's silence. I stand in front of a tall, heavily laden bookcase breathing in the cinnamon-scented incense that burns in a little elephant-holder on one of the shelves. An elephant. That brings a smile to my lips. I imagine my own elephant sitting there waiting for me every night as I step in from Paris — as I step in from the rigours of the rue de Rivoli to this pretty oasis of calm and light. I turn back into the room. I can hear my blood racing. I breathe in the worn, hand-laid parquetry floor, the white marble fireplace, the high ceilings, and the long French windows. I marvel at the ancient wooden shutters that sit on the edges of the wide windowsills, framing the wooden leaning rails and the curling-ivy iron lacework. And the sky. There's so much sky. I struggle for composure because I must be certain — and I am.

'Très joli,' I say, at last. 'C'est très, très joli.'

I escape into the next room. Too little praise? Too much? I know it's incumbent upon me to go through the process properly. They've made some polite concessions to my nationality (I've insisted upon being addressed by my first name, and my too-complimentary observations about the small wooden aeroplane that sits on the mantelpiece have been indulged), but I know I must not worry les propriétaires. There's a lot at stake. I'm expected to convey the air of a considered, competent purchaser.

I'm grateful to be alone for a minute or two in the master bedroom. I look at the fireplace, the beautiful proportions of the room, the window, and more sky. A bedroom with space and sky and an armoire, a chaise longue, impossibly long curtains, and deep-blue walls. This is a real bedroom. I resist an urge to leap onto the big brass bed. I want to lie down and look at the sky. Maybe I just want to lie down. I wish Jack was here. The apartment is threatening to overwhelm me. I mustn't be rash, but I'm feeling so light-headed. It's been nearly forty hours since I last slept. The bed looks so inviting. I'd never get away with it. All the bears are home.

Athina and Madeleine stand in the doorway.

'Have you seen the next room, Elle? It's the best.'

Madeleine allows Athina to lead me into the adjoining room. It's smaller, almost triangular in shape, with a pretty, antique wooden desk floating in the middle. It needs nothing more because nothing could compete with the view. The room's angled corner window looks straight down along the rue de Rivoli. An exclamation of surprise escapes from me.

'C'est incroyable, n'est ce pas?' says Madeleine.

Yes. It's incredibly incredible. Madeleine stands at the window and points across the street.

'Regardez. There's the BHV. The best store in all Paris. You can buy everything you need for an apartment at the BHV. Even wood for the fireplace.'

I laugh, but it's not a joke.

'C'est vrai,' says Athina calmly.

What's true is that even in my wildest imagining I never dreamed we would find an apartment this wonderful, in this position, with this view. I beam at Athina. Madeleine can sense a sale. She shows me the built-in robe and the bathroom-cum-laundry. We return to the living room. Paris Combo's song sings inside my head. I throw caution to the wind.

'It's lovely. It's absolutely lovely,' I say as we pass Luc and Sébastien, who are still locked into their position at the fireplace. They smile at me uncomfortably. I suppose it must be awful watching strangers appraise your home. The charming little room off the other end of the living room was once a dining room, but now it's a second bedroom. It's small and bright and also has windows overlooking the street. Perhaps the story about the owners wanting to move into a smaller apartment is true. At eighty square metres, this is the largest apartment I've seen, but I wasn't expecting this much space. I stand in the middle of the room imagining it as a dining room again with everything white.

I can see us sitting at a white, wooden table on smooth, sculptured chairs eating from large, round white plates. Here we could stare across tall candles and small rosebuds, dreaming into a white luminous future. The barely audible classical music, something French and complex — Satie perhaps — crescendos in the salon.

I move to the window. In the building opposite, office workers sit at desks. On the ground below, people and cars stop and go, stop and go. Lights change from red to green and back again. Sirens wail. Pigeons coo. Silent rain dribbles down from the sky. Athina was right. Luck does seem to be following me around. This apartment is in the centre of everything.

The tour is finished. We are back in the entrance where we began. I try to map the rooms into my mind. I must remember them. I must remember every wonderful detail to describe to Jack. I'm ready to leave, though. The forced politeness is asphyxiating. And I need some distance, some space from that hammering voice in my head that keeps on nagging me about why. Why are they selling this gorgeous apartment? Sébastien is saying something to Athina about the pantry in the kitchen. Luc is explaining about the courtyard and when the renovation will commence. The trouble a friend of mine had buying a flat in London springs into my mind. When she took possession there were no curtains, no light fittings, no stove. Does the apartment come with chattels? That's a bit tricky. I'll have to be specific. I ask about the curtains and the stove. Frowns all round. Not the curtains but, yes, they may leave some of the light fittings. Ça dépend. They're happy to leave the new stove and the dishwasher, though. Très bien. Très généreux. I avoid their eyes because now they've put the word leaving in my head it won't leave me alone. Why are you leaving? That's all I have to say. But I can't. It's not an innocent question. Perhaps I could risk a where question. And where are you moving to? I'm sure that wouldn't hurt.

'Are you staying in Paris?' I ask civilly.

Luc's peaceful eyes blink at me shyly. 'Yes,' he says, 'we are moving around the corner to rue des Lombards.'

'Rue des Lombards!'

So much for civility. I'm yelling across the room.

'That's where we first rented an apartment. That's where I first came up with the plan.'

'Plan?'

'To buy a piece of Paris.'

Luc looks confused. Athina interprets quietly, under the volume of my new enthusiasm.

'There was a butcher's shop. On the corner. Do you know it?'

Luc and Sébastien look at one another then turn back to me, shaking their heads.

'Well, that's where we stayed. When I first imagined buying an apartment in Paris.'

'You weren't staying at the butcher's shop,' says Athina gently.

'No. Directly opposite. I would have liked to stay there, though. It was the most beautiful shop in all of Paris. It's gone now.'

I look around with exaggerated sadness at my surprised audience.

'I wasn't expecting that.'

'Paris is changing very quickly,' says Sébastien. 'Things become more and more expensive. It is difficult for little shops.'

I don't know what surprises me more: Sébastien's English or his sentiment. What is he talking about? Paris is too old to change quickly. Of course, some things have to change. I've conceded that, but architecturally it's locked into the nineteenth century. Frozen in time. Isn't that the whole point? It stays just like this apartment, with parquetry and marble and curling wrought-iron. Anyone can see that.

'Many restaurants and cafés are closing, too. There is no loyalty anymore. People drift from one place to another.'

I look at everyone agreeing with Sébastien. Drift? Parisians don't drift. They move with purpose — from somewhere to somewhere else. I've stood and watched them. I couldn't be that wrong. I want to push past him and run the length of the apartment back to the study. I want to stand in the window and point down at the rue de Rivoli and say — see, see all those people out there going about important, particular Paris business. There's no drifting. There's no drifting, disloyalty, or change. Things are as they have always been. People here are treading the same paths they have trod for twenty or thirty or hundreds of years. They're eating in the same restaurants for lunch and dinner day after day. They're living in apartments their parents lived in and their parents before them. Paris is permanent. Luc holds out a glass of water to me. Where did that come from? I didn't even notice him leave the room.

We stand on the street looking up at the window that looks down on us. It's hard to imagine all that lies behind that narrow piece of glass. Athina takes my hand. Her liquid eyes smile at me.

'You do like it, don't you, Elle?'

'I can't believe it. It's the same as the apartment in my head. Exactly.'

'I think you mean heart,' she says sagaciously.

Madeleine stands patiently on the footpath waiting. Now what? Do I say yes? Just like that? Yes. This is the apartment we want to buy. Does she really think I'm going to fly halfway around the world, dash in, take a look at an apartment, rush out, and make and offer on it? Just like that?

It's five to five. In Melbourne it's five to one in the morning. It's too late to ring Jack. My heart starts slapping my ribcage. I have to decide by myself. I never imagined that. The rue de Rivoli roars around me. A church bell sounds. Is that Notre-Dame? My ribcage is starting to hurt. I'm standing on the same marvellous street as the Louvre, listening to bells peel from Notre-Dame, and wondering if I'm going to buy this piece of Paris. What is there to think about? I tilt my face at Madeleine and hold her with my eyes.

'Très bien,' she says.

Thirty-three

Madeleine sits us at her desk and hands me a form. It's a *Proposition d'achat*, a proposal to purchase. I fill it out in Jack's name. It seems prudent to put his power of attorney to the test. I leave Madeleine to fill in the description — four pièces, fourth arrondissement, fourth étage — while I try to concentrate on the sums. On the short walk back to Immo Flamel I've moved the figures around and around in my head, and I'm still not sure what our offer ought to be. Madeleine is looking at Jack's power of attorney. She notices we have different names; she thought we were married. I wave my marriage certificate in the air. Athina assures her that in Australia it is legal to keep your own family name. It's pas de problème. Bon. D'accord. Everything seems to be in order.

The asking price is four hundred and forty-two thousand euros. I think I'll offer twenty thousand less. That sounds about right. So why does the Egyptian tailor and his galabiya keep popping into my head? Because the asking price here is perfectly reasonable, too — that's why. Should I offer the exact asking price? Probably not. They must have to factor in some room for negotiation. That's how the system works. The neck of my jumper is pressing tighter and tighter against my windpipe. I thought I was over all this mortification with money. Madeleine tries to help out.

'Qu'est-ce que vous proposez?'

What am I proposing? That everyone sit here all afternoon waiting for me to open my mouth? Twenty thousand less is not a *vexer* amount. It's what they'll be expecting.

'Je propose quatre cent vingt-deux mille euros.'

'Très bien.'

Four hundred and twenty-two thousand euros. Madeleine is writing the amount down. My jumper stops choking me. I wasn't trying to offend that tailor. It's just that I was new to the rules of bargaining. Immo Flamel seems smaller than it did in summer. The terms and conditions of the proposal float around the modest office. I look around me. Who would have thought it would all end here? I notice a partitioned office at the rear of this one. The distorted shape of a person is just discernible through the frosted-glass window. Athina is writing out the declaration in French for me to copy onto the document. It's the same as the one we wrote when we made our offer for the museum apartment. 'I have read and approved my proposal to purchase for the amount of …'

Monsieur bursts suddenly out of the small rear office and stands over Madeleine, glaring at us. He snaps something at her, and she looks down at her desk. He says something else, and she whisks the form away from me and hands it to him. He looks at it, and then he looks at me as though I have just materialised. Athina's sharp intake of breath distracts me. I look at her and then I look at him. Something like fear flickers across his face, and as we lock eyes in mutual contempt I can see that Monsieur is a bully.

What prompted Monsieur's ill-tempered arrival? Our volume?

Our Franglais? Our general amiability? Madeleine introduces us. Monsieur Hasselmann. For the first time in my life I am tempted to say g'day. Or hi Bob! If I had to bet, I'd say his name's probably not Bob. The way he's snarling at Jack's power of attorney is very unBob like and more than a little unsettling. I decide to err on the side of caution and opt for a fulsome 'bonjour, monsieur' instead. Monsieur grunts at me and waves the Proposition d'achat form across the desk.

'Qu'est-ce que c'est? Qu'est-ce que c'est ça?'

Madeleine fiddles with some papers. Athina's eyes cloud with concern. No one says anything. Monsieur slaps the form down on the desk and points to Jack's name.

'C'est qui?' he bellows. 'Ce n'est pas vous.'

Athina begins to explain, but it is clear that Monsieur is not interested in explanations about nationality or marriage certificates. What he wants to know is why Madeleine has allowed me to make an offer for an apartment in someone else's name. He doubts the authority of the power of attorney. It doesn't look like a real document. Athina swears to its veracity. She tells him that my husband is an advocate — that it is a legal document. She volunteers to translate it, but translation doesn't interest him either. He drops the document on the desk, looks at me accusingly, and says, 'Il manque un tampon.'

It lacks a tampon? The power of attorney lacks a tampon? Athina and Madeleine stare at the guilty document in alarm. Monsieur bangs his fist, gavel-like, upon the paper. We all jump. Madeleine opens a drawer, grabs a couple of rubber stamps, and sits them in front of us.

'Voici les tampons,' she says gravely.

Tampons are stamps? I turn to Athina. She nods.

'Yes, Elle,' she says. 'The power of attorney doesn't have a stamp.'

'Ah, oui. Je vois,' I say pleasantly, nodding comfortably as though I'll be able to clear this up in two seconds. I'm about to speak when something in the atmosphere tells me that perhaps this lack might be just a tad more serious than I imagine it to be. Athina has moved up a notch from concerned to worried, and Madeleine has moved from confident professional to picking nervously at her shirt sleeve. I lower my eyes, cross my legs, and lean back in my chair.

'In Australia,' I say smilingly, 'we don't have stamps.'

Monsieur Hasselmann stares at me.

'Tous les pays ont des tampons.' Monsieur is certain on this point. I pretend not to understand him. I wave his concerns away and embark on a convoluted monologue about Australia being a young country and not having yet realised the intrinsic value of stamps. I throw in something about rubber being difficult to get in warm climates. The more I speak, the more furious he becomes. I build to an impressive finish and throw in a 'voilà' just to round everything off. Monsieur is forced to look to Athina for translation. She improvises impressively. She assures Monsieur that everything I have said is true. There are no stamps in Australia. Monsieur Hasselmann is certain he has seen a stamp on something from the Australian government. He demands to see my marriage certificate.

Zut. I fish it out of my documents again. Does it bear a stamp? Monsieur's self-satisfied look tells me he's confident that it does. I unfold it slowly. Imagine being condemned by your own marriage certificate. But I'm not. He's wrong. It bears the Australian emblem and four lavish signatures, but no stamps. Not one. I love a sunburnt country. I hand it to him. Monsieur sneers at it. He seems to consider it a poor excuse for a marriage certificate. He wants my *livret de famille* next. He thinks this is a trump card, but we've already been through all that with the bank. We don't have those in Australia either. Who ever heard of a country that doesn't have family books? C'est pas possible. Monsieur throws my marriage certificate on top of the doubtful power of attorney.

'We're only twenty million,' I say cheerfully. 'We have ways of keeping tabs on people without paperwork.'

Athina decides not to translate. Monsieur is going to phone the Australian embassy and check up about the family books. Bon. Go right ahead. They're very nice at the Australian embassy. A good friend of mine works there. Monsieur loses interest in the embassy. He wants to know our professions.

'I'm an actress,' I say vivaciously, 'and my husband is an avocat de la couronne.'

Madeleine looks mildly scandalised. Monsieur glares at me, and then gnaws on the inside of his bottom lip. Clearly he has no sense of humour. He's still glaring. Perhaps my offhand exuberance is a mistake, but Monsieur looks like the sort of man who might just benefit from a little contempt. He picks up the power of attorney and holds it aloft as though he is going to read from it aloud.

'Madame,' he barks, 'if your husband is counsel to the queen he will have no problem to get a stamp from the government.'

'C'est vrai,' I say, straightening up in my seat and adopting a more conciliatory tone. 'C'est une très bonne idée.' I think it could be time to appeal to Monsieur's better nature, even though I'd bet that Monsieur Hasslemann doesn't believe in the rights of appellants, either. What I really need is something to divert his attention from the offending documents.

'Perhaps, monsieur, it would be better if the Proposition d'achat was in both our names. My husband and myself.'

Monsieur takes a slow intake of breath at this suggestion. 'Peut-être.'

I nod contemplatively and then steer my passport carefully across the desk to him. He opens it roughly, and stares at the kangaroo and her friend the emu on the opening page.

'Regardez. Regardez-vous,' he says, bashing at the Australian emblem with his index finger. 'Voici un tampon.'

'Vraiment?' I feign surprise.

'Bien sûr, madame.' He holds my passport up and open for us as though he's conducting a show-and-tell class.

'Ah, oui, je vois. Je comprends maintenant. Pardon, monsieur. Je suis très desolée.'

He looks at the three of us. We lower our eyes in unison. He takes this as a clear sign of deference to his superior knowledge. Now he can afford some largesse. We will start again with a new Proposition d'achat and, in the interest of international relations, he will, on this occasion, even make an exception for the power of attorney.

'That was close,' I say as we walk along rue de la Verrerie, weaving our way around people and puddles and traffic.

'Real estate must be quite stressful,' says Athina.

'Yes. I think I can vouch for that.'

We're heading towards La Belle Hortense for a well-earned drink. We've decided we need a coupe du champagne before heading home to dinner. It was to be celebratory (the signed copy of my Proposition d'achat sits in my documents folder alongside my deplorable Australian papers), but now we need something to calm our nerves as well. We turn into rue Vieille du Temple. It's much quieter than it was in July; the seats outside the café L'Etoile Manquante are empty. I suppose the sodden footpaths and the damp afternoon air keeps everyone inside. I scan the street for Monsieur le Painter. He and his canvases are where? I look across at the Pâtisserie. It seems so long ago that I stood here on the hot street watching Monsieur at work. Now I'm disappointed not to find him here. That can't be right. What was I going to do? Rush up and tell him that I'd bought an apartment? That I'd finally found what I was looking for? How ridiculous. We don't even communicate. Athina asks if I'm alright. I'm looking lost. It's lack of sleep. Too much excitement. I'll be fine after a glass of champagne.

It's warm and familiar inside La Belle Hortense, even though Monsieur, who I hope takes me for a foreign correspondent, is missing, too. A madame makes coffee for the only other patron — a small man with ancient scars smiling on his left cheek. We perch on the high barstools and wait. The coffee smells wonderful. Maybe we should have coffee instead. Athina is looking at me sceptically. We're supposed to be celebrating. You celebrate with champagne, not coffee. Funny how I don't feel like champagne any more. I don't feel like I ought to at all. I ought to be elated. Instead I feel flat and torpid — like someone let all the air out of me.

I should go to bed, but I have to ring Jack before tomorrow. He answers the phone sleepily. I apologise for the early hour and walk him through the apartment room by room. I highlight all the good points — the size, the light, the new kitchen and bathroom, the windows, the position, and the view. It seems insane to give all those up for an ill-placed bathroom, a crumbling (soon to be restored) courtyard, and irrational speculation about why the owners are selling.

Far away in Melbourne, Jack listens carefully. There's silence on the line. Athina's telephone is heavy in my hand. I describe the rain and the bus ride, Luc and Sébastien, grumpy Monsieur Hasselmann, coffee at La Belle Hortense, and Monsieur le Painter's absence. I wish you were here. I really, really wish you were here. That's what I keep telling him. That's what I say in between rooms and people and drenched streets and the swirl in my head.

'You really think we should buy it?' he asks.

'Yes. I've offered them four hundred and twenty-two thousand euros.'

I put my hand on my chest to still my breathlessness.

'Okay. They'll probably counter-offer with four thirty-two. That sounds a fair price. Hello. Are you still there?'

'Yes.'

'Make sure that business with the courtyard is right. We don't want to be stung with an enormous bill for restoring it after settlement.'

I can see myself reflected in the window. I look weary. I'm dully aware of Athina in the kitchen clearing dinner away. She and Yoann are talking in excited whispers. Jack is talking contracts and signatures and money transfers. He's making inquiries about an accountant. Then there's insurance. There's so much to do. I'm suddenly exhausted. I promise to ring again as soon as I hear from Madeleine.

'Goodnight, darling,' he says. 'I'm so proud of you.'

That wakes me up. It's amazing what you can do when someone believes in you.

Thirty-four

I wake early and eat an enormous breakfast with Athina and Yoann before they leave for work. After that I pace around their living room, waiting for the phone to ring. Aristote sits on the windowsill. It's fair to say that, even though I've always admired him, Aristote and I have never been close. He flicks an ear at me. I'd love to flick one back. I sit on the end of a row of discarded theatre seats, nursing a cold cup of coffee. Aristote keeps me and the street below under vigilance. He's always on alert. I suppose he has to be. He used up eight of his nine lives when he leapt from a fifth-floor balcony. I wonder if I should risk a pat. I wonder how a cat actually measures distance. I wonder what time Madeleine will phone.

It's mid-afternoon when Athina returns. She brings the autumn sunshine with her. She can tell by looking at me that there's been no phone call. She makes peppermint tea and tells me not to worry. It's Friday afternoon. Madeleine has to confer with Luc and Sébastien. These things take time. I've just poured the tea when the phone finally rings. Athina answers it and hands Madeleine over to me.

The owners have declined my offer. Their counter-offer is, as we imagined, four hundred and thirty-two thousand euros. She waits for my response. I ask if this price includes the agent's commission. She assures me it does. With the sale price, the agent's commission, and twenty-six thousand euros for stamp duty, the apartment will cost four hundred and fifty-eight thousand euros. I close my eyes against the enormity of the sum.

'Okay. We accept.'

I replace the phone slowly in its cradle. Athina pulls down a theatre seat and sits beside me.

'You've done it, Elle,' she says.

I take her steady hand in my shaking one.

'I have, haven't I?'

We spend the rest of Friday on the phone. Athina rings Amandine, our banker. She's overjoyed. An apartment on the rue de Rivoli — c'est superbe. Insurance will be très facile. She makes an appointment for next week. À bientôt. Bon week-end. I phone Jack. A babysitter tells me he's out for dinner. I phone Julia. She's playing a gig tomorrow night somewhere in the Odéon.

We should all go out to celebrate. I can't reach Jack on his mobile either. Claude is out, too. I leave her a message, and she phones back and invites us to lunch. It is just after midnight in Melbourne when I reach Jack. He's thrilled to pieces. He tells me he's been celebrating in advance. He sounds as though he has, too. He's added up the figures. Everything is fine. Settlement will be some time in December. That means we ought to return in January. He'll book the flights and call again in the morning. I put the phone down, overjoyed. Everything has changed. My world is suddenly bigger. From now on, I'm part of two universes.

We meet Julia for a drink before her gig. She's playing at Le Mazet, a new bar on rue Saint-André des Arts in the sixth. She strides in, wearing long, black boots and a denim miniskirt. She drops her bag on the floor, kisses Athina and Yoann, hugs me, and orders a glass of red.

'Finally,' she says, 'I'll have somewhere decent to stay in Paris.'

Then she tells me that, really, she and her band are off to Ireland for a month, and that she intends to come back to Melbourne for Christmas — probably longer.

'You're leaving Paris?' I look over my drink at her, amazed.

'Not forever, but there's a lot happening in the music scene in Melbourne. It's probably time to go home and give it a crack.'

She asks Athina and Yoann about their holiday in Greece. Their conversation hums around me: France, Ireland, Australia, Greece. How easy it is to pretend today that the world fits in the palm of a hand.

Julia's band plays folk-rock music that tonight's audience is going mad over. There are people everywhere. We're squashed in beside the bar until I spy a small, vacant table near the door. It's an effort to push through the throng and claim our seats. It's impossible to talk. I didn't even know they had bars like this in Paris. It feels like Melbourne. I listen to Julia's haunting voice taming the crowd. It must be wonderful to sing like that. Yoann says something, but I can't hear him above the music. It swirls around and through me. I miss Jack and Ellery. I wonder when Julia and I will be in Paris together again. Her song is about a painter's palate and the colours of love. I wonder if Monsieur le Painter has sold his paintings, and has moved somewhere warmer for the winter. In four days' time I sign the contract to buy our apartment in Paris. Two days after that, I'll be flying home again. Cigarette smoke drifts past my face, journeying into the ether, into nothingness. I suppose that's why we do it. It's really our journey that shows us who we are — the destination, after all, is the same for everyone.

Sunday afternoon drizzles softly down the windowpane. I'm sitting in Athina's living room, listening to Patricia Kaas singing 'Autumn Leaves' on the CD player. We're eating Twistie sandwiches — the French version with Twisties squashed inside baguettes, not sliced bread. They're delicious. I stare happily out at the rain. It's luxurious to be in Paris for only seven days and have all the time in the world.

Yoann is in the kitchen, making Australian meat-pies. Claude is coming for dinner. I'm supposed to be making pavlova. Perhaps the Australian cookery book wasn't such an intelligent gift after all. Athina and I talk about Melbourne. It's been four years since she's been back. She misses her family terribly, but her mother is coming to visit in November. I listen to her list the Melbourne things she misses most: sunshine, the beach, sausage rolls and fish and chips, magpies, visits to Healesville Sanctuary, Cherry Ripes, and Twisties — of course. I agreed with all of these except for magpies. How could anyone miss magpies? They dive-bomb you in spring.

Yoann is ready to put the meat into the pastry cases. We go in to watch. The rich aroma of the meat mocks what's left of our humble Twistie sandwiches. I grab my camera and take a photo of Yoann and the finished meat-pies. They look wonderfully exotic lined up in a Parisian kitchen. We assemble the ingredients for the pavlova. I don one of Athina's aprons and set to work happily. Never did I imagine myself standing in a Parisian apartment making pavlova. I try to beat the egg-whites in time to Kaas singing 'The Windmills of Your Mind'. It doesn't work.

Claude leans tentatively over her pie and asks what it is. Yoann explains in careful detail the type of pastry, the cut of meat, and the method for assembling and cooking. I smile into my red wine. What serious scrutiny for a humble dish. The pies are rich and succulent. My pavlova is a brave effort. It looks lovely, though, decorated like Christmas with bright-red berries. I ask after Josephine and Jean-Louis and the apartment with the ornaments. I like to think that Madame managed to sell it for a better price than we were offering. Claude doesn't know, but she does know that the apartment on the rue de Rivoli is a rare find. We were very lucky. Athina looks at me. I agree wholeheartedly this time.

'You will have to paint it.'

This is not a suggestion. It's an imperative. I fiddle with my water glass. Claude is waiting for a response.

'Yes,' I say at last. 'We'll have to try and organise that.'

'It's not difficult to paint an apartment,' says Claude. 'You just have to find a good painter.'

'Yes,' I say again.

'I think the apartment's just been painted,' says Athina.

'Yes, but in the wrong colours,' says Claude, 'and you must have it painted before you furnish it.'

Of course, I have to agree with that, but I can't think how it's going to work. I suppose we'll only be here for two or three weeks in January, and there are beds to find and white goods and kitchen things and …

'There's a lot to do, of course,' says Claude, energised by the idea. 'But we can all help. You must start with the dépôts-ventes.'

'What's a dépôt-vente?' I ask, sipping my wine.

'Places that sell second-hand furniture,' says Yoann. 'You can find all sorts of very good things in the dépôts-ventes. We found this table in one of them.'

We stop eating and examine the table. It's an oval gate-leg in heavy oak.

'It's lovely,' I say, leaning back into my seat. Dépôts-ventes. I run the words around my tongue. There's so much to look forward to.

I yawn as I help Yoann put the last of the dishes away. The dinner was a great success. I've definitely overeaten.

'I think I'll go for a long walk tomorrow,' I say. 'I might wander over to the Place des Vosges and browse through the art shops. Not that we can afford to shop there, but it might give me some ideas.'

'Maybe photographs would be better,' says Yoann. 'There is in the fourth a very good photograph shop that is not too expensive.'

We finish clearing the kitchen in silence. Claude's been gone about an hour, and Athina is in the living room on the phone to her mother.

'I have to get some things for the theatre at the BHV tomorrow,' says Yoann. 'Maybe I could meet you over there to show you where it is.'

'That'd be great. What if we meet at L'Etoile Manquante, on

rue Vieille du Temple? I might even get you to buy something from Monsieur le Painter for me, if he's back. I'd love to have one of his paintings in the apartment — something to keep me thinking about how crazy life's rules are. It's funny, but every time I see him that's what I think about.'

Yoann closes the kitchen dresser and runs his hand slowly along its ancient wooden surface. He doesn't speak.

'That's only if you have time.'

'Ellie …' His eyes are full of anguish.

'It doesn't have to be tomorrow. I'm here for another four or five days.'

'I have to tell you,' he says looking directly at me, 'it is very sad, but the painter … he has died.'

'Died!'

I yell the word across the kitchen.

'Are you certain?'

I look up at Yoann. He looks back at me. My mind flies around inside my head. Died. That means dead. Not just dead drunk on the street in the afternoon sun. Not alive. Not living. The man who knew who he was. That man? I thought he'd managed to escape. I thought he'd managed to find a way to live outside the rules. I thought he was free. I slide into a chair. Yoann sits down next to me. He looks at me, concerned. I make no attempt to wipe away my tears. He goes all blurry.

'I thought he was happy,' I say hoarsely. 'I must have been wrong.'

Yoann traces his cheek with the tip of his thumb. 'You think happiness protects us from death?'

I stand and move towards the window.

'It could do,' I say, wiping my face roughly with the backs of my hands. 'It could do.'

I hear Monsieur le Painter's voice ringing through the early morning. Of course he was wailing. Of course he was lonely. Of course he was holding high his bloodied, broken heart for the dawning day to see. I lean against the window. Yoann offers me a glass of water. We stand side-by-side and stare out into the dark night.

'It is not what you think,' he says slowly.

I grip my water glass. The night beyond this kitchen seems so far away.

'It was a motorcycle.'

'What?' No, that's not what I thought, and now I don't know if that makes it better or worse.

'What happened … what happened … to his paintings?'

'I am sorry to say it, but I do not know,' says Yoann dejectedly.

The dull ache of 'Ne Me Quitte Pas' drifts through to the kitchen. If you go away. I always thought 'ne me quitte pas' meant 'don't leave me'.

'Athina must be off the phone,' I say needlessly.

We turn away from the window and look towards the music.

Thirty-five

It's time to create a dress code of my own. Something that matches the occasion is all that's required. Something Monsieur Hasselmann would approve of. Hmmm … perhaps that's aiming a bit high, especially as my concentration is suffering from a very late night. Yesterday, Monday, the day for starting again, I walked from Montparnasse to Montmartre. It took me hours and hours. I caught the métro back home, ready to collapse into an early bed. Instead I stayed up until two in the morning, drinking Ouzo with

Athina and talking and talking, then finally dancing and singing along with Kylie. So now the sun is already brilliant in the sky, and if I don't choose soon I'll be late.

I throw a pair of jeans onto the bed. They're a yellowy-mustard colour and covered in aubergine mermaids. Très original. That's what the mademoiselle in Vaison-la-Romaine who sold them to me a couple of years ago said — and they are, too. I team them with a pale-green long-sleeved t-shirt and a battered, brown leather jacket.

'Wow, Elle,' says Athina as I waltz into the kitchen. 'You look amazing.'

'Shows you what a night with Kylie does for you.'

I pick at my breakfast. I'm too restless to eat. I check and recheck my documents. Today is the day. We're ready.

We breeze confidently into Immo Flamel. Luc and Sébastien are already there. They're dressed in sombre suits. Monsieur Hasselmann and Madeleine wear dark suits, too. The whole effect is funereal. Except for me, of course. I'm glowing like the southern sun. We greet each other cordially, leave Madeleine at her desk, and crowd into Monsieur's box-like office.

Monsieur opens the file on his desk and extracts a large document. It's the contract of sale, the 'promesse de vente'. He looks uncomfortable. What a shame it's not Monsieur Impeccable with his charming smile and stories about the airline in his place. Monsieur Hasselmann makes a lengthy speech about the procedure for signing a contract of sale. Athina translates. Everyone waits patiently. Even Monsieur. He's a bit more subdued than he was last Thursday, but then I haven't really said anything yet.

We start with the length of the contract. Ninety days. Everyone seems content with that. That will make settlement just before Christmas. An apartment in Paris was number one on my

Christmas-present list for years, but I decide not to share this thought with the group. Monsieur declares that it's incumbent upon him to read through the contract page by page, aloud. No wonder everyone's looking so serious — it's at least twenty pages long. He starts with the cost of the apartment, the agent's commission, and the deposit. That's all in order, so why is everyone so tense? Monsieur has asked me a question. How am planning to pay the deposit?

I whisk my chequebook out of my documents' folder.

'By cheque,' I say proudly. 'We have an account at the CCF.'

Monsieur looks at my chequebook in disbelief.

'It opens the French way,' I add cheekily. Even though I'm dying to give a demonstration, I leave it at that because I think I know what's happened. I know why everyone is nervous. Monsieur has no faith in my ability to carry out this transaction. I feel a bit responsible. Maybe I overdid the flibberty-gibberty last time.

Monsieur dismisses my chequebook by ordering me to sign the bottom of the first page. Page one. Only nineteen more to go. I write the comprehension clause down first and then sign my name. Voilà. We're on our way. I throw Monsieur Hasselmann a small smile. He ignores me. Luc and Sébastien are bent over the desk, signing their copy. I turn to Athina. She meets my disappointment with an encouraging look. It shouldn't be this hard. It's a contract of sale we're signing, not a death warrant. Then I remember that French history is a bit different from Australia's, and make an effort to defer to their tone.

The next page is about the restoration of the courtyard. Monsieur explains that Luc and Sébastien have already paid their apartment's share of the costs. Athina reads the page and confirms this. Their share is twenty-four thousand euros. Zut. I can see why it's important to make sure that there are no misunderstandings. I direct my question to Luc.

'So that's all finalised? We don't have to pay anything else for the courtyard?'

He looks down at the desk. 'Oui. C'est vrai,' he says shyly.

Monsieur slaps at a tome on a shelf behind him. He tells me importantly that, under French law, it is always the owners who must pay for renovations. When this decision was made I was not the owner. I am not the owner now. His outburst is rather convincing.

We continue on through the remaining pages in much the same way. Monsieur Hasselmann waits for someone to make some comment about the clauses and conditions, and then he corrects them. There are three or four tedious pages covering government regulations for checking the building. The office is hot and airless. I'm so parched, my tongue sticks to the roof of my mouth. There are checks for everything: caveats, impending caveats, plumbing, chimneys, termites, tunnels. Tunnels?

'What do you mean, tunnels?'

As a time-saving strategy, I was trying not to ask non-essential questions, but this one gets the better of me.

Monsieur sits back in his chair. A tiny sneer hides in the corner of his mouth.

'Tunnels are passages that link one apartment with another.'

Athina, Luc, and Sébastien look at the floor. I look directly at Monsieur.

'Sounds more like a secret passage than a tunnel,' I say flippantly. 'Something you'd expect in a medieval building, not a nineteenth-century one.'

Monsieur straightens up. He takes a long, Pinteresque pause before speaking.

'There were tunnels,' he says, choosing his words carefully, 'built to help the persecuted escape during the war.'

'Oh,' I say, chastened. 'I didn't think of that.'

'That is the difference between an old country and a new one,' he says. 'In a new country, you don't have to think about the past.'

He's happy now. He moves his pen around the desk in a little victory march.

At the end of an hour-and-a-half we have finished reading and signing the contract. Madeleine brings us some water. Her eyes flick quickly around the room. Assessing the damage? We drink in silence. Monsieur regards us with a satisfied air as he gathers up the papers. He asks for Jack's power of attorney. I hand it to him with a copy of our marriage certificate. He smoothes them out and puts them in a file. He says nothing about stamps; he just flattens his hands on the desk and asks for the deposit.

There's an etching of the Arc de Triomphe on the cover of my chequebook that I've not noticed before. I have taken note of the *Madame Nielsen E. Australie* that's printed in the left-hand corner, though. I've looked at that again and again, imagining myself as I am at this moment — writing my first cheque. When I come to sign it, Athina suggests a photo. We must have a photo of me buying an apartment in Paris. Everyone agrees. Even Monsieur.

Luc and Sébastien rearrange the office because Athina has the good idea of including the Immo Flamel calendar that hangs on the wall behind us. Monsieur Hasselmann tidies his desk, smoothes his hands through his hair, and flicks at his lapels. He says he wasn't expecting to have his photo taken. He's not the only one. He moves his chair closer to the calendar. Athina clambers around the furniture, trying to get the best angle. I hold my pen poised, wondering why Monsieur is so keen to be photographed, and smile into the lens. As Athina takes the picture, I sneak a look at him. J'y crois pas. He's smiling twice as broadly as me. Real estate agents are definitely an enigmatic lot.

Thirty-six

Luc and Sébastien invite us back for a drink and a last look at the apartment. We step through the blue door and cross the courtyard. Julia was right. It is derelict — wonderfully, wonderfully derelict.

Luc offers us orange juice or Coke. I'm unsure. I was expecting … what? Champagne? Wine at least. I opt for orange juice. I hold my glass in the air. Félicitations. The juice tingles down my throat. It tastes like champagne. Of course it does. I smile around the room. It's just occurred to me: there's a special measurement for time spent in Paris. These are our champagne hours. That's the name for all the heady, sparkling days we'll spend here.

Luc is saying something about Australia. About how he completed a Masters in anthropology at Sydney University in Aboriginal artefacts. Now he's in aviation. Aviation? I guess he's still in the letter 'A'. I ask if he's been to Melbourne. He smiles at me apologetically. No. But he would like to go.

'You'd love it there,' I say. 'It's very … European.'

Sébastien asks if I would like to take some photos to show to Jack and Ellery. I hesitate. Is it impolite? It's not really my apartment yet. They insist. I take a couple of quick shots to move me to where I really want to be — standing in the little corner room staring out at the rue de Rivoli. I stare at myself reflected there in the window's pane, suspended in the heart of Paris, dreaming. Deux pièces. Trois pièces. One million pieces of Paris collapsed into this one apartment. I focus my camera and frame my lens around the window frame that frames my future. Snap.

It's getting late. It's time to leave my champagne hours behind. I tell Luc and Sébastien how much I love their apartment. That I'll take good care of it. That I look forward to seeing them again. I linger in the dark-green entrance hall. Luc promises that in January we'll drink champagne in their new apartment opposite the butcher's shop that isn't there. We kiss each other au revoir. It's strange how, now I'm at the end, it feels like the beginning.

Silently, we close the door onto the street. I touch Athina on the arm. She stops and looks at me and smiles.

'Don't worry,' she says. 'You'll be back sooner than you think.'

'It's not that. It's just the opposite.'

'What?'

'All that worry about coming and going and time and distance that's in the past. From now on, I'm only a day away. I've shrunk the world.'

'You know what I love most about you, Elle?'

'My brilliant capacity with languages?'

'Your optimism. It's so Australian.'

We walk towards the métro. A woman walks past me, effortlessly trailing a tartan shopping trolley.

'That's the very first thing I'm going to buy when I get back.'

'Le caddie?' asks Athina. 'The shopping trolley?'

'Yes. I love those. I'll need one for Picard. I'm going to get one in blue tartan to match our door.'

'N'importe quoi,' she laughs.

We take the steps down to the métro two at a time. Every Paris dream I've ever had sings inside my head. I'm at the barrier searching in my bag for my ticket. I'm on the train; it's speeding me towards the butcher's shop. The butcher's closes early on a Tuesday. I jump off the train and run as fast as I can. It's still open. I burst through the door. Bonjour, madame. Bonjour, monsieur. Breathless, I purchase half a rabbit, two canettes, and some andouille. Then I outline my weekend cooking plans to Monsieur le Butcher, and he tells me about his.

Acknowledgements

I would like to thank the following people for their generous assistance and warm encouragement in the writing of this book: Kirsten Abbott, Clare Baker, Louise Bellamy, Boris Brkic, Belinda Burke, Maurice Byrne, Merrin Canning, Anne-Laure Cavigneaux, Anne-Sophie Delemer, Paul Disspain, Kyriaki Efstathiou, Rodney Eggleston, Jim and Wendy Forrest, Lisa Gorton, Matt Gurry, Sarah Gurry, Jennifer Hansen, Kristin Keam, Diane Kirby, Michael Mannion, Barbara Nielsen, Jim Nielsen, Kerry Nielsen, Marielle Rebbechi, Bob Sessions, Christopher Sinn, Liz Skobel, Carole and Roger Stoddart, and Dianna Thomas; Tim and Tricia Gurry for generously lending me their beach house to write in; the staff at Lina's, particularly Sara, Elana, and Sarah, for always saving me the window seat; my fellow students at RMIT's school of Creative Media, for your support and camaraderie; and the university for granting me exceptional leave to enable me to meet my deadlines.

I am also greatly indebted to Antoni Jach, whose tutelage, wisdom, and unwavering confidence guided me through the travails of a first manuscript; and to Athina and Yoann who, in the midst of their own punishing workloads, painstakingly corrected my French and some of my English, too. I am similarly indebted to everyone at Scribe who have generously given of their time and expertise — particularly Aviva Tuffield, who first read my manuscript, and my publisher, Henry Rosenbloom, without whose faith, guidance, and exquisite timing this book would never have happened.

Ellie Nielsen

I would especially like to thank my husband Jack and our son Ellery, for always being there to hold my hand when things became a bit shaky; and most especially, to Julia Gurry, my reader and inspiration, who was by my side, word by word, from first to last, please accept my love and heartfelt gratitude.